First published 2016 by Legend Media Ltd
ISBN 978-0-9538689-1-9
Copyright © 2015 Stuart Logan
All rights reserved. No part of this publication may be reproduced, stored in a retrieval system or transmitted in any form or by any means (electronic, mechanical, photocopying, recording or otherwise) without the prior permission of the publisher except for the use of brief quotations in a book review.
Illustrations are the copyright of people and organisations indicated throughout and are reproduced by their kind permission.
The moral right of the author has been asserted.

Edited and designed by Legend Media Ltd.
Printed by Calverts Co-operative using FSC paper and biodegradable inks.

This book is sold subject to the condition that it shall not, by way of trade or otherwise, be lent, hired out, or otherwise circulated without the publisher's prior consent in any form of binding or cover other than that in which it is published and without a similar condition being imposed on the subsequent purchaser.

The CAT and the Hamsters

Stuart Logan

LEGEND
MEDIA

Dedication

To my dear nonagenarian parents John and Glad Logan.
You have always been a source of love and support.

The College of Air Training crest had
valuable advice for pilots

Contents

Acknowledgments 8
Prologue 12
Chapter 1   A background to pilot training in Imperial Airways 16
Chapter 2   A background to pilot training in BEA and BOAC 33
Chapter 3   A short history of Hamble Airfield 50
Chapter 4   College of Air Training aims, intents and setting-up 60
Chapter 5   Selection procedures 67
Chapter 6   Learning to fly — and the aircraft employed 77
Chapter 7   Ground-based training 121
Chapter 8   Accidents and incidents 130
Chapter 9   The denouement 155
Epilogue 163

Appendices

The CAT courses 167
Instructors 192
Apache flying exercises 194

Acknowledgements

Almost every author has a chapter in their book acknowledging the people who have helped make the project possible. This is only right and proper but how many readers bother to study the acknowledgements section, especially when it consists of a well intentioned but prosaic list of people they've never heard of? That's a shame because, although writing a book is a multifarious process for the author, it's almost impossible to do it well without some help and support and if nobody reads the author's acknowledgements, then those deserving of thanks receive no plaudits.

Accordingly I'm going to present my acknowledgements as a story. I'll tell it just like it happened and you can see how people became involved. From that you will be able to see what part they played in this book, how they helped me, and why they are deserving of my heartfelt thanks. They are mentioned in bold type but the story begins in a slightly serendipitous way!

For many years, even when I was flying full-time for British Airways, I'd been interested in horticulture and used the spare time on airline nightstops to study for the Royal Horticultural Societies 'Master of Horticulture' qualification. During that time I shared my horticultural thoughts with readers of my regular column in the international renowned **Newbury Weekly News**.

About five years ago a man telephoned and introduced himself as secretary of a local horticultural society. 'Would I like to deliver a lecture to his society?' he asked. I replied that I would be delighted and enquired what subject would they like me to address? 'Well!' he said 'My children used to go to school with your children and if I remember correctly you were an airline pilot.' I confirmed that was so, but added that I been retired from airline flying for a decade. 'Never mind,' he went on, 'I think it would make an interesting lecture, if you could explain to our society just how a pilot gets to become a gardening correspondent.' I said, tongue in cheek, that it was a well-deserved promotion and eventually told him that I'd entitle the lecture 'From Sky to Earth.'

In the course of finding photos for the Powerpoint lecture I needed a picture to illustrate my time at the College of Air Training. Surely a quick browse of the web would suffice. To my surprise, Wikipedia carried only a short stub of an article and no pictures. The sole website with any detailed information — http://www.delscope.demon.co.uk/personal/hamble.htm — was run by a gentleman called **Derek Haselden**, who was 'ground crew' at Hamble during the last years of CAT. His site is very informative and carries an eclectic collection of information concerning Hamble but not too much detailed information on the college itself. The British Library database drew a complete blank. Amazon proffered *A Short History of Tractors in Ukrainian* but I've no idea why! Thus it began to dawn on me that there was no extant history of CAT and that I might have to try to put that right myself.

I began the project by contacting Derek in April 2011 and he was most helpful and encouraging. Fortuitously there was a CAT reunion due the next month and he circulated a request for assistance which led me to **Phil Nelson**, who organised the reunions. They had originally encompassed staff and instructors who had worked at the college but latterly as numbers thinned cadets were included. As a result of the reunion I was contacted by **Milos Liskutin** on behalf of his father **M.A. (Tony) Liskutin D.F.C. A.F.C.**, a popular flying instructor. Other instructors' names followed and I spent many interesting hours with a tape recorder in the company of **Cecil Pearce**, **Dave Lewry**, **Brian Buswell** and **Barry Byrne**.

Perhaps the biggest stroke of fortune was to make contact with **Ian Underdown**, the chairman of Hamble-le-Rice Parish Council and son of my old meteorology instructor. **Roy Underdown** had gone on to become principal of the college in its last years and had collected material to write a book on the place. Ian told me that his father strove valiantly to keep the establishment going and his book would have told that story. Sadly he died before he could begin the book but his unique archive of material has proved to be invaluable and I give special thanks for its generous loan. I believe that Ian will secure the archive with an aviation museum in the future.

There are other similar research materials at the **British Airways**

The CAT and the Hamsters

Heritage Collection online at http://www.britishairways.com/en-gb/ information/about-ba/history-and-heritage/heritage-collection and also by prior request at British Airways Heritage Collection, Waterside, Speedbird Way, Harmondsworth, Middlesex, UB7 0GA. I should also like to record my thanks for their permission to use many of the old BEA and BOAC photos of CAT. Even so there was no eye-catching contemporary photo that was suitable for the dust jacket. That particular problem was solved by my very talented stepson **Andrew MacGregor** who drew me a beautifully evocative picture. Hardly surprising it is so good, because Andrew works as a professional illustrator http://www.andymacgregor.com.

Early in the project I discovered the excellent Flightglobal Archive which comprises every issue of Flight Magazine published between 1909-2005, digitally scanned and fully searchable. It is an invaluable resource and I drew on it extensively.

The next reunion was in 2012 and I attended. Just inside the entrance was a tall, middle-aged man dressed in full CAT cadet uniform of blazer, white shirt, tie and grey flannels. I chided him for not having put on weight like the rest of us and told him that even my old college scarf was a tight fit these days. He was surrounded by a cornucopia of college memorabilia ranging from old course notes and study documents to items of crockery bearing the CAT crest. **Trevor Hughes** 743C allowed me to borrow his extensive collection and it proved to be very informative.

Another source of original documents turned up in a much more unusual manner. After the college was closed and the demolition men moved in, it was still possible to use the airfield. So two ex-cadets landed quite legally, parked their aeroplane and began to take a look around their old training establishment. It was in a sorry state and many buildings were either demolished or in the process of being knocked down. Within the ruins of Ara House they climbed to the top floor and found that all of the filing cabinets had been emptied of their contents and removed. The files and records strewed the rubble-covered floor. They scooped up an armful of papers each so that those artefacts at least, should be saved from destruction. Thanks to them!

As the project accumulated data, the issue became not what to put in but what to leave out, so if I've omitted anybody who offered assistance please forgive me. During the writing period I tried to interview a range of cadets, with a view of taking verbal snapshots of the 20 year span of CAT's existence. My thanks to the following men who patiently submitted to interviews and in many cases lent personal letters, photographs, records and documents: **Peter Hunt** 602; **Tom Weller** 603; **Alan Robinson** 604; **Rick Reayer** 604, Hector MacLean 631; **Jerry Latham** 644; **Mick Tarry** 653; **Bruce Garner** 654; **Roger Guiver** 661A; **Pete Clements** 672B; **Mike Bannister** 674C; **John Russell** 694A; **Steve Leniston** 694A; **Dave Such** 702C; **Laurie Ayres** 702C; **Jim Bounden** 704A; Trevor Hughes 743C and last but not least BA Flight Manager Tridents **Gil Gray**.

Most writers are indebted to their partner, who acts as muse, confidante, unpaid sub-editor and general displayer of great patience when the whole spare bedroom is filled with dusty cardboard boxes full of old documents. So to my dear wife **Sue** — thank you darling.

It's oft said that everyone has a book in them. That may be so but getting a first book published is damnably difficult. If publishers wrote back saying that the best thing to do with this manuscript is light the fire with it, that would be disappointing but one would know where one stood. But to promise considered perusal once, twice or even three times and then break each promise is rude, time-wasting and very disheartening. Eventually my bacon was saved by an event just as serendipitous as that which conceived the original idea.

I was playing golf with a journalist friend and between shots, moaning about publishers and their shortcomings. He then surprised me by saying that he and his wife ran a small publishing business and could they help? Thank you **Shane McGarvey** of **Legend Media Ltd**, you've helped me bring the whole project to a concrete conclusion. I just hope that it won't behave like concrete when we launch it!

Stuart Logan. September 2015.

The CAT and the Hamsters

Prologue

UNLIKE the Universe, the College of Air Training did not emanate from the Void. It coalesced from a hazily perceived, gradually evolving requirement but in trying to give a public voice to those perceptions, the civilian and military branches of British aviation ended up in a literary dogfight.

It came to the fore on October 16, 1953 in the august pages of *Flight* magazine, which carried a three-page article by David Brice, an associate member of the Royal Aeronautical Society. The article, entitled *Pilots for the Airlines*, provoked a furious response. John Bishop was a serving RAF officer and just three weeks later his published rebuttal of Captain Brice's views stated: 'his arguments are in many ways so illogical, and his premises so unsound...' and 'paragraphs two, three and four are largely platitudes' and later on 'in paragraph ten we are told, in effect, that the ex-short-service pilot is a rejected and redundant animal; a mere driver. This is not only insulting because of its lack of truth but in fact the civil airline pilot is much nearer to being a mere driver than the Service pilot, though the distinction is so slight in degree that I would be loath to return the insult.'

This is strong stuff and *Flight* presaged Bishop's piece with a mild health warning: 'The criticisms (in places a little severe) which we print below...' Captain Brice was not only a senior BOAC captain but during the currency of the spat was installed as Master of the Guild of Air Pilots and Air Navigators of the British Empire (GAPAN) by no less a personage than HRH The Duke of Edinburgh. That didn't stop further robust debate on his article. *Flight* printed five or six articles and a couple of letters on the subject in a six-month period but none quite matched the personal passion of Squadron Leader John Bishop.

World War II was a conflict in which fewer than 3,000 RAF Battle of Britain pilots engendered the warrior's ultimate commendation from Sir Winston Churchill: 'Never before in human conflict...'. Yet here were two pilots engaged in a bad-tempered, public conflict of opinion, despite having

The CAT and the Hamsters

been fighting on the same side a mere eight years previously. What on earth — or even in the air above it — had brought about this dichotomy?

Flight set the scene in its leading article of October 30, 1953, relating to the GAPAN meeting mentioned above. 'It is no exaggeration to say that this country is going through one of the most crucial periods in its long history. The retention of the nation's position as a first-class power and one which exercises the most mature and well-balanced influence on world affairs is going to depend to an increasing extent upon the development of air power in the Royal Air Force and in British air commerce.' Also: 'Recognition of the importance of the air can be followed — on the part of the Government and the industry — by actions to place the nation, militarily and commercially, in an unassailable position during the coming decade.'

In part, the need to train sufficient pilots to meet the separate needs of the RAF and commercial aviation had been highlighted by the Wilcock Committee in 1950. Group Captain Clifford Arthur Bowman Wilcock, OBE, AFC, FRAeS, was given the task, among other things of comparing 'the standards required of aircrews and ground personnel for Service and Civil Aviation purposes and to make recommendations with a view to enabling competent personnel of all categories to be available for Civil Aviation from Service sources after as little training as possible.'

It was the start of a debate over pilot training which would rumble on until September 1960, when the College of Air Training at Hamble accepted its first cadets. Various arguments had been put forward during the ten intervening years. Some advocated that the state-owned corporations BEA and BOAC, who were by far and away the largest employers of civil pilots in the UK, should accept ex-RAF pilots. In the industry these chaps were jokingly termed 'Retreads', an epithet they later countered by calling Hamble graduates 'Hamsters'.

Notwithstanding that friendly rivalry, the demands on military and civilian pilots had become increasingly divergent as passenger traffic burgeoned and the bomber-based airliners of the early post-war years were consigned to history. Sure enough, if you'd piloted a Lancaster or Wellington during the War, then it was a cinch to fly their peacetime equivalents the York and Viking but what about the new turboprop Viscount or the pure-jet Comet?

Additionally, the RAF was facing financial and operational strictures. It

The CAT and the Hamsters

avowed that missiles were the thing of the future and the need for human pilots was diminishing. Furthermore it was phasing out its short-service commission in favour of career officers. National Service was also coming to an end so that by December 31, 1960 the last servicemen had been conscripted. Flying training was becoming increasingly expensive and the RAF's budget didn't run to providing free flying training to men whose ultimate ambition was to be a civil airline pilot. Those occurrences reinforced the opinions of a body of advocates for exclusively civilian training for commercial pilots. *Flight* said as much in a leader of January 2, 1953. This was something of a shift in position from September 28, 1951 when the leading article was calling for something more akin to a short-service commission precursor to a civilian flying career. The former view was reinforced by detailed proposals published on July 3, 1953. Their author was principal of the London School of Air Navigation Mr. I L S McNicol, whose initials alone constituted a good approach.

In truth all they had to do was to gaze across the North Sea to Rijksluchtvaartschool (government civil flying school) at Eelde airfield, near Groningen, in the north of Holland. The Dutch were the first in the world to set up a state-sponsored training facility such as this and virtually the whole of its output went direct to KLM. As the Dutch flag-carrier was the oldest airline in the world still operating under its original name, this seems apt. *Flight* was most enthusiastic about the facility in its article of May 24, 1957 and went so far as to say: 'Those who talk about this country's civil aircrew problems do not have far to look for a sensible example of airline pilot training in practice.'

Gradually the consensus was urging HM Government in favour of a national University of the Air and the intention to form the College of Air Training (CAT) was finally announced in Parliament on May 6, 1959 by Mr. John Hay, Parliamentary Secretary to the Ministry of Transport and Civil Aviation (MTCA). Air Service Training (AST) based at Hamble was to be purchased as the nucleus of the new facility, which would be jointly owned by BEA, BOAC and MTCA.

Thus the argument between Captain Brice and Squadron Leader Bishop had been settled and even though teachers at my small nursery school in southern Hampshire hadn't seen fit to draw the attention of us seven-year-

The CAT and the Hamsters

olds to the debate at the time, it would have a profound effect on the future of one of that youthful cohort. Accordingly, the objective of this book will be to briefly explore the background of those individual components mentioned by Mr Hay, before delving more deeply into how CAT functioned in practice.

To that end we can explore how Imperial Airways and its primitive approach to training and flight safety was mutated by World War II into the nationalised carriers; how the latter drew on the seemingly inexhaustible pool of ex-wartime fliers and how the realisation began to crystallise that demand might soon exceed supply. It will also be instructive to cast a fleeting glance over the airfield boundary and see how Hamble evolved from a farmer's field into the second busiest aerodrome in the country.

Chapter 1

A background to pilot training in Imperial Airways

ON AUGUST 25, 1919 a De Havilland DH4a left Hounslow Airport for Paris Le Bourget. On board was a passenger, the day's newspapers, some mail, a quantity of Devonshire cream and several brace of grouse. Certain authorities assert George Stevenson-Reece was the very first passenger on the very first international scheduled civilian flight. He arrived, alive and well, some two and a half hours later. Unfortunately the same could not be said for the grouse, which had been shot several hours before take-off.

To illustrate how auspicious undertakings have burgeoned from small beginnings it's sometimes said 'mighty oaks from little acorns grow'. Well if the flight in 1919 was the allegorical acorn, by the start of World War II civil air transport was still a small, ungulate-gnawed sapling.

Among the pioneer air transport operators prior to 1920 were Daimler Airway, Handley Page Transport Ltd, British Marine Air Navigation Co. Ltd, the Instone Airline Ltd and Aircraft Transport & Travel, who had carried out the first flight mentioned above. Their vicissitudes are well recorded elsewhere. Suffice to say there was widespread financial difficulty, exacerbated by state subsidies paid to competing foreign operators.

Some British pilots even offered to work without pay, an idea which was to be enthusiastically advocated by some latter-day airline managements but opposed by the British Airline Pilots Association (BALPA). Despite the altruistic sentiments, all scheduled services operated by privately-owned British companies had ceased by February 1921. His Majesty's Government stepped in a month later with its own piecemeal state subsidy and each of the operators mentioned previously received financial support in return for operating an assigned route.

None of this really addressed the Government's desire to support and foster air travel within the far-flung British Empire. Indeed, in 1919 an 'Advisory Committee on Civil Aviation' had recommended the establishment of 'trunk routes' to Canada, India, South Africa, Australia and New Zealand, even

The CAT and the Hamsters

Aircraft Transport and Travel (AT&T) — Airco DH.16 circa 1922 Croydon
Flight via Wikipedia

though the aircraft to operate those potential routes were not yet even a gleam in the eye of an aeronautical engineer.

What the country really needed was another committee. Step forward Sir Herbert Hambling (a good name but in no way connected to the airfield at the centre of our story — still it's a favourable omen). Sir Herbert's 'Civil Air Transport Subsidies Committee' — CATS for short and another portent — was appointed in January 1923 and recommended rationalisation of the existing air transport operators into one company.

In Parliament on July 2, 1923, the Secretary of State for Air, Sir Samuel Hoare, was asked 'if he will state the number of men trained in the art of flying with the commercial air service?'. His answer was as follows: '... whilst 704 civilian pilots' licences have been issued during the last few years, only 104 of these licences are still current...'. Although the nascent RAF had expanded markedly during the First Word War, few of its pilots saw their future in civilian skies.

However rationalisation was effected by March 1924 when Imperial Airways Ltd was brought into being and afforded an initial Government subsidy of one million pounds. It inherited 16 assorted aircraft and 250 staff, 19 of whom were pilots (Munson, 1970, p20). Things began inauspiciously with the pilots of the merged airlines refusing to fly for the terms and conditions on offer but eventually agreement was reached. As reported in *Flight* on April 3, 1924, the airline was offering a starting salary of £400 per

The CAT and the Hamsters

annum rising to £500 after five years with flying pay of one and three-eighths pennies per mile. The magazine estimated that if flying an average of two hours a day at 85 miles an hour, the emolument would be worth £355 a year.

In its editorial, *Flight* went further. 'Without wishing to take active part in the controversy, we do feel it our duty to point out that what has been accomplished in the past has been in a very large measure due to the skill, determination and loyalty of the pilots who have operated the air-liners from the days of the A.T. & T. up to the present time. Theirs was the duty to show that flying was safe, and until that fact was demonstrated, obviously, the most splendidly-organised and economically-run air service could not hope to carry on...

'Safety and regularity are still primary considerations and in the development of new routes and the extension farther afield of present lines, the question of skilled pilots will still remain one of the most important. In other words, for several years to come these pilots will still be doing pioneer work and the day when an airline pilot is nothing more than an aerial chauffeur is still a very long way off. That being so, it is essential that the scale of pay should be such as to attract the right kind of pilot, so as to ensure highest efficiency and, therefore, safety, and that he is not worried by financial considerations during the relatively short period of his flying days.'

Two years earlier, on June 19, 1922, *Hansard* recorded the then Secretary of State for Air, Captain Guest MP, giving the following answer in the House of Commons: 'The question as to whether the provision of an assistant pilot should be made compulsory is under consideration. It is a complicated question, and cannot be decided hastily; meanwhile, the carriage of passengers seated beside the pilot has been forbidden.' This necessity for a co-pilot, coupled with the new airline's policy decision in 1925 to operate mostly multi-engined aircraft imposed some financial pressure but eventually it had a beneficial impact on safety.

In line with the new policy, the airline ordered three Armstrong Whitworth Argosy aircraft, the first of which operated to Paris on July 16, 1926. Four more of the type were to be ordered within three years. Apart from the French capital, there were additional cross-Channel routes, in all totalling 1,760 air miles, but, as yet, none of them were Empire-bound. However two Short S8 Calcutta flying boats were bought around the same time as the Argosy.

The CAT and the Hamsters

Imperial Airways
— Armstrong
Whitworth Argosy
over Croydon
Brirish Airways

These would be delivered two years later, along with three more of that type, but for the moment the route network comprised a handful of European and Scandinavian cities.

Croydon was the main base for Imperial Airways and as such had a regular feature in *Flight* called 'Croydon Weekly Notes'. It employed a light gossipy style to inform readers about the iconic British airport of the inter-war years. However, many interesting insights can be gleaned from careful perusal of the excellent *Flightglobal/Archive*. For instance this snippet from June 6, 1930 about landing in limiting conditions catches the prevailing attitude and, reading it from the point of view of a modern professional pilot, it's disquieting to think that we weren't able to reproduce this performance safely until over 50 years later and that needed sophisticated Category 3b ILS and autoland-equipped aircraft.

'Sabena pilots seem to be catching all the bad weather lately. This time it was M. Cocquyt, who at 2am on Tuesday morning ran into a thick fog, which came up suddenly at Croydon, Kenley and Biggin Hill, and although he could see the lights of these three aerodromes from above, it was impossible to distinguish anything near the ground. After making several unsuccessful attempts to land amid 'salvos' of star shells, he finally adopted a clever piece of strategy—flying very low near the south-east corner of the aerodrome, where he knew there were no buildings or obstructions, he crossed Purley Way at right angles, and taking a line on the Neon ' Tee 'dropped in below the Neon Beacon, and gradually flattened out, knowing he had best part of

The CAT and the Hamsters

a mile of clear ground in front of him. His landing was perfect, but so thick was the fog, that he had to await the arrival of the aerodrome tender to show him the way to taxy to the Tarmac. A wonderful effort of piloting, but, oh! the suspense to the onlookers.

If airline managements were prepared to see this risk-taking publicised as 'a jolly good show', just imagine what pressure they put on their pilots in private to emulate the feat.

Hansard reveals that in Parliament there was much debate and searching questions were asked of the Secretary of State for Air, especially at the annual occasion of the Air Estimates. MPs were concerned about multiple issues: airships versus aeroplanes; value for money of the Imperial Airways subsidy; new air routes into the Empire; availability of civil pilots and machines to the military in the event of war; how to maintain a pool of qualified pilots for civil aviation and the RAF and was Great Britain keeping up with the French? So no change there, then.

Sir Samuel Hoare was an intrepid Air Minister, for not only did he propose an annual subsidy of £93,600 for Imperial Airways to develop a route from Croydon to Delhi but he and his wife undertook the 6,000 mile journey in early January 1927. Captain F L Barnard (the Chief Pilot) flew the first half of the route across Europe and North Africa. Thenceforth Captain Wolley-Dod followed an easterly route across Arabia, Persia and India. The aircraft involved, G-EBMX, was a newly-built, seven-seat De Havilland DH66 Hercules. To the uninitiated, in other words most of the UK population, this bore a striking visual similarity to the Argosy. According to the account Sir Samuel gave to the House of Commons, during the journey the Bristol Jupiter VI engines 'purred like three kittens'.

Despite the success of this ministerial foray, the air route was truncated at Basra until 1929 due to Persia's refusal to grant overflying rights because the Germans had secured a monopoly for flying over what is now Iran. Further officialdom still affected flights across India but by 1933 the route was up and running. During that period three of the original five Hercules had been crashed. Only the first caused fatalities but the airline still needed two more new aircraft as replacements.

Useful revenue was gained from the first Empire air mail link to India on March 30, 1929. Letters travelled by Argosy to Basle, thence by train under the Alps to Genoa (aeroplanes didn't do mountain crossings in those days). Here the postal missive was transferred to the Short Calcutta, which hopped around the Mediterranean coast to Alexandria. From there the Hercules, permanently stationed in the Middle East, carried on across the desert to Karachi. Only official passengers were permitted at this stage but 364lbs of mail, equivalent to 1,200 letters, was carried.

On the return journey the aircraft gained a passenger at Alexandria in the form of the redoubtable Sir Samuel Hoare, who had accompanied an aerial survey to the borders of Uganda and back in connection with the proposed African air route. This time he regaled his audience not with the sounds of purring kittens but with 'hippopotami snorting in the Nile'. The intention was to link London with Cape Town via Nairobi, a massive undertaking of logistics which had been initiated by the RAF as early as 1919.

On May 9, 1927 a paper had been put before the Royal Aeronautical Society by Mr. F Tymms, MC, AFRAeS. It bore the title 'Civil Aviation Prospects in East Africa' and received a rapturous endorsement by *Flight*. Its depth and attention to detail showed that plans to operate a regular commercial service down the eastern side of the continent were viable but without the initial profit potential of the Indian route.

Late in 1929 Imperial Airways captain Wolley-Dod was sent on a fact-finding mission to South Africa in the company of fellow captain Gladstone. The former Chief Pilot, Captain F L Bernard, who had flown with Wolley-Dod in the pioneering Hercules to India, had been killed in a crash only six months later on July 28, 1927 while practicing for the King's Cup Air Race.

The route to the Cape opened sector-by-sector down the Nile Valley from Cairo, calling at Khartoum, thence south to the African Great Lakes at the head of the river. Each of Britain's three East African colonies was linked by stops at Kampala, Nairobi and Dodoma in Tanganyika. The route headed southwest to Broken Hill (now known as Kabwe in Zambia) before swinging south-east towards Salisbury. Another long south-westerly flight visited various regional capitals before terminating at Cape Town.

Here again a mixture of aircraft operated the routes. Initially, the Short Calcutta flew from the Cairo hub to Mwanza on the southern edge of Lake Victoria. This was 5,114 miles from Croydon. The first service departed on February 28, 1931. Just over a year later the final link from Kisumu, on

The CAT and the Hamsters

the eastern shore of Lake Victoria, to Cape Town was inaugurated using the landplane Hercules. Passengers could leave Croydon on Saturday and be at Africa's southern tip 10 to 12 days later.

The Empire Air Mail was to play a vital part in augmenting the airline's revenues. A scheme was announced at the end of 1934 to carry any letter weighing ½ an ounce to anywhere in the Empire for the price of 1½d. Wherever possible the letters would be carried as air mail. In response to a written Parliamentary question in November of that year, the Assistant Postmaster General indicated that although there was no absolute monopoly, it was Government policy 'to utilise the services of Imperial Airways for the carriage of mails to Empire countries so far as is reasonable and practicable'. This led to the airline becoming the world's largest carrier of external air mail by 1938.

The assured revenue and need for increased capacity had naturally set in train a search for larger and more efficient aircraft. However, even in the early 1930s some British aircraft manufacturers were still refining the stick-and-string biplanes derived from the Wright Brothers' early efforts but loyalty to outmoded designs did not feature in new airliners emanating from German and American manufacturers. The policy of purchasing multi-engined aircraft had been followed on the most part but Imperial's new specification called for four engines to be used.

The thinking was that although a two- or three-engined aircraft could safely carry out a forced landing after an engine failure, a four-engined aircraft could carry on to a designated airfield or even to its destination. Simply put, because of this presumed availability of 'full-length' destination runways, designed landing speeds could be increased. This in turn could usher in the era of the monoplane. At last British aeronautical engineers could try to catch up with their foreign competitors.

Accordingly eight of the Armstrong-Whitworth AW15 Atalanta were ordered. Delivery was completed by 1933 and the aircraft were pressed into service on the African routes. They proved to be too small for the traffic load, which was good news and bad news. Good that loads were high but bad that an inadequate specification choice had been made. They were withdrawn from African service in 1937. Perhaps because of that setback, the manufacturer was asked for a bigger, better aircraft. The result was

The CAT and the Hamsters

an AW27A Ensign, more than twice as heavy with almost three times the power and hence the potential to carry up to 40 people. Unfortunately the manufacturer was necessarily concentrating on producing the AW38 Whitley bomber and the Ensign production was fostered out to a satellite production facility at Hamble. So although it's not yet time for its starring role to begin, the Hampshire airfield is already intent on edging into the footlights.

As to the Ensign, like so many foster children in literature, it was subject to conflicting inputs. For the first time but regrettably not the last, the national carrier had an undue influence on the manufacturer's design process. This led to delays and the first airliner was not delivered until early 1938. Initially it operated in Europe but was found to be underpowered. After engine upgrading improved performance somewhat, 11 were in service by the time WWII began.

Armstrong Whitworth A.W.27 Ensign Mk 1 at Hamble
Unknown

It was around that time the iconic and dependable Handley Page biplanes were retired from civilian service. The HP42 and its more powerful sister the HP45 had been delivered from November 1930 onwards. For the first time the pilot had an enclosed cockpit, a feature which must have assisted greatly with reading a large map and doing the crossword. These 10-ton, 130ft span aircraft were so sedate in the cruise (100mph) that the Dutch aircraft designer Anthony Fokker is reputed to have asserted that each Handley Page airliner came equipped with its own headwind.

Not so the pioneering Empire Class flying boats, which cruised at double that speed and established themselves as aircraft which flew into the public's

The CAT and the Hamsters

mind whenever Imperial Airways was mentioned. The Short Brothers had as much experience of aviation as anyone in Britain and had been responsible for a series of biplane seaplanes. The airline was familiar with the manufacturer's S8 'Calcutta' and also the later S17. The latter was a four-engined flying boat termed 'Kent' and it had a landplane equivalent 'Scylla'. These aircraft provided their pilots with an enclosed cockpit and some of aviation's first civilian autopilots. However in 1936, only two years after the Scylla were delivered, Shorts rolled out — or floated out, to be more accurate — the S23. With a similar span to its large biplane predecessor and only five feet longer, the monoplane astonished customers by being 26mph faster than the RAF's contemporary Bristol Bulldog frontline fighter.

Imperial Airways — Short S23 C Class Flying Boat at Hythe
British Airways

With the Empire air mail monopoly firmly in mind, Imperial Airways ordered 28 of the behemoths straight off the stocks and named them Empire or 'C' Class. From July 1936 when 'Canopus' joined the fleet, new aircraft arrived at fortnightly intervals. Their main base was at Hythe, just across the Solent from Hamble. These stately flying boats avoided the need for expensive runways and their longer range enabled them to circumnavigate trouble spots on the routes to Australia, the Far East and southern Africa. The age of intercontinental air travel had arrived but one obstacle still remained. — the Atlantic Ocean.

The 'C' Class boats were fine for the shortish sector lengths of the southerly and easterly routes but the western ocean was a no-holds-

The CAT and the Hamsters

barred 2,000 mile sea crossing, even between Shannon and Gander. Several ploys were tried: an uneconomic payload and extra fuel tankage; in-flight refuelling and even piggybacking a smaller aircraft on a large one and air-launching it when well out over 'The Pond'. None really answered the question before global events, in the shape of World War II, overtook the scenario.

Before that momentous event, in the smaller pond that was the domestic and European market, Imperial Airways had been somewhat innovative and had also set high standards of service and reliability. Yet it's possible to hold the view that these services closer to home were the poor relations in the mind of the airline's management. Lacking the glamour of far-flung destinations and competing with subsidised continental competitors, perhaps the shorthaul routes were where the company took its eye off the ball. As so often happens in commerce, another business saw an opportunity to be exploited.

British Airways Ltd coalesced into being during the early part of 1936. They had no connection with the modern BA but did use smaller, more nimble aircraft to operate European services in competition with Imperial Airways. This aggressive policy culminated in the Government-sanctioned, purchase of 10 Lockheed Electras. These modern American monoplanes knocked spots off Imperial's pedestrian biplanes by almost halving sector times on the prestigious London to Paris route and to add insult to injury, the new airline only charged 85 per cent of the larger airline's fare. Questions were asked in the House.

What the country really needed was another committee.

Step forward Lord Cadman, who, in November 1937, proposed that two British airlines should not compete with one another on any route. Accordingly, although Imperial Airways could continue to concentrate on its longhaul routes, it should also work closely with British Airways on the shorthaul sectors.

However, there was a sub-plot providing impetus for Cadman's report. That was the issue of Imperial Airways safety record, and the airline's unwillingness to invest money in modern developments which would assist its pilots in carrying out safe all-weather operations. Airframe and engine de-icing systems were available but not fitted to the airline's trans-European

The CAT and the Hamsters

aircraft. Likewise back-up wireless sets, which added to weight and expense, were also absent. Full panel instruments for flying in non-visual conditions were still not standard. Under these circumstances pilot dissatisfaction re-emerged, particularly in respect of Major George Woods-Humphrey.

Having been an ex-Royal Flying Corps pilot and involved with the management of two of Imperial's precursors, Woods-Humphrey was seen as something of a martinet by the pilots. He was pivotal if not causal in the strike at the very beginning of the airline in 1924 and was the focus of pilot disquiet. Nevertheless, the board of the company kept him on as General Manager but appointed the respected Herbert Brackley as Air Superintendent, as a concession to the aggrieved pilots.

Later on, when giving a lecture to the Royal Aeronautical Society, Major Brackley said that it had been thought that the business life of a commercial pilot would be comparatively short but experience was causing this view to be modified: there were already captains in Imperial Airways with more than 10,000 flying hours and whose physical condition suggested that they were fit to continue for many years to come. Indeed, in 1936 eight of Imperial's original captains were still flying with the company after 12 years. Aged between 37 and 44, their total hours were between 8,000 and 12,000.

Both of these managers and the newly-formed Guild of Air Pilots and Navigators (GAPAN) were to have a defining influence on the training and standards of conduct for the nascent air transport pilot's profession.

This is a direct quotation from the GAPAN website, accessed on January 19, 2012: 'Before the Guild was established in 1929, the future status of air pilots and air navigators was very much in doubt. The small group of commercial pilots who formed the Guild were virtually responsible for ensuring that their successors enjoyed a professional status and one of the Guild's objectives has been to foster and improve that standing.'

GAPAN began on February 1 with 50 members, 26 of them from Imperial Airways. One month later the Air Ministry issued Air Navigation Directions (A\D7A) laying out conditions of experience for upgrading the commercial 'B' licence to a Master Pilot Certificate (the 'A' licence was the private pilot's licence of its day and the 'B' the commercial). At that time Britain had only 19 commercial aircraft and a mere 35 pilots with navigators' certificates endorsing their 'B' licence. The USA and Germany both possessed more than 10 times that number of aircraft.

There is an interesting insight into the Imperial Airways management thinking concerning pilot training and selection in a letter from Brackley to Woods-Humphrey on May 6, 1930.

● He felt that pilots should have a forum where they could input their views on the selection of new aircraft.

● He wanted to monitor technical development which could enhance safety and regularity of the airline's services.

● With regard to night flying, he wanted to instigate training and maintenance of currency of experience.

● He was also concerned to oversee standards of facilities at the company's landing grounds.

To the modern aviator these seem to be worthwhile and prudent points but he expands on training and selection thus:

● All pilot applicants should be carefully considered and an efficient personal record maintained after joining the organisation.

● They should have experience of most of the following: multi-engined operation; night flying; cross-country navigation; familiarity with several commercial types; flying-boat procedures; 1,000 hours in command.

● In addition be in possession of the 'B' licence and second-class navigator's certificate. Be of steady and sober habit without the responsibilities of a large family.

These are exacting requirements for male pilot applicants (and it was only men who were considered) given that commercial aviation had been in operation for little more than a decade. Imperial had no training scheme of its own and expected to import pretty much the finished article. That degree of experience would most likely be found in ex-RAF pilots and Brackley urged that close contact be kept with the Air Ministry to get advanced notice of suitable candidates who might be approaching the end of their service career.

Even so the new entrant pilot was hired on sufferance.

● Aptitude would be tested by the Air Superintendant or the Chief Pilot. Only then would introductory ground school lectures be given on aspects of airline operations.

The CAT and the Hamsters

● For the first month, flying would be undertaken as co-pilot to an experienced captain, who would write reports on performance and this would naturally limit flights to aircraft fitted with dual controls.

● If that probationary period was satisfactory there would be further lectures on pilot's direct responsibilities, traffic and engineering, company policy, international legislation, and rules and regulations at foreign aerodromes.

● This would take about a month and be followed by an exam.Successful pilots would then get a further month of intensive co-pilot flying experience. Only then could command be offered on short sectors within Europe and preferably on cargo-only flights.

● After completing a further three months of this, the probationary, prebendary pilot could be offered a job. To continue with the ecclesiastical analogy, it must have felt a bit like canonisation!

It's remarkable to note that no mention is made of type conversion, instrument flying (although night flying would have necessitated at least basic skills in this art), or route experience. In retrospect, the aircraft types available were all fairly basic machines with manually-operated flying controls and a limited range of engine styles. Autopilots were in their infancy and the modern 'T' shaped arrangement of essential instruments was not introduced in the RAF until 1937 and even later in transport aircraft. Even enclosed cockpits were a relatively recent innovation.

Parliament saw the first stirrings of a civilian-based training system on April 27, 1936 when Captain Harold Balfour MP asked the Under-Secretary of State for Air: 'What is the average time which elapses between the first application by a civil pilot for a 'B' licence and the granting of such licence.' In addition he wanted to know 'whether he (the Minister) will consider the desirability of freeing civil commercial air pilots, applying for a 'B' licence, from having to attend at the Royal Air Force service station, Hendon, for general flying and cross-country flying examination tests and whether he will consider the advantages of having a civil test system for civil transport pilots divorced from Royal Air Force work?'

Sir Philip Sassoon replied: 'The average time taken to obtain a licence where the practical tests have to be completed is from two to three months from the date of first application. This period may be exceeded as result of

The CAT and the Hamsters

weather conditions and of having to wait for a suitably dark night for the night flying test. It is agreed that the present system calls for review, particularly on the point whether the flying tests should continue to be conducted at Hendon. This is already under consideration.'

Certainly, if examination is made of the airline's crash record, it is obvious that something was amiss throughout this period. In 1929 the Handley Page W10 G-EBMT crashed in the English Channel. Seat belts were not fitted but probably would have reduced the death toll. At first, contemporary reports in *Flight* were at pains to stress that prior to the accident some 3,800,000 miles had been flown in the four years since 1925 without a fatal accident.

The same magazine also noted, in a separate issue, that it was not editorial policy to cover air crashes. That might be considered evidence that an undercurrent of collusion was abroad, so as not to unduly alarm the public, but with the third fatal accident of the year questions began to be asked, beginning with an editorial on November 1, 1929.

However, by February 21, 1935 the magazine was saying: 'That far too long a period still intervenes between the occurrence of an accident and the issuing of a report on it.' Concern was also beginning to surface in higher quarters. In the House of Commons on March 18, 1936, Mr. C Wilson asked the Under Secretary of State for Air: 'Whether he can state the number of lives lost through accidents to aircraft during each of the last five years?'

Sir Philip Sassoon answered: 'The lives lost through accidents to United Kingdom civil aircraft during each of the years 1931 to 1935 are as shown below. (These figures include accidents abroad in the case of air transport services operated from this country.)1931 = 24; 1932 = 20; 1933 = 38; 1934 = 43; 1935 = 47.'

Fire extinguishers, seatbelts, de-icing equipment and blind flying instrumentation were not made mandatory until after the 1937 accident to the Short 23 'C' Class G-ADVC in Phaleron Bay but by the late autumn the Under Secretary had decided to inaugurate the Cadman Committee. The seatbelts paid dividends on May 5, 1939 when G-AAXC encountered turbulence which caused injuries to the crew. The legendary Captain O P Jones was launched out of his seat into the cockpit headlining where he made another deep impression. None of the strapped in passengers was injured.

The CAT and the Hamsters

Imperial Airways pilots had been inexorably bound up in these events, often finding that the demands the company made on their professionalism and innate skill were not made easier by the equipment the company provided. All too often the pilots felt that they were pressured to operate in exacting conditions in primitive aircraft and their reward for getting it wrong was the sack or a one-way sector to the big crew room in the sky.

A mass meeting of pilots on June 27, 1937 led to the formation of the British Airline Pilots Association (BALPA). *Flight* briefly outlined the objectives of the Association on October 14, 1937.

● To maintain the status of the transport pilot's profession and to protect individual members from any possibility of unfair treatment.

● To ensure that such pilots have some say in the choice and equipment of the machines which they are expected to fly.

● To correlate the opinions of pilots on such matters as flying pay and to see that an equitable arrangement is reached.

● To operate its own pension scheme.

The Cadman report was duly published on February 8, 1938 and it raised Government eyebrows by suggesting an immediate doubling of the £1.5million subsidy. It also pointed to the futility of subsidising two operators who were in competition on the same route. In an exercise of stating the obvious, it pointed out the paucity of British-manufactured medium-sized airliners. Nor did Imperial Airways management escape unscathed. Adjectives such as defective, intolerant and unyielding peppered the narrative. The company were also cited for conceding 'uncontested monopoly' to the Americans in the Pacific and West Indies and utilising obsolete aircraft on the Empire routes.

Even their most modern type, the 'Empire' flying-boat, was experiencing a torrid time. Between its introduction in the autumn of 1936 and mid-summer 1939 no less than eight had either been destroyed or severely damaged in flying accidents. In its issue of July 6, 1939, *Flight* reported that captains Horsey and Bailey had been taken off the line in order to take charge of flying instruction of the company's pilots and crews. Horsey was to be at Croydon and Bailey at Hythe. Crews, mainly from the East, who had been flying Hannibal and Atalanta types, were to be trained on Ensigns at Croydon. The

The CAT and the Hamsters

correspondent trumpeted 'this is quite probably the beginning of something big in British Civil Aviation; it may even develop, in years to come, into a sort of commercial Cranwell'.

Captains Horsey and Bailey were the first two commercial pilots in Great Britain to obtain commercial tickets for marine aircraft and they both went to Imperial in 1924 from the British Marine Navigation Company. Each had more than 10,000 hours of flying experience.

As a consequence of the report, the Government announced the formation of a single, state-subsidised airline, British Overseas Airways Corporation (BOAC). Changes to the management structure of the moribund Imperial Airways resulted in the appointment of the ex-BBC supremo Sir John Reith, and the departure of the controversial Woods-Humphrey. The editor of *The Aeroplane* magazine, C G Grey, spoke up in favour of the latter and tried to apportion the blame towards Sir Eric Geddes, the airline's chairman.

Despite the hiatus in the management structure, existing schedules were operated and pioneering flights made to America utilising the Short–Mayo composite (the piggyback solution). In addition, the Far Eastern and Pacific route structures were cemented and on May 19, 1939 Imperial Airways placed an advertisement in *The Times* listing their long-haul destinations.

In line with the Cadman report, the upstart British Airways began to handle the short-haul destinations within Europe and the UK.

Nationalisation bills had passed through Parliament and BOAC was scheduled to come into existence on April 1, 1940 but the dark clouds of war enveloped the company before it could begin peacetime operations. All civil aviation was suspended at war's outbreak but BOAC operated in a quasi-military role until the end of hostilities.

DESTINATION	DURATION	FREQUENCY
Egypt	28 hours	6 services a week
East Africa	3 days	3 services a week
West Africa	4.5 days	1 service a week
South Africa	5 days	2 services a week
Malaya	5.5 days	3 services a week
Hong Kong	6 days	2 services a week
India	3 days	5 services a week
Australia	10 days	3 services a week

The CAT and the Hamsters

It could be said that the start of World War II brought about the demise of Imperial Airways, just as the end of World War I had led to its birthing pains but there was more to it than the military conflicts.

The airline had done sterling pioneering work but it had been hamstrung by mismanagement and poor staff relations allied to lack of direction and financial backing by HM Government, leading to unsuitable aircraft procurement.

By modern standards the airline's safety record was appalling. Of 169 hulls employed by the company more than one third were crashed or involved in incidents which severely damaged them. Luckily, perhaps due to low airspeeds and light passenger loads, the death toll of these five dozen incidents was 'only' 109 souls. Pilot training and procurement had undoubtedly progressed but in the impending and more exacting post-War era there was much room for improvement.

The CAT and the Hamsters

Chapter 2

A background to pilot training in BEA and BOAC

FOR Britain's airlines, World War II started on September 1, 1939 with the Air Navigation (Restriction in Time of War) Order 1939 but the official declaration of war, by Neville Chamberlin, came two days later. All scheduled services to Europe were suspended and some aircraft were flown to Exeter to operate National Air Communications flights on behalf of the Government. There was a desultory trickle of flights to the Continent but the German advances snuffed these out and also led to the loss of two Short S30s and two Armstrong Whitworth AW27s. No passengers were hurt but the wartime attrition of Imperial's fleet had begun even before BOAC took over officially on April 1, 1940.

The new nationalised carrier operated the rump of the Empire services but the entry into the conflict by Italy and eventually Japan effectively re-drew the map of the world's air routes. During hostilities BOAC operated a variety of unarmed aircraft. Initially the flying boats emanated from Lisbon to West Africa and thence via the Cape to Ceylon and Australia. Although Sweden remained neutral, it supplied Britain with vital ball bearings. The

Imperial Airways
— Short Empire
Class - Cavalier
at Bermuda circa
WW2
Tyrell family

The CAT and the Hamsters

airline flew more than 1,200 times between Leuchars and Stockholm in an eclectic collection of aircraft, including DH98 Mosquitos and Armstrong Whitworth AW38 Whitleys. However the most significant of its wartime exploits was the taming of the North Atlantic.

A service to return ferry pilots to the USA was started in May 1941 using Consolidated LB-30A Liberators. With its 2,100 mile range, the aircraft was just what the airline needed to gain invaluable experience for the post-war years. Three Boeing 314A 'Clipper' flying boats were also purchased at £259,000 each. This leviathan had a 3,500-mile range and could lift double the weight of the pre-war 'Empire' Class. It operated the Foynes to Lagos sector of the so-called 'Horseshoe Route' to the Antipodes. The Boeing was also used on the North Atlantic.

At the outset of the conflict, the Secretary of State for Air had officially pinned BOAC and its assets to the war effort. Now on October 16, 1943 the airline assumed responsibility for the general administration of the Air Transport Auxiliary. Male pilots who were not fit for operational service and female pilots, who were not allowed to fight, contributed greatly to the war effort by positioning military aircraft around the British Isles.

These might be new aircraft which needed delivery to their squadron, or damaged operational aircraft which needed to visit the repair shops. In all, 650 pilots delivered 147 types of aircraft during the war and Hamble was one of the 22 ferry pool airfields used by the ATA. The idea had originated with the pre-war competitor to Imperial: British Airways — and by the War's end 308,567 aircraft had been ferried by ATA pilots. Sad to say, 173 died carrying out this vital function.

By early 1943 Britain was allowing itself the luxury of gazing into what Winston Churchill had called three years earlier the 'broad sunlit uplands' of a future peace. Late in the previous year Parliament set up the Brabazon Committee to consider 'what new types of civil aircraft were required for the post-war period and what types of military aircraft could suitably be converted to meet civil needs when the war came to an end'.

Another straw in the wind was seen in *Flight* when a military pilot enquired how he might qualify as his civilian equivalent after the War. Mr T R Thomas of the Air Registration Board replied as follows: 'He should consult the Statutory Rules and Orders and Air Navigation

The CAT and the Hamsters

Directions. He will find all the information he requires in the latter and if he can pass the medical examination, details of which are given in paragraph 94, he should make application to the Secretary of State for Air, 25, Julian Road, Bristol, for an application form. He will find that a Royal Air Force pilot may be exempted from the practical flying tests but must pass the technical examination.

'Particulars of this are given in the second part of paragraph 99. The issue of these licences is not a particular interest of the Board; except that it carries out part of the technical examination on behalf of the Secretary of State, but I would like to take this opportunity of assuring your correspondent, and other pilots and engineers in the Services, that considerable thought is being given to ensuring that they will be able to use the knowledge and experience gained in the Royal Air Force to help them to qualify for work in civil aviation after the war.'

After a titanic and bloody struggle, the conflict finally came to a close with the surrender of Japan on August 15, 1945. Having been instrumental in winning the War, Churchill then lost the election and a new Labour Government announced its plans for post-war air services.

These would be provided by three state corporations: BOAC, which would continue to operate routes to the Empire, Far East and North America; British European Airways (BEA), which would operate services to Europe and within the United Kingdom and British South American Airways (BSAA) to operate new services to South American and Caribbean destinations.

The corporations started operating with an eclectic mix of aircraft and in its 'Statement of Accounts for 1946/47', BOAC revealed: 'At the beginning of the year the fleet strength was 207 and the main operating fleet comprised nine different types' and added 'with the exception of the Constellations, the majority of aircraft were obsolescent and nearly all military conversions. They were of relatively small capacity, needing a large number of aircrews, and with the limitations imposed by the length of stages on the Corporation's routes payloads were small in contrast with operating costs'.

The Lockheed Constellation was BOAC's first four-engined, American, land-based airliner and the company made an initial order for five. Bi-weekly transatlantic flights began on July 1, 1946. BEA had begun under its own auspices six months earlier, again with a mix of

The CAT and the Hamsters

pre-war British twins and some ex-military Douglas DC-3s. Even when the Vickers Viking entered service in the autumn it was still a development of the Wellington wartime bomber.

Consequently, with the RAF contracting and most of the airline types in service being ex-military, the corporations had a plethora of experienced pilots to choose from. In 1945 the RAF and BOAC jointly formed a four-engine flying school at Ossington, with a radio navigation and twin-engine flying school at Whitchurch (Bristol). However in May 1946 all facilities were amalgamated and moved to Aldermaston in Berkshire. A retrospective *Flight* article of April 15, 1948 stated: 'Accommodation was scarce, and the intensive flying programme caused some congestion but 1,066 ex-RAF pilots were passed out on Dakotas, Yorks, Vikings, Haltons and Oxfords in 18 months.'

Keeping to the time-honoured principle that the number of landings in the log book of a careful pilot should always equal the number of take-offs, the magazine also reported: 'During this time 16,164 hours were flown, which involved 29,543 landings and as many take-offs, with only one damaged undercarriage.' Other training covered: 561 first and second-class navigation licences; 493 R/T licences and 112 aircrew were given radar courses. Apparently 'at some periods during that intensive 18 months, there were 500 pupils at the school at one time'.

It's hardly surprising that this intensive scheme soon began to fulfil the operational requirements of the airlines. Nevertheless, on April 30, 1947 they formed a new company, Airways Training Ltd, to deal with the training of air and ground crews. The facilities of the school would also be available to all other civil air transport operators. It was acknowledged that basic training could be centralised up to a point but advanced training would be undertaken 'on the line'. Despite these developments there were still concerns within the industry about a future pilot shortage.

What the country needed was another committee!

This time it was chaired by Group Captain Wilcock, MP, who gave his name to the working group.

Flight had written a leader on July 31, 1947 when the committee was announced saying: 'Recruiting and training of personnel for civil aviation will assume increasing importance. One phrase in the terms of reference of

The CAT and the Hamsters

RAF Aldermaston on August 19,1943 — 3 years later civil pilots were being trained there.
USAF via Wikipedia

the Wilcock committee is significant: "To compare the standards required of aircrews and ground personnel for Service and Civil Aviation purposes, and to make recommendations with a view to enabling competent personnel of all categories to be available for Civil Aviation from Service sources after as little training as possible".

'If the Royal Air Force were a large and expanding Service, the theory behind that phrase would be sound but as things are, and with the uncertainty of how the RAF will develop during the next few years, it appears to us unwise in the extreme to rely upon a flow of Service personnel into civil aviation. The two branches are tending farther and farther apart, and surely the time has come when civil aviation should cease to depend upon military aviation in this respect.'

However by April 1948 another *Flight* editorial was reproving the concept of a training school at Aldermaston that took pupils from the wider pool: 'It has now been found that the requirements of the corporations have been met, and that they have almost enough fully-trained personnel for present needs.'

The CAT and the Hamsters

It continued: 'There is no reason to doubt that the courses will be good ones. What is doubtful is the principle of State-owned monopolistic corporations entering into direct competition with private enterprise.' In particular AST at Hamble was mentioned, as was Straight Aviation Training and the London School of Air Navigation.

Flight's main area of concern seemed to be potentially unfair competition but it was worrying unnecessarily, for within seven months the newly-formed establishment was being closed down. Apparently, the response had proved unsatisfactory and in the interests of economy the corporations decided to shut up shop and carry on with training at their own bases. Within two years the site was to be taken over by the Ministry of Supply, who had a much more glowing future in mind: the Atomic Weapons Research Establishment (AWRE).

Even when the Wilcock report was published in the summer of 1949 its findings were somewhat diaphanous. However it did highlight how very expensive it was to learn to become a pilot from scratch, especially to a standard acceptable to the corporations. Wilcock estimated the cost at £1,200 to 1,500 (on October 16, 1947 an industrial court had recommended a salary scale of £600 to £1,650 per annum for corporation pilots). The group captain also predicted future pilot shortages in the period during the early to mid-1950s and recommended state sponsorship of cadets to ameliorate the problem. The Minister of Civil Aviation did not agree with some of the findings, especially state sponsorship and prescient souls were already beginning to question the wisdom of closing Aldermaston.

Late in 1947 the Government had announced that a limited number of National Service pilots, called up to the RAF, would be accepted for pilot training. The entry would be restricted to cadets holding the Air Training Corps (ATC) Proficiency Certificate and who had obtained the School Certificate. After training, and on completing their period of whole-time national service, they would be required to enlist in one of the Air Force non-regular forces for a period of reserve service.

Then on January 29, 1948 *Flight* reported Minister of Civil Aviation Lord Nathan stating in the House of Lords that during the last year, aircrew training had cost BOAC £1,095,000 and BEAC £590,500. In their next annual report BOAC confirmed that sequence of events:

The CAT and the Hamsters

'Some of those RAF pilots who had been seconded to the airline during the war returned to peacetime occupations, whilst others were unsuitable for employment, owing to age or for other reasons. Thus fresh aircrew had to be recruited and trained. In March, 1946, a Central Training School was opened at Aldermaston, and a total of 847 aircrew were trained during the year.'

These were confused and confusing messages for the British taxpayer. Apparently the Government didn't want to fund or sponsor training of civilian pilots for the state airlines and the same airlines didn't want to run a dedicated school training pilots for themselves or other people. Aircrew training was a major factor in the substantial losses made by the airlines and these losses would only increase if predicted shortages affected operational efficiency. In that case the Government would be forced to cover the losses from state funds. It was the familiar story of piecemeal, make-do-and-mend governance with no-one taking a lead or looking at the big picture.

Other Government activity also affected civil aviation in post-war Britain. Firstly, new classes of licensing for pilots and aircrews were introduced in April 1949, giving effect to the country's obligations under the International Civil Aviation Organisation (ICAO). The principal change was the replacement of the commercial pilot's old 'B' licence by a graduated system of three commercial licence categories. They bestowed privileges which related more closely to the flying experience of the licence holder. The licences were, in ascending order: commercial (CPL); senior commercial (SCPL) and airline transport pilot (ATPL). In simple terms the holder of an ATPL was deemed fit to fly any size and weight of aircraft in command, while the CPL permitted only command of aircraft less than 12,500 lbs in weight (effectively a light twin). In addition to the basic licences, endorsements were required for each commercial type flown and an instrument rating (IR) was needed to fly in controlled airspace. Regulation was beginning to exert its constraining influence on the erstwhile, blithe spirit of pre-war airline operations.

Post-war aircraft were also becoming more complex, in turn demanding more of pilots and aerodrome facilities. Some of this development was a direct result of the Brabazon Committee. That had been formed on December 23, 1942 under John Moore-Brabazon, (Lord Brabazon of Tara) to investigate the future needs of the British Empire's civilian airliner market.

The CAT and the Hamsters

The committee identified five categories of potential development. The first category (type I) was the Bristol Brabazon. Here again the state airline tail was allowed to wag the aircraft industry dog and the mammoth eight-engined airliner was designed to satisfy BOAC's specific requirements. In the event it ended up satisfying no airline's requirements and was a spectacular flop. BSAA and later BOAC were in receipt of the four-engined Avro Tudor. It too suffered from meddling at the design stage and was delivered late (nothing had been learned from the AW Ensign). Thus the type III requirement was not a success. Nor was the type Va but the type Vb became the delightful De Havilland Dove and Heron feeder-liners. Limited success accrued to the type II, Airspeed Ambassador, which was ordered and operated by BEA. The same airline was overjoyed with the type IIb Vickers Viscount and the

Ex-BOAC Avro 689 Tudor 2. Now Air Charter — Stanstead April 10, 1955.
RuthAS - own work. Licensed under CC BY 3.0 via Wikimedia Commons

aircraft went on to be one of the most successful all-British airliners. Last but not least was the hubristic De Havilland Comet I. BOAC and the British aircraft industry had a global, five-year, technical lead before metal fatigue tore the world's first jet airliner and British hopes into small pieces.

In autumn 1950 the Ministry of Civil Aviation issued its second biennial report on British civil aviation in the post-war period. The 100-page booklet, entitled *Civil Aviation, 1948-49* contained a comprehensive review of all aspects of the Ministry's work. It confirms much of what has been stated above.

'At the end of 1949, BOAC had 11 Constellations, 22 Argonauts and

The CAT and the Hamsters

five Stratocruisers (five more Stratocruisers followed in the early months of 1950). Solents, introduced in April 1948, are now being progressively replaced by Hermes. BEA continued to operate a fleet of Vikings, Dakotas and Rapides, but by the end of 1949 the long-term types conceived by the Brabazon Committee were coming into sight. An order was placed for 28 Ambassadors in 1948 and subsequently a number of Viscounts have been ordered. Comets and Bristol 175s (Britannia) will supply the future needs of BOAC, while 25 Hermes IVs will be used as 'interim' aircraft.'

This new equipment would bring its own influences to bear on the cockpit environment. The crowded 'office' of the four-engined bomber and its civilian offspring was likely to become a thing of the past. Modern VHF radio telephony, radio-based navigation aids and up-to-date systems panels were foreshadowing the demise of the dedicated navigator, radio operator and flight engineer. It was already possible to see that in the future, pilots would do the R/T and navigation, especially on short-haul sectors.

It was slightly surprising then that the long-haul carrier (BOAC) made the first move. They offered a scheme to their 200 or so navigators, which would allow suitable candidates to retrain as pilots. The thinking was that although navigators would slowly be phased out, it would be profligate to lose all their accumulated flight time and route experience. In addition it would produce a ready supply of new pilots for the right-hand seat during a period of paucity.

Originally 117 navigators applied to take part in the scheme and, of those, ten were rejected because of their age. A further 28 subsequently dropped out for family reasons or because of unsatisfactory progress in early flying lessons, leaving 79 in the scheme. The rump of 112 navigators would retain their original positions for the foreseeable future. Training was expected to take about 18 months and the airline agreed a form of financial sponsorship. The majority of the neophyte pilots would become available to the corporation during 1952 when it expected to need their services. Early graduates might be transferred to BEA, whose need was likely to be urgent in the spring of 1951.

That proved to be the case and BEA was forced to not only wet-lease capacity from BOAC to operate the London to Nice service but it also put in place a new pilot training regimen. Instead of the previously stringent requirements on recruiting only previously-qualified pilots, BEA began

The CAT and the Hamsters

recruiting men without valid licences. Some, but not all, had considerable previous flying experience. Under the new scheme the corporation bore the initial cost of obtaining the necessary licences and the employee repaid the money in instalments from his salary, which was between £500 and £700 pa during the cadetship.

At the beginning of 1951 the airline employed about 470 pilots but it deduced a requirement for 616 by the year's end. This was met but wastage during the previous two years had been approximately 30. Even though 132 pilots were recruited during the year, this number was six per cent less than 1950. Twenty-eight training captains were needed for the new pilots and also to deal with the normal routine of command courses, conversion courses and routine six-monthly proficiency checks. They served alternate six-month periods 'on-the-line' and with training flight. Flying training was concentrated at Blackbushe but synthetic training and some of the ground subjects were dealt with at Northolt.

Synthetic training was a relatively new concept in the 1950s and is

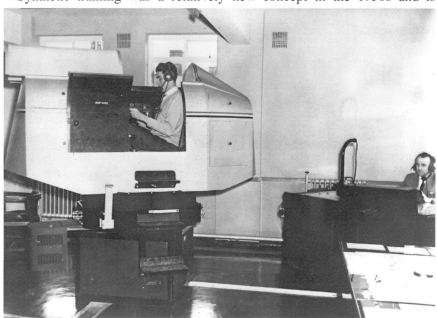

Link trainer at Hamble with the cockpit hood open   *Hamble pictures BOAC*

The CAT and the Hamsters

nowadays referred to as simulator training. The rather quaint pre-war term came into use in the late Thirties, with the American-designed Link Trainer. Referred to by generations of tortured pilots as 'the sweat-box' this ingenious machine helped to teach the skill of 'blind flying'. Fixed firmly to the ground, this synthetic, generic cockpit was coaxed around an imaginary sky by a pupil with reference to the trainer's flying-instruments panel.

By the early 1950s BOAC had purchased a much more sophisticated, type-specific trainer for their Boeing Stratocruiser fleet. The British firm Redifon supplied the airline with a modified version of a Curtis-Wright product for about £100,000. It relied on electro-mechanical wizardry to accurately replicate the performance of the real aeroplane.

Pilots reading this will be depressed to learn that an instructors 'trouble panel' was fitted as standard. This, in now time-honoured tradition, allowed the introduction of faults and failures just when the trainee thought that it was all going so well. Approximately 16 periods of two hours each were anticipated as part of a type conversion onto the 'Strat'. The 'flight-simulator' had arrived and could only get more Machiavellian as computers became more powerful.

Aldermaston's closure led to considerable diversification of the corporation's training efforts. That BSAA had been absorbed into BOAC didn't preclude the use of at least half-a-dozen airfields for line and conversion training. Whitchurch, Blackbush, Cranfield, Southampton, Shannon and Hurn were all used at one time or another. However there was no dedicated training school to foster a new generation of pilots in readiness to command the new generation of corporation aircraft arriving in the 1960s: Trident; Tristar; VC10; Vanguard and Britannia as well as the Boeing 707 and 747.

Early in 1950 the Ministry of Civil Aviation approved a new CPL course given at Air Service Training, Hamble. Students completing the whole of the curriculum at AST could be granted licences on a basis of 150 hours flying instead of the normal 200 hours. It was the first Ministry-approved course for a would-be commercial pilot. In the following year the MCA went further by announcing that ex-National Service pilots would be encouraged to convert their RAF hours into a CPL, with the hope that the airlines would sponsor their further training to SCPL and IR standard.

None of this satisfied *Flight* magazine, which was beginning to become

The CAT and the Hamsters

exercised on the topic of a civil pilot shortage and in a leader on October 28, 1951 called for an integrated scheme. In this system a young man would join the military for a short period after his schooling finished and learn to fly. Then in his late 20s he would convert to civilian licences and finish his pensionable career with the airlines. It was neat enough, as long as the needs of the RAF and Fleet Air Arm ensured a surplus of ready-trained candidates for civvy street. Sure enough, just over a year later, the magazine had begun to have its doubts: 'But this remedy may not in any case be a lasting one, because of the already foreseeable changes in the RAF's aircrew structure and requirements; even today the Service will naturally seek to retain the cream and release only pilots of average or mediocre ability. This is not an encouraging thought for civil operators.'

Step forward Mr I L S McNichol. He was the principal of the London School of Air Navigation in 1953. It was his opinion that civil aviation could not continue to rely on a supply of Service-trained pilots and anyway the divergence between a Service and a civil flying career was growing wider.

He also thought that what the country needed was another committee.

The Minister of Transport and Civil Aviation (MTCA) would be its ex-officio chairman and membership of the committee might be as follows: one representative from each of the two airways corporations; one representative of the independent operators (through BIATA); a spokesman for each of the professional bodies (GAPAN and BALPA); a delegate from the civil training organisations and a representative from each side of the House of Commons (helping to ensure that the policy would stand in the event of a change of government).

McNichol proposed that applicants should have demonstrated previous commitment to aviation by being in possession of a PPL and that, if selected, they would be state-sponsored. However the cadets would be expected to repay their £1,500 to £2,000 training costs once in gainful employment. Although parts of the course would be carried out at diverse locations (one being the London School of Air Navigation perhaps) cadets would all leave with a CPL and IR to become junior airline officers. It wasn't a bad template and had the virtue of utilising many facilities already in existence but the initial £200 to obtain a PPL might prove a stumbling block for some young men. This led to a robust debate concerning the origins and hence financing

The CAT and the Hamsters

De Haviland Trident at Farnborough on September 8 1962. G-ARPC was the third production aircraft. The first Trident flew on January 9 1962
Trident 62 by TSRL — own work. Licensed under CC BY-SA 3.0 via Wikimedia Commons

of future *ab-initio* civil pilot training. It was foreseen that between 70 and 120 new pilots would be needed annually and these could be supplied from an initial intake of 400 young men, a horrifying attrition rate of between 70 and 82.5 percent. All this might cost in the order of £250,000 a year. This much was set down in a memorandum of June 16, 1954, presented to the Minister of Transport and Civil Aviation, Mr. A T Lennox-Boyd by Air Marshal Sir Guy Garrod, chairman of the Air League of the British Empire. The document's clarion call — 'It is now urgently necessary to place the recruitment of pilots for civil aviation upon a firm and permanent basis' — was the result of several months' study by a working party representing the most important bodies in British civil aviation. Those bodies, fully supportive of the proposals, were the Air League; Airwork, Ltd.; BEA; BIATA; BOAC; BALPA and GAPAN.

By March 1959 *Flight* asserted that no less than five proposals had been turned down by the Government. In response, Mr. John Hay, Joint Parliamentary Secretary to the MTCA said: 'The Government do not wish to sponsor training under a State contract.' France and Holland both had national flying schools which fed trained pilots into their state airlines and such a scheme could be realised in the UK by setting up a board of directors, the members of which would be senior executives of BOAC, BEA and the

The CAT and the Hamsters

British Independent Air Transport Association, and on which the Ministry of Transport and Civil Aviation would be represented.

Flight reported cagily that training for a commercial pilot's licence and instrument rating at a British national school could be accompanied by additional training of both a character-building and professional nature and that the course would take two years and would cost about £5,500. The periodical continued: 'How such a sum would be found, or how support for the scheme would be apportioned, is not yet clear but it may be that each student would be aided by a specific grant from the Ministry of Education and by the award of various scholarships. Air Service Training at Hamble has been mentioned in connection with the scheme (it is also the school chosen by General Air Training) but since contract arrangements are viewed with disfavour by the MTCA, it seems that a fairly drastic reorganization of AST might be involved before a national school could be established. Reports that AST might be taken over by a BOAC-BEA board have neither been confirmed nor denied. Although the details remain to be decided—they may, in fact, not be finalised for some considerable time.'

This caginess and the denials by a Government minister were good signs. No visible, particulate-emissions without conflagration, as the old adage puts it. Sure enough, on May 6, 1959 the same John Hay made a statement to Parliament. It is reproduced here in full from Hansard Author's bullet points: HC Deb 06 May 1959 vol. 605 cc388-9

● *The college, to be called The College of Air Training, Hamble, will open in the autumn of 1960 at Hamble aerodrome using facilities at present owned by Air Service Training Ltd.*

● *The facilities are to be purchased on behalf of the Board by the Airways Corporations at a price already agreed.*

● *The college will be administered by a Board of Governors embodied under a Trust Deed and nominated by the Chairmen of the Airways Corporations and the Minister of Transport and Civil Aviation. The British Independent Air Transport Association has agreed in principle to participation in the scheme.*

● *It is proposed that the Board of Governors will be composed of the following members: one from the Ministry of Transport and Civil Aviation, one from the Ministry of Education, one representative expert on educational administration, three from British Overseas Airways Corporation, three from*

The CAT and the Hamsters

The 'Leo House' block of cadet study bedrooms *Author*

British European Airways Corporation.

• *There will also be a provision to enable the British Independent Air Transport Association to nominate a governor.*

• *The training will consist of a course of about two years duration in which flying instruction will be integrated with a thorough grounding in navigation, aerodynamics, meteorology, engineering and other aspects of airmanship such as aviation law.*

• *The aim is to develop to the fullest extent possible in each cadet those qualities of self-reliance and dependability which go to make a good airline pilot.*

• *The cadets will be expected to live in. First-class sports and recreational facilities will be provided.*

• *Fifty cadets will be sponsored by BOAC for the first year.*

• *Cadets will be sponsored by the airline operator requiring their services. During the four following years the Airways Corporations are expected to sponsor a maximum of 110 new cadets each year. In the third year and onwards therefore, the students will number about 220.*

• *The requirements of the independent airline operators and others cannot at this stage be precisely foreseen but the college will be open to the nominees of all British airlines as their demands require.*

• *The cost of training each pilot is expected ultimately to approximate £4,000 (excluding fees and board and lodging in the college against which it is possible that maintenance grants from local education authorities may*

The CAT and the Hamsters

be available in appropriate cases; my Right Hon. friend the Minister of Education is consulting the local authorities associations about this).

● *During the first two or three years, however, the cost per pilot will exceed this figure. The Government will contribute a grant of £1,000 per pilot trained with extra assistance to meet the additional costs during the first two years. The sponsors will find the remaining sum of approximately £3,000 per cadet. State grants to the scheme are estimated to total approximately £100,000 to £120,000 per year from the outset.*

● *An announcement will be made in the near future explaining how prospective candidates should apply and the conditions of entry to the college.*

In the autumn of 1959 *Flight* reported some more details of the scheme. The College of Air Training (CAT) would cost about £400,000 per annum to run. It's difficult to know exactly how that would translate at today's values, but by using the historic inflation calculator at www.thisismoney.co.uk the running costs would be about £8.4million per annum, a 21-fold multiplier at 2014 calculations. However in 1960 a senior captain's salary in the corporations was about £4,000 per annum, equivalent to about £176,000 using inflation on average earnings, so accurate money comparisons are questionable.

During the first five years cadets were expected to repay £200 per annum to the Corporations. This total of £1,000 towards their training costs would initially be costing newly-appointed second officers about 20 per cent of their annual salary. In addition, if they were not in receipt of a local education authority (LEA) grant (available dependant on parental circumstances) they would have had to pay £380 each year in tuition fees whilst at Hamble.

It's interesting to remind the reader at this point that, due to an administrative inconsistency, the courses 611 to 646 inclusive were able to issue a successful BALPA-supported legal challenge to the repayment of the £1,000. These lucky gents didn't have to repay the money and were refunded the sums already paid. However courses from the first year and those half dozen cadets who insisted on going to BOAC did not receive refunds.

So with the cadets finding £1,760 and the Government chipping in £1,000, the airline's share stood at £1,240 per successful cadet. It was still taxpayers' money, indirectly, but the corporations certainly didn't want the sort of

The CAT and the Hamsters

attrition mentioned above. Therefore academic requirements were set as passes in five different subjects at GCE (English, maths and a science subject were mandatory) with two passes at A level. Airline sponsorship would only be given to prospective pilots who could pass the aptitude, fitness and intelligence tests. Age limits at entry were 18-20, although candidates with university degrees could be accepted up to the age of 23.

Thus the foundations for a University of the Air had been laid at last. The first cadets would attend the college on Thursday September 15, 1960. There would be 21 of them, all destined for BOAC and all expected to be inducted onto the new Boeing 707 in two years' time. In the event none of these things came to pass but that shouldn't come as a big surprise to any assiduous reader of the narrative so far.

Chapter 3

A short history of Hamble Airfield

ALFRED HARMSWORTH was the 1st Viscount Northcliffe. Between 1907 and 1925 his newspaper, the *Daily Mail*, awarded numerous prizes for achievements in aviation. These prizes are credited with advancing the course of the industry during its early years and considerable sums were offered to the pastime's pioneers. So it's not surprising that in 1912 the paper sponsored a 'waterplane' tour of the British Isles and what better place to start than Hamble?

The airfield has already had mention in several of the previous chapters but it's now time for a more detailed exploration in relation to history of the venue which hosts our story. It was already familiar to Winston Churchill, Alliot Verdon-Roe, Amy Johnson, Sir Alan Cobham and the author Neville Shute but to me, as a boy planespotter in southern Hampshire during the late 1950s and early 1960s, it was unknown.

That was surprising, because there were few local airfields that didn't get a visit from my like-minded friends and me. We would avidly 'cop the regs' in J W R. Taylor's book of *Civil Aircraft Markings* (price 2/6 and published by Ian Allan abc). Akin to trainspotting, the books listed the five-letter registration that adorned the fuselage and wings of every aircraft. To see and identify the machine in flight or on the ground was to be able to underline it in the book and annotate the empty column, where and when seen. Confident in the knowledge that G-EEKS wasn't a valid registration, we derived much harmless fun from the pastime.

In one of my old books is an entry which reads: 'G-ALTR — A.S. 40 Oxford 1 — Air Service Training Ltd. Hamble 21-05-60'. I vaguely remember that visit for its disappointment. The airfield sits at the end of Hamble Lane, which is called the B3397 nowadays. It probably was then,

The CAT and the Hamsters

but I didn't notice that.What I did notice was that when we eventually gazed over the grey, bleak grass-covered aerodrome from the top of the adjacent railway bridge there was a paucity of aircraft. Just the one Airspeed Oxford doing circuits and bumps. Disappointed and disheartened, we cycled back through the farmland and smallholdings towards Northam and Swathling among the north-eastern outskirts of Southampton. My best friend and I used to regularly cycle the 20 miles from our homes to Southampton (Eastleigh) Airport and back, but this almost futile excursion had been an extra 14 miles of pedalling for just one 'cop'.

Six months late I 'copped' G-ALTP, another Oxford, flying over my parents' house. Coincidentally this was three weeks after the first cadets were welcomed through the portals of the College of Air Training by Air Vice Marshall E C Bates, the Principal. None of the first cadets would be doing any flying for another three weeks (six weeks into their course) but there was a rump of foreign students from the old ATS establishment finishing off their own courses. By the time the next issue of Ian Allen's publication came out, the Oxfords were designated as being owned by College of Air Training (Properties) Ltd and joined by De Havilland DHC1 Chipmunk 21s. Flying over my home these provided more 'cops' through the binoculars, without the effort of having to cycle anywhere all thanks to my future colleagues, who were in the process of earning their wings.

The epicentre of Hamble village hasn't changed too much since those days. It couldn't really, constrained as it is by the River Hamble to the east and the marshy Hamble Common to the south. Further north, much of the agricultural land has been inundated by a flood of housing estates. These are incorporated into a larger village that now calls itself by its 19th-century epithet: Hamble-le-Rice. However, it was not until the early years of the 20th century that this sleepy waterside settlement began to play its part in the historic flypast of British aviation.

Nobody knows if the early waterplane flight inspired the local boat builders, but what we do know is that two firms — Luke & Co and Hamble River Engineering Co. designed and built a large seaplane, the HL1. The firms' premises were then requisitioned by the Admiralty at the start of WWI to augment their own land aerodrome called 'Browns'. Whether the name had anything to do with the cows that previously used the field isn't recorded;

The CAT and the Hamsters

what is known is that no less a person than Winston Churchill flew from the field during 1913 in a Sopwith biplane.

During the war the Admiralty offered the facility to Fairey Aviation to facilitate the building and testing of their float-planes. The firm maintained an association with the venue until the late 1950s. Activity was carried out on a slipway south of Hamble Common right at the point where the river joins Southampton Water. The original buildings at Hamble Point were destroyed by fire in 1932 and had to be replaced. The site is now occupied by the Hamble Point Marina.

Another famous name in British aviation also occupied premises in the area. In 1909 Alliot Verdon-Roe was the first Englishman to fly an all-British aeroplane. His early manufacturing efforts were carried out in Manchester under the name Avro and more than 8,000 Avro 504 biplanes were sold during the First World War. In 1916 the proprietor moved to Hamble, purchasing 300 acres to the north and west of the Fairey site. Forty skilled technicians came with him but were disappointed by the lack of gas and mains drains in their accommodation.

The Avro holding also abutted Southampton Water so the firm applied to build a garden city of 350 houses half-a-mile north of the factory. Due to a shortage of materials only 24 houses were built and these now adorn Verdon Avenue on the north side of Hamble Lane. In 1917 Avro also built a number of spartan accommodation blocks. These single story buildings eventually became 'Gemini', 'Lupus' and 'Virgo' houses, providing lodgings for CAT cadets until the 1980s.

Cessation of wartime hostilities brought the building to an end but not before a light, branch-line railway was constructed. It ran south from the mainline station and can often be seen in photos, curving across dispersal and along beside the airfield control tower. Shell Mex & BP took over the terminus of the railway in 1926, consequently building a petrol and oil depot.

After the war the Hampshire Aero Club had set up home on the airfield and one of their notable pupils was Don Juan de la Cierva, a wealthy Spanish civil engineer. He designed and named an early form of rotary-wing aircraft which he called an Autogiro. In Britain the machine employed an Avro 504 fuselage and was constructed at Hamble during 1926. Avro's chief test pilot was 'Bert' Hinkler, the famous Australian pioneer of long-range flights.

The CAT and the Hamsters

Edwardian postcard of Hamble from the river. The Bugle pub was not unfamiliar to cadets.
Hamble pictures

Hinkler taught Cierva to fly his own Autogiro.

It needed little space to land and take off but this could not be said of contemporary landplanes. Accordingly, in 1926 Avro purchased 200 acres of land east of Hamble Lane and delineated further to the east by Satchel Lane, an older coast-hugging thoroughfare. The LSWR railway between Southampton and Portsmouth formed the northern boundary of this 'North Airfield'. Thereafter, aircraft built at the smaller 'South Airfield' would be taxied across Hamble Lane to the bigger field for a less hairy take-off. Any attempt to taxi across Hamble Lane nowadays would be thwarted by a procession of yachtsmen in big BMWs. They're usually on their way to the numerous modern marinas that have replaced the old seaplane slipways.

The aero club also took the opportunity to relocate to the north airfield and some of the buildings associated with this period became the CAT cinema and its adjoining facilities. In 1928 Vernon-Roe sold his interest to John Davenport Siddeley of Armstrong-Whitworth Aircraft Ltd. They produced the AW27 Ensign for Imperial Airways and the prototype eventually flew from 'across the road' on January 24, 1938.

In 1931 Mr. Frederick Handley Page (chairman of the Society of British Aircraft Constructors) described Siddeley as 'the mainspring' of a new venture called Air Service Training. This was on Thursday June 25 when HRH the Duke of Gloucester formally opened the AST school at Hamble. Before a distinguished gathering, the royal guest of honour asserted that he 'felt quite certain that it would be the finest school in the world, and that all

The CAT and the Hamsters

The light branch railway circa 1983
Hamble pictures

nations would be interested, particularly as excellent facilities were available for flying training both on land and sea machines'.

The school was set up to train overseas pilots to a standard at least as good as Cranwell and some of the new buildings were constructed to the same pattern. Instructors were expected to possess the RAF A1 certificate of competency. Particularly notable was the main administration block (ARA House), also the adjoining mess and bar, both of which were later to become features of a CAT cadet's life. Although it has to be said that most of us preferred to visit the bar rather than the admin-building, because the latter only housed trouble. The commandant at the time was Group Captain R J F Barton, aided by Flight Lieutenant H F Jenkins at CFI. The latter had made a speciality of instrument flying or, as it was known at the time, 'blind flying'.

More land was added to the aerodrome during the early Thirties but the local farmer was still permitted to graze stock on the parts of the airfield not operational on the day. Increasing numbers of foreign cadets attended the school by now and a new sports field was created for their divertissement. At one time over 400 students from 33 countries were present. Among them were aviation pioneers Amy Johnson and Sir Alan Cobham, author Neville Shute, who later featured Hamble in several of his novels and, among the military, future VC recipients Lieutenant Commander Eugene Esmonde and Wing Commander Guy Gibson. Cobham inaugurated in-flight refuelling trials from Hamble in 1937 but around this time the Hampshire Aero Club moved to Eastleigh.

The CAT and the Hamsters

Hamble was used by a wide variety of aircraft up to and during the war. Not only did AST have basic trainers such as Miles Magisters, Tiger Moths and various pre-war Avros but the advanced training fleet included Avro Ansons, Airspeed Envoys and the Westland Wessex. Military aircraft included the Hawker Hart, Hind and Audax, while down on the slipway Short Calcutta and Rangoon types trained Imperial Airways pilots for the new Short Empire Class boats. It was a busy time and things got busier.

British Marine Aircraft Ltd had been formed in February 1936 to produce Sikorsky S42-A flying boats under licence in the UK. The company built a factory on the western side of the Hamble peninsula with a slipway to Southampton Water. New hangers were built aplenty but the fledgling company was not on the Government's list of approved contractors and found it difficult to acquire materials. Henry P Folland, who had been chief designer for the Gloster Aircraft Company, acquired the struggling company and endowed it with his own surname.

Folland became part of the Hawker-Siddeley Group and still operate at Hamble under the aegis of British Aerospace. For a while after the death of Folland in 1954, the company was managed by W E W 'Teddy' Petter, designer of the Westland Lysander and Whirlwind as well as the superb English Electric Canberra. While he was at Hamble, Teddy designed the very successful Folland Midge and Gnat. Although it never flew from the

Hamble airfield in the 1930s
Hampshire Airfields (via J. Booth).

The CAT and the Hamsters

North Airfield's grass runways, the Gnat will forever be associated with the old Folland works. To that end Gnat T1 XM697 (originally XM693) is on display outside the BAE Systems factory and opposite a Hamble pub confusingly named 'The Harrier'.

At the outbreak of the Second World War, RAF volunteer reserve flying training was stopped and the facilities were employed to train instructors for the RAF. Then, on January 1, 1940, all AST staff were mobilised and largely dispersed to other training airfields. The airfield began to assume a new responsibility, repairing Spitfires under contract to the Air Ministry. On September 26 the nearby Supermarine works at Woolston was destroyed by German bombing. In response AST had to quickly expand their operations and by the end of the war 2,575 Spitfires had passed through the repair shops. So frequently did ops controllers vector the damaged aircraft direct to Hamble, to save time, the guidance became informally referred to as 'going home to mother'.

Aircraft which had been returned to servicability were reunited with their squadrons by the Air Transport Auxiliary (ATA), under the organisational auspices of BOAC. Hamble had its own ATA unit called No15 Ferry Pilot Pool and in September 1941 this became an all-female unit using the accommodation immediately east of ARA House. Twenty years later those same buildings housed the CAT pilot selection centre. Perhaps the time interval was just as well, because those brave and glamorous ATA women would certainly have disturbed the concentration of the young men trying to get themselves selected as cadets. Indeed, after the war it took another 35 years before the gentle sex got airborne regularly from Hamble's turf. That occasion was the training of the first female cadet at CAT, Miss L M Barton. Her date of entry with the rest of Course 792 was February 12, 1979.

The wartime repair facilities dealt with a wide range of allied aircraft but suffered only one enemy attack, on February 9, 1943. Unfortunately one man was killed in the hanger but compared with other south coast facilities Hamble got off comparatively lightly. Quite possibly it was the uncamouflaged bulk of a Boeing B17 Fortress, parked in dispersal while radar installations were carried out, which attracted the opportunistic German attack.

From a student pilot's point of view, Hamble airfield sometimes seemed 'a bit tight'. Even the longest runways were little more than 1,000 yards long.

The CAT and the Hamsters

Back row: Maureen Dunlop (Argentina), Roberta Leveaux (USA), Doreen Illsley, Rosemary Banister, Kay van Doozer (USA), Emily Chapin (USA), Mary Wilkins. Third row: Vera Strodl (Denmark), Betty Hayman, Grace Stevenson (USA), Jackie Sorour (South Africa), Margaret Duhalde (Chile), DB, Dora Lang (killed). Second row: Anna Leska (Poland), Rosemary Rees, Margot Gore (CO), Philippa Bennett, Veronica Volkertz. Front row: Anne Walker, Taniya Whittall (killed), Mardi Gething (Australia). All rows left to right.

Some of the brave ATA women who flew from Hamble   *Via Maidenhead Heritage Centre*

So, even though they were not fully laden, to land and take off in large four-engined aircraft such as the B17, Avro Lancaster or York were skilful feats. Notwithstanding that fact, aircraft came to be mended or converted and went away whole, until the war's end when they came to be scrapped. Gradually the pace of work slowed so that during the 1950s production was more concerned with manufacturing components rather than treating entire aircraft.

Not so the training side of the business, which restarted on August 1, 1946 with six Tiger Moths, two Avro Ansons, two Airspeed Oxfords, a Percival Proctor and a Miles Whitney Straight. There were now four departments — aircraft engineering, radio engineering, radio and navigation/flying. *Ab initio* pilots were mostly from overseas but a scheme to convert ex-RAF pilots to civilian licences also started in 1946. Pre-war staff were re-engaged and augmented by surplus RAF trainers from Shawbury (Empire Air Navigation School) and Cranwell.

The CAT and the Hamsters

Hillier WH 12B hovers next to a Chipmunk   Hamble pictures

Such was the prodigious output that the Ministry of Transport and Civil Aviation (MTCA) agreed that AST at Hamble could become a second examination centre, where pilots and navigators could sit their licence exams instead of having to travel to London. The airfield also became home to No14 Reserve Flying School, which helped the RAF volunteer reserve (RAFVR) maintain its standards. Southampton University Air Squadron operated in conjunction with them as well. This, coupled with a Royal Navy air signals school and a RAF basic air navigation school, meant that the Hampshire airfield was at full capacity. Accordingly, Pegasus House was build to the east of the main drive in 1950.

Although waterplane training did not recommence after the war, Aquila Airways was formed in May 1948 and equipped with ex-BOAC Sunderland flying boats. The company took part in the Berlin Airlift of 1948-49. Thereafter it operated as a normal scheduled civil airline from Southampton Water, to Lisbon, Madeira and the Channel Islands. AST's involvement was limited to servicing and maintenance from the old south airfield slipway. The airline ceased operations in 1958, even though its fleet had at one time comprised 18 Short Brothers variants.

The land-based aircraft fleets were also burgeoning during the 1950s as the De Havilland DH82A Tiger Moth primary trainer was replaced by another

The CAT and the Hamsters

De Havilland aircraft. The DHC1 Chipmunk (Chippie) began to arrive in 1952, registrations were G-AMMA, along with G-AMUC through to UH. I mention the registration marks because some saw service with CAT and not because I underlined them in my planespotter's book. AST also used Dakota aircraft to convert BOAC's surplus radio operators to navigators. A sharp-eyed planespotter would also have noticed Auster Aiglets and some Hillier WH12B helicopters during 1955.

As the ancillary military units were disbanded, taking their specialist aircraft with them, movements at Hamble became dominated by the 'Chippie'. A further batch of ex-RAF aircraft arrived during the winter of 1956-57 and these were registered as G-AOUN to UP as well as G-AOZP, G-AOTZ, G-AOJY, G-AOZU & ZV and G-AOTX. The following year AST decided to replace the Oxfords with new, American, twin-engined, Piper PA23 Apache aircraft G-ARJS to JX but in the event these did not arrive until after CAT was in operation. Chipmunks belonging to No2 Air Experience Flight were also based at the airfield from June 1958. In these aircraft Air Training Corps (ATC) cadets had their first taste of flying.

Much of the infrastructure, some of the instructors and many of the aircraft, later to become familiar to CAT cadets, were now in place at AST Hamble. The company and its airfield had been associated with BOAC training from time-to-time during the previous two decades. Everything was ready for Mr John Hay, Joint Parliamentary Secretary to the MTCA, to make his statement to Parliament on May 6 1959, as mentioned in Chapter Two.

The CAT and the Hamsters

Chapter 4

College of Air Training — aims, intents and setting up

THERE were two recurrent themes running through the storyline that preceded the inauguration of the College of Air Training. The first was the impending pilot shortage and the second the question of who was going to pay for the substantial cost of training the new pilots. College of Air Training (Properties) Ltd did pay £340,000 for the entire AST installations as a going concern. £42,000 of that was for an extensive inventory of chattels, exclusive of aircraft. (Underdown, 2012).

On December 18, 1959, *Flight* reported that 'plans are now complete for the transfer to Airwork Services Training at Perth in Scotland of the engineering school that has formed part of Air Service Training Ltd. at Hamble for the past 30 years. The move of technical staff and facilities from Hampshire northwards is to take place during next year's Easter Holiday, when the present Hamble organisation gives place to the new Government-sponsored College of Air Training, which is for pilots only. Engineering students will thus be able to continue work after the holiday without any break in their curriculum. So far, 107 students have been enrolled for the first term at Perth, where Airwork have operated a flying school since 1932. Plans are afoot to adapt existing hangars and buildings as extra classrooms and workshops and some new buildings are to be erected to house extra living accommodation and recreation rooms.

In an article dated May 15, 1959 entitled *A British University of the Air*, *Flight* magazine referred ironically to the deficiency that had been 'just around the corner since 1947' and reinforced the observation by reporting that 'BALPA estimate that about 80 of their members (the largest number since just after the war) are at present looking for a job'. There had been one of Britain's recurrent periods of recession in 1958 and there was a backlog of redundant pilots seeking employment but normal attrition was expected to erode that surplus over the coming years. In addition, ex-RAF pilots would probably be in short supply in the future, due to the exigencies of service contraction.

The CAT and the Hamsters

Additionally, the complexity and specialist nature of civil airline operations had rendered the ex-military pilot of diminishing value to the airlines until he had been subjected to a prolonged period of retraining. Nevertheless the matter would be a serious issue throughout the existence of the college, when the inability of the corporations to match their training programmes to their real needs almost beggared belief.

At the outset, the cost of putting a cadet through the two-year course was variously estimated at £4,000, exclusive of board and lodging (John Hay MP, 1959) to a total of £5,000 (Stevens, 1961) or £8,000 (BEA, 1961). What we can know for certain was that the Government was committed to subsidise each cadet by £1,000.

On April 1, 1960 *Flight* reported that 'a sum of £110,000 is provided for in the 1960-61 Civil Aviation Estimates as a contribution to the new College of Air Training'.

Also not in doubt is the £673/10s cost to the cadet (College of Air Training, 1960). This included £60 per annum tuition fees and £254/5s maintenance costs. Also required was a one-off sum of £45 to cover books, stationary; publications and uniform. At the end of the course a refund of £10 might be had for returning certain items in good condition. Against the costs, cadets would be eligible to apply to their Local Education Authority for grants on a par with those offered to university students. The 'liberal studies' element of the course was an important element in achieving eligibility for these LEA grants.

In examining these costs it should be noted that £1,000 in 1960 equates to roughly £17,500 today, using the GDP deflator. So the tranche of costs expected to be paid by the cadets themselves was to prove contentious. In 1960 cadets had been informed that they would have to repay £1,000 over a period of five years at £200 per annum. The information was contained on page five of the *Fly with BOAC* brochure but a letter dated August 18, 1960 from public relations officer Wing Commander A H Abbott informed cadets that the repayment requirement should be considered cancelled.

Then 18 months later, on February 5, 1962, in a letter from the College Principal, cadets were informed 'It has always been the view of both corporations that it is reasonable, in view of the expensive training provided to cadets, that some of the cost should be contributed by individuals.' (Reayer, 2012).

The CAT and the Hamsters

Unfortunately not all the cadets had been told the same thing, so the Principal's letter was an attempt at fence-mending and obfuscation. In it he stated that it was the intention to create a separate, lower pay scale for Hamble graduates: one that would automatically allow the repayment of the £1,000. The prospectus had held out the promise of an approximate salary of £1,000 per annum, so to lose one fifth of that was a substantial imposition. Air Vice Marshall Bates concluded by informing the cadets that 'discussions were proceeding to determine the precise salaries which shall be effective and, immediately these have been decided, you will be informed.'

The confusion was to lead to a legal challenge from the cadets on the early courses and a waiving of the repayment. Later courses were told categorically, that the repayment was necessary and would be deducted from salary. I believe that courses 651-656 were the first ones to have to pay the monies.

The next intake (661a-661b) was asked to report to Hamble between 2pm and 6.30pm on December 31, 1965. When they got there they were told two things: 'Sorry nothing's going to happen until January 2, so come back then'

Hamble Airfield at the start of CAT in 1960
CAT Prospectus in the 1960s

The CAT and the Hamsters

and 'be advised you will have to pay back £1,000 out of your salary.' The college official might have added 'Oh and have a great New Year's Eve' but then again he might not. Two years later, after their graduation to BEA, one of their number asked BALPA why he was making repayments after tax had been deducted and not before. He was told the association did not want differential pay scales within the corporations as a matter of policy.

If all this detail leads the reader to believe that the protagonists were making up the rules as they went along, that's not an unreasonable viewpoint. After his flying selection one young man was congratulated on obtaining a place by the Principal, only to receive a letter from BOAC saying that his acceptance would be subject to 'A' level results. As the man was already in receipt of the necessary 'A' level certificates this small incident is indicative of flawed liaison between the nascent college and BOAC.

AST had been in the business of training pilots since 1931. A. H. Abbott had been chief instructor in the late 50's. Now he was the public relations officer. Air Marshal Sir Hugh Walmsley had been managing director of AST and became *de jure* Principal of the new college on May 1, 1960. By the time it opened he had resigned 'for personal reasons' and his deputy E C Bates had taken over. Five years later that man failed to make a favourable, initial, impression on us. He addressed the first assembly of our intake with an uninspiring message which went something like this: 'It's good to see you all here together today for the first time. Unfortunately this is probably also the last time I shall speak to you all together, because several of you will have failed the course by the time our next meeting comes around. Work hard and make sure it's not you who goes!'

Because of his antipodean background he was christened 'Abbo-Jim' by the earliest cadets.

In 1931 the RAF had offered some of the best flying training in the world and, in setting up the AST College, J D Siddeley was keen to emulate Central Flying School standards. To that end ex-RAF instructors were employed and the quasi-military ethos retained. It's probably insightful that the Principal and his senior instructors were keen to retain their military ranks on official communications. Quite what the Board of Governors made of this when they took over is difficult to ascertain.

Initially there were 10 Chipmunks, two from Airways Aero Associates

The CAT and the Hamsters

and the remaining eight from AST, but it was planned to eventually increase the fleet to 21. As to the Apache; six were to be delivered between June and September 1961 and by August 1962 the planned fleet strength was to be nine (*Flight* staff reporter, 1960). Squadron Leader G C (George) Webb was retained as Chief Flying Instructor and was assisted by nine other instructors during the induction of the early intakes of cadets. It was anticipated that as the college expanded the number of flying instructors would rise to 21.

On October 28 1960 the following appeared amongst the situations vacant pages of Flight:

> **COLLEGE OF AIR TRAINING, HAMBLE** VACANCIES exist for Flying Instructors. Minimum qualifications are CPL with I/R and Instructor endorsement. SALARY: £1,660-£1,960 with contributory Pension Scheme. APPLICATIONS to: Bursar, CAT etc (Situations vacant, 1960).

The rates of pay were to become an issue as time went on and this snippet from *Flight's* 'Brevities' page dated January 15 of the same year may be a clue why:

'New rates of pay offered to BEA pilots of Comet 4B services are now under negotiation with BALPA. The maximum rate of pay for a senior captain under the offered scale would be £4,200 a year.'

Using calculations based on inflation of average earnings that equates to £181,000 in 2011 (Measuring Worth, 2011).

Twenty one (Chippies & instructors) was obviously somebody's lucky number because 21 young men (aged between 18 & 24) arrived at Hamble on Thursday September 15, 1960 to be the first cadets. They were joined by a second tranche of 20 some six weeks later. The six- week interval was significant because the first batch would concentrate exclusively on ground-school throughout the initial period.

BOAC stated that when the formation of the college was announced it was in receipt of 1,500 letters of enquiry. It called in 260 potential cadets for interview and the 41 mentioned above were the chosen few (*Flight* staff reporter, 1960). Two years later the first intake graduated. Eight of the original number had fallen by the wayside. Two had failed on medical grounds and six had 'not made the grade' as the Principal put it in his speech. We cadets

The CAT and the Hamsters

had a more brusque view than that: the unfortunate men had been 'chopped'. Sir Matthew Slattery (Chairman of BOAC) stressed that the object of the College was to train captains and not chauffeurs and that they should remember that they, their company and their country would be judged by their personal deportment and behaviour. There were 'other crews'— not in the corporations—who took over aircraft after only a cursory look at the necessary reports and documents, and then stepped out of the aircraft at the end of their flight 'to go ashore for 36hr, when the time came to fly on somewhere else'. In the corporations, the graduates would be expected to be on duty all the time, acting always in the highest traditions of discipline and deportment. (*Flight International*, 1962).

He went on to say that despite what was proposed at the start of the college, the graduates would not be joining BOAC as Boeing 707 pilots, because the company was in no hurry to absorb them. BEA on the other hand was desperately short and would welcome 26 of the intake. The remaining seven would join BOAC as navigators on the older aircraft that still required them. Only 12 years earlier the corporation had been encouraging navigators to become pilots. Is there a bit of a pattern developing here?

In the words of AV-M Bates, 'it was a relief that the headaches and anxieties of the first courses were over.' There were to be others but Hamble had done its job well and those graduates joined the corporations as some of their youngest employees, having been transformed from schoolboys to qualified pilots in two years. Accordingly they were not boys among men, from the aptitude point of view, but many of their captains would have seen active

BOAC chairman Sir Matthew Slattery with Rick Reayer at the graduation ceremony for the first courses on October 26,1962
Rick Reayer

The CAT and the Hamsters

service in the Second World War. A few could even date their experience back to Imperial Airways, meaning that many knowledgeable senior pilots would be watching this first invasion of 'hamsters' with a dispassionate professional interest.

Furthermore; from the outside observer's viewpoint, simple arithmetic will show up a failure rate of 19.5 per cent. That was a distressingly high figure after all the weeding out in the four-stage selection procedure. In simple terms it was a lot of wasted money and effort, as well as the smothering of much youthful aspiration: although, to the CAT Principal, the chopped cadets had merely fallen by the wayside. To produce 35 second officers for the airlines from an original pool of 1,500 applicants was setting the bar very high from the outset and were there enough young men in Britain to satisfy the future demand for 100 cadets each year?

So now we need to examine how applicants were tested during the selection procedures and ask if those tests the best method of both assessing their suitability for the college and their likelihood of graduating successfully once they got there.

Chapter 5

CAT — selection procedures

AFTER BOAC had cleared its backlog of 1,500 existing letters of enquiry, young men who wished to become cadets at the College of Air Training would have responded to adverts such as this one from *Flight* magazine.

> **TRAINING AS AIRLINE PILOTS**
> **COLLEGE OF AIR TRAINING**
> Applications are invited for cadetships at The College of Air Training for entry commencing September 1961. The course is for 2 years. Cadets, on graduation, will be guaranteed long-term engagements as pilots with the British Airline Corporations.
>
> Applicants must be unmarried British Subjects over 18 years old and under 20 on entry. University graduates under 24. They must have obtained, or be likely to obtain before entry, a General Certificate of Education or Northern Ireland Grammar School Senior Certificate in at least 5 subjects, including English Language, Mathematics and a Science subject. At least 2 of the passes must be at A Level. Applicants from Scotland should have obtained the Scottish Leaving Certificate with passes in either 3 Higher grade and 2 Lower grade, or 4 Higher grade subjects, including in both cases English Language, Mathematics and Science.
>
> University graduates and undergraduates need not necessarily have obtained these GCE qualifications. Applications from those who are otherwise suitably qualified will be treated on merit. Applicants will be required to pass a medical examination at least to the standard of the Airline Transport Pilot's Licence.
>
> Cadets will be resident at the College. They will receive no pay during the College course and will be required to meet maintenance and other expenses, of approximately £675 over the 2 years. County Education Authorities will consider applications for grants to defray all, or part of these expenses.
>
> For prospectus and application form, write to: The Principal, College of Air Training, (Department 'S'), Hamble, Hampshire.
>
> (College of Air Training, 1960)

If the completed application form was satisfactory they could then expect a further four stages of the selection procedure. Prior to CAT, Air Service Training had been operating a pay-as-you-go establishment since the early 1930s. Now, however, the corporations and the state were the main sponsors

The CAT and the Hamsters

Cadets from course 635 had all passed selection but two of them would not graduate
Hamble pictures, BOAC

of the flying training and they had definite views on the sort of graduate they wanted the new college to turn out.

It would not be sufficient for cadets to graduate with bare minimum passes in a commercial pilot's licence (CPL). The avowed aim was to train captains of the future, equipped with a deferred airline transport pilots licence (ATPL), instrument rating and personal leadership qualities of the highest order. Furthermore the successful cadets would have assimilated advanced technical tuition, covering a wide and comprehensive aeronautical syllabus. Last but not least, a broad general studies curriculum and physical training would add gloss to the neophyte airline officer. (Prospectus, 1960). With such exacting standards demanded, the selection process itself was necessarily exacting. Hence the need for four stages, each more challenging than the previous one.

There was a medical questionnaire included as part of the initial application pack and applicants also had to send a letter from their GP after a rudimentary check-up. This was because something neither the candidate nor the college could do anything about was the physical fitness to hold an ATPL. Good eyesight and hearing, freedom from degenerative disease and a host of other medical parameters were basics. Candidates were either fortunate enough to have the health requirements at application or not but as an additional stringent criterion the Corporation doctors would try to assess whether that level of health was likely to be maintained during a 35-year career. Of the thousands of young men who were in receipt of the requisite educational

The CAT and the Hamsters

qualifications and minded to apply for selection, a large proportion would be ineligible on medical grounds. Nevertheless over the 20-year life of the College and despite these exacting standards; there was still an attrition rate of about one per cent on medical grounds.

In the early 1960s I attended the RAF centralised pilot selection centre at Biggin Hill to obtain a 'special flying award' (in other guises this was termed a flying scholarship). Then a year or so later, after successfully completing the flying scholarship at the Hampshire Aero Club, I applied for and completed the CAT selection procedure at Hamble. I mention this for comparison purposes and, although it's only a subjective opinion at some distance from the past, it seemed to me that the CAT process was more rigorous. For a start, it included flying selection which, at that time, the RAF process did not but also on page seven of the 1960 Prospectus it stated: 'On arrival at the College the cadet must be in possession of an accurate watch with a centre second sweep.' Now there was one requirement I could be certain of satisfying — and I've still got the watch.

On December 9, 1960 *Flight* reported that Air Marshal Sir Hugh Constantine, Air Officer Commanding-in-Chief of Flying Training Command, made a speech at the annual dinner of the Association of British Aero Clubs in which he reported that 'the AOC stated that 3,012 flying scholarships had been awarded since 1950 and over 1,200 of those scholarship pilots had joined the services. Furthermore, compared with aircrew entrants without previous experience the 'wastage' rate for scholarship pilots was only one sixth. On that basis Flying Training Command was thinking of introducing the Chipmunk (flying selection) into the initial selection process'.

This was entirely in accord with Philip Cleife who, during his RAF service, was in command of the Training Research Squadron of the Empire Flying School. On February 26, 1960 he had written a two-page article in *Flight* asserting: 'Now it is a known fact, incontestably established during nearly half-a-century of flying training, that aptitude to fly and command an aeroplane is one of the most difficult of all human accomplishments to predict on the ground. The complex combination of personal qualities needed is such that there is no simple yardstick by which they can be measured during an interview or test.' He developed his argument by saying that under the duress of airborne instruction the most likely and promising cadets could 'crack up'

The CAT and the Hamsters

and fail to make the requisite progress. He continued: 'A most effective way of making the best final selection is to train students in sufficient numbers to allow for wastage, and then eliminate those who are discovered to lack pilot aptitude — the greatest proportion of all wastage occurs during the early stages of training.'

However he submitted that this would be a most undesirable way for the college to proceed for three reasons: the college was a University of the Air and should not concern itself with the 'prep school work' of *ab initio* training; it would be hopelessly uneconomic to squander expensive, high-quality training on large numbers of candidates in order to pick out the exceptional ones; the companionable atmosphere of a flying school might not engender a sufficiently ruthless regime to weed out the lower percentile among otherwise enthusiastic and likeable young men.

Future experience would show that he had no need to worry on the third count where CAT was concerned. In conclusion, Cleife advocated some form of pre-entry, flying training as a part of the selection procedure.

In the event that is more or less what the college governors instigated. The first 260 cadets completed their selection for BOAC sponsorship on the airline's premises. Initially this was at Building 219, Harrington Square, London Airport (Heathrow) and the subsequent, residential selection at

Tubby Fieldhouse (centre) was the face of flying selection   *CAT photo DVD*

The CAT and the Hamsters

Dormy House, Sunningdale. Here candidates were informed that although meals were free 'gratuities to the catering staff were entirely at their own discretion'. In addition they could use the bar, provided they satisfied the licensing conditions by 'signing in' and paying one shilling membership. Presumably the bar steward was an informal part of the selection team.

Success in the residential selection process would lead to a requirement to complete the full ATPL medical with the Ministry of Civil Aviation at the candidate's own expense. In the same letter that required one of the initial cadets to take that medical, J M Abell (Recruitment & Postings Superintendent (Flying Staff)) wrote: 'It is quite possible that a flying grading course will be will be introduced into the procedure for those who have passed into the same phase as yourself, but this is not yet certain, and I can give you no details until the College comes into being. Should this happen you will appreciate that final selection will depend on success in the flying test'. This letter was dated March, 29, 1960.

Then on May 5 the same candidate received a letter from the College Principal inviting him for flying selection. This would take place over a five-day period and be limited to ten hours with a qualified flying instructor (QFI). AV-M Bates went on: 'This test, in addition to those you have already taken at Dormy House, is designed to indicate your general aptitude for flying, and will give the final guidance to the Selection Board in making its final selections for the first College entry.'

Thus it is evident that although BOAC had initially opted to follow the two-stage interview procedure plus a medical, it decided fairly late in the day to include flying selection. It was a policy that endured throughout the early life of the college, albeit with flying selection reduced to less than five hours for some later candidates, and then was abolished altogether by 1970. Perhaps this was a sign of impending financial pressure and was well below the number of hours recommended by Philip Cleife.

An insight into the pros and cons of flying selection is thrown up when the governors were considering the implications of Paper GB.408 and expansion plan 'Golf'. The Principal prepared a paper highlighting that if the Chipmunks were all replaced, not only would there be an absence of aircraft to teach the spinning and aerobatics aspects of the syllabus but the four dedicated aircraft used for flying selection would be lost.

The CAT and the Hamsters

He notes that in the selection year September 1965 to August 1966 some 242 candidates were tested, assessing how they responded to the five hours of dual instruction on the Chipmunk. Of those; 8.6 per cent (21 boys) were deemed to lack 'sufficient aptitude for flying to have a reasonable chance of success in training'. These 21 young men were considered hopeless but an additional, unlisted number, were borderline cases. Curtailing of flying selection would result in 'wastage in training being increased'. His habitual use of the epithet 'boys' in the document, when referring to potential cadets, can perhaps be explained by the social attitudes of 50 years ago.

My own flying selection at Hamble hasn't left any lasting impression on my memory except that it was conducted by 'Tubby' Fieldhouse. Perhaps time has eroded the fine detail but I seem to remember him taking me out to a parked Chipmunk — without much formality — and saying: 'Well you've got a PPL (Private Pilots Licence), take me flying!' The fact that this was going to be a different experience from my training at the nearby Hampshire Aero Club was brought home by my being attired in CAT's flying overalls. At the aero club, flying was conducted in casual clothes. Furthermore the Chipmunk seemed to be lacking a nosewheel, a fact that it reinforced by trying determinedly to ground-loop during the take-off run. Luckily I'd been warned about this tendency by my aero club's Cessna instructor, who I'd employed to give me a pre-selection refresher.

The selection analysis document quotes previous flying experience as giving an average of 28 per cent rejection rate for candidates with previous flying experience compared with 54 per cent for those without. This seems to bear out Cleife's assertions. However, some ex-instructors have told me that it was more difficult for them to teach a cadet with previously ingrained bad habits than to start with an *ab initio* man.

The document seems to bear out the instructors' subjective analysis with the tabular analysis on the following page.

Additionally, the total percentage figures shown are for the first seven years of CAT's existence and contrast unfavourably with lower numbers of suspensions from Perth, Kidlington and Carlisle. (*The Air Corporations. Report on selection procedure 1967-68*)

Before this final stage of flying selection the prospective cadet would have been interviewed, re-interviewed, weighed up and assessed. These

PREVIOUS FLYING HOURS	SAMPLE	SUSPENDED FROM TRAINING	FAILURE RATE
35+	84	15	18%
11-34	150	23	15%
2-10	86	23	27%
Less than 2	287	83	29%
TOTAL	607	144	23.72%

procedures form part of a selection battery (Hunter & Burke, 1995). Some candidates said that it felt more like assault and battery. The processes involved date their beginnings to just after the First World War and came to be called aviation psychology. Earliest tests measured general cognitive ability but it was reasoned that some measure of personality would be useful. The question researcher had first to answer was: what measure of personality?

A biographical inventory tries to determine a list of events or activities in a candidate's past, on the basis that 'past behaviour is the best predictor of future behaviour'. So that was included in the battery. The Minnesota Multiphasic Personality Inventory (MMPI) has been considered the gold standard in personality testing ever since its inception as an adult measure of psychopathology and personality structure in 1939 (Wikipedia, 2012). Something akin to this was added to the battery. Last but not least electro-mechanical apparatus (CVT & SMA to the initiated) (Hunter & Burke, 1995, p. 117) was used in an effort to determine the reaction time, balance and hand-eye co-ordination thought essential in the ability to fly an aeroplane.

Candidates on later courses completed these and many more tests at Hamble in the selection-centre at the north-western end of the main driveway. Among the ex-cadets I have interviewed for this book, it's striking how random memories of the process become after 50 years. In my own innocence I quite enjoyed the challenge of trying to keep an electronic dot in the centre of a square on a TV screen by using a rudimentary stick and rudder (SMA) but I didn't understand the significance of answering dozens of questions which seemed preoccupied about whether I was concerned about catching diseases from door knobs (MMPI). Ignorance was bliss! However the mechanical aptitude tests (if cogwheel 'A' turns clockwise, in which direction does lever G move?) were meat and drink to a chap who owned a Number 9 Meccano set.

The CAT and the Hamsters

The Selection Centre produced its own report in September 1968 — *The Air Corporations Joint Pilot Training Scheme, Report on Selection Procedures*. The report drew no conclusions but was rather a statistical analysis of the various criteria used during the selection process. For instance, a simple four-column table relates to the SMA test mentioned above and notes that at the top end a score of 0-11 yielded a later failure rate of 17 per cent of cadets, while a score of 36 or above resulted in more than twice as many failures. I'm sure that it was fascinating reading at the time but leafing through the dry statistics now, it's difficult to see any real patterns, other than an increase in failure rate as the test result scores declined but that's hardly surprising. Even less astonishing was the fact that flying selection scores did seem to be a useful predictor of success. There were four assessment bands, with the lowest echelon being over six times more likely to fail than the six per cent failure rate of the highest band.

The table on the previous page highlights just how shockingly inefficient was the selection procedure. Even after all the tests, CAT didn't manage to consistently achieve graduation for more than five out of six cadets. Until the twilight years of its existence, that is!

One cadet I interviewed from that era (743) was surprised when I asked him about 'chop rates'. He didn't understand what I meant. 'Suspensions or failure rates,' I said but he was still mystified. Further questioning established that nobody from his intake of 41 cadets was chopped and that the CAT instructors persevered with them until they achieved the required standard. This took 753 days, yet barely a year earlier a similar sized intake (731), lost five cadets but graduated in only 606 days.

Perhaps this was a result of the college suffering a hiatus of 18 months, caused in part by the newly-formed British Airways reducing its requirements for pilot graduates. When 743 eventually graduated they were offered alternative non-flying posts in BA but eventually most of them decided to take the hint and apply for jobs with carriers such as Britannia, Virgin and Cathay Pacific — all of whom were keen to assimilate these high-quality recruits. No new cadets were taken on by CAT until February 13, 1978. The reader can only surmise what the chop rate might have been if every cadet had been given that bit of extra time?

Unfortunately the system wasn't set up in that way. Previous intakes had

The CAT and the Hamsters

been at a time of perceived pilot shortages. That had the college striving to shorten courses and make graduates available to meet Corporation deadlines. As a consequence, the number of enquiries from schools was not sufficient to service demand after wastage and so entry parameters were modified over time — firstly to attract university graduates and later female applicants. These new contenders were soon subject to the selection department's dry analysis of their performance.

The aforementioned 1968 report was able to contrast the educational background of candidates. This was particularly germane because of the university graduates who had become eligible to apply for a foreshortened course that began on July 9, 1965. Only two graduate courses, G1 and G2, were effected at Hamble; subsequent graduate training was carried out at Kidlington. In the year 1967-8 there were 11,011 enquiries to the college producing 1,372 acceptable applications, of whom 293 were graduates being admitted to the selection procedure.

In September 1977 CAT governors considered an additional report on the selection of female cadets. In the 16 previous years of the college's existence, applications from females had not been considered. The report mentions 200 enquiries which transmuted into 24 firm applications. Four ladies were too small, being under 5'4" in height, one was too young and one too old. Seven others were deemed unsuitable and the report saw fit to give a slightly disdainful mention of their hobbies such as 'riding, patchwork, smocking, renovating furniture, growing plants and jumble sales.' Had the news been leaked it would have been enough to make some male candidates cancel their subscriptions to *Good Housekeeping* magazine. Eventually only four young ladies were brought to the secondary stage of selection but none achieved a score of five or above — the minimum requirement on the seven-point scale for the award of a cadetship at that stage.

The selection board was a product of time and place with firm ideas of what they wanted. One graduate of course 644 tells of a lengthy interview in front of a pair of senior captains, one BEA and one BOAC, and the head of selection, A H Abbott. Before his own interview, and during a coffee break, he surreptitiously asked the previous interviewee what questions were being asked. He replied: 'They asked me which aircraft are operated by BOAC?' and my man was mortified — he didn't know the answer. Helpfully his informant

The CAT and the Hamsters

recited a list, which was hastily committed to memory and repeated during the interview when the question duly came up. Unfortunately the Boeing 707 had been omitted — both from the original candidates list and consequently from his own answer. The interviewers were onto the omission like a flash: 'Did you ask the previous candidate what questions we were asking?' Hopelessly exposed, he answered: 'Yes, sir!' and still firmly believes that a negative answer would have scuppered his chances.

Unfortunately one's future at Hamble very often rested on such happenstance as described in that anecdote! Thank goodness they never found out about my needlework.

Embroidery was a different matter! Fellow attendees on one selection course were appalled when, during a group discussion, I mentioned reading something in my father's *Daily Express*. Later one advised me: 'You should only tell them that you read *The Times*, or better still the *Telegraph*.' When I said that would have been a lie, he shrugged his shoulders and advised me to tell the selectors what they wanted to hear, not the inconvenient truth.

Chapter 6

Learning to fly at CAT — and the aircraft employed

EVEN when I'm otherwise engaged in the garden, or on the golf course, the sound of an old Gypsy Major engine will cause me to break off what I'm doing and cast my gaze skywards. That's not so important when sowing a row of carrots but it's not to be recommended in the middle of taking a putt. I'm often rewarded by the sight of an Auster or Tiger Moth but the most evocative observation is of a Chipmunk. From most angles it looks as if it has only one main undercarriage leg but 146 hours 35 minutes of Chipmunk experience (certified in my logbook as 'flying times correct' by N Manning) reassures me that there are two.

The De Havilland Canada DHC-1 'Chipmunk' was designed to succeed the classic 'Tiger Moth' elementary trainer. The DHC-1A-1 flew for the first time from Downsview airfield, Toronto on May 22, 1946 — three months before I was born. In all, 218 Chipmunks were built at the airfield in the period up to 1951. These tandem seat, stressed-skin monoplanes were powered by a 145hp Gypsy Major 1C engine but were only partly aerobatic as this variant.

Interest in the aircraft was shown by British Aeroplane and Armament Experimental Establishment, based at Boscome Down in Wiltshire and they acquired two of the aircraft for evaluation. The outcome of their testing was specification 8/48 for a fully aerobatic Chipmunk T. Mk 10 powered by a

De Havilland
DHC-1 Chipmunk
Trevor Hughes

The CAT and the Hamsters

Gypsy Major 8. The RAF ordered 735 of this variant for use by 17 University Air Squadrons, many RAFVR flying schools and also as an *ab initio* trainer at Cranwell. Production was carried out in DH factories at Hatfield and Chester. In all 1,014 were manufactured in the UK until production was ended in 1956.

Looking in my own logbook I can count 32 individual aircraft, ranging from the Mk21 — a total of 28 were built as a civilian version of the Mk20, which itself had originally been built for export — to the Mk22, a civilian conversion of the military T10 and the Mk 22A with fuel tankage increased from nine gallons per side to 12 gallons per side. The oldest CAT Chipmunk was G-OTX rolled out on December 19, 1949 and the youngest was G-APSB on September 4, 1953.

Registration	Mark	Gypsy	Major	Usage
G-AMMA	Mk21	Mk10 series II		MoA then Luton Flying Club
G-AMUC/F/G/H	Mk21	Mk10 series II		Originally AST
G-AOJY/Z	Mk22	Mk20		Ex-Air Navigation Training/Airwork
G-AOTX/Z	Mk22A	Mk20		Ex-Airways Aero Associations
G-AOUN/O/P	Mk22A	Mk20		Originally AST
G-AOZP	Mk22	Mk20		Originally AST
G-AOZV	Mk22A	Mk20		Ex-Airways Aero Associations
G-APSB	Mk22A	Mk20		Ex-Dacier Ltd
G-ARMB/C/D/E/F/G/	Mk22A	Mk20		CAT (ME- crashed onto I.O.W.)
G-ATDF/P/X/Y	Mk22	Mk20		Ex-RAF
G-ATEA/B	Mk22A	Mk20		EA- had mid-air over village with WZ864
G-ATHC/D	Mk22	Mk20		Ex-RAF
G-ATJJ/K	Mk22	Mk20		Ex-RAF

Table of Hamble Chipmunks circa 1965/6 after (Taylor, 1961-2004)

The first courses in 1960 began their flying training after six weeks of intensive ground-school instruction, while my own intake started on September 3, 1965 but didn't begin flying until early December. The CAT Governors' financial estimates for July 21, 1960 estimated a requirement for ten Chipmunks in that year; then 14 in 1961-2 along with six Apaches and 21during 1962-3. Apache numbers were to be 21 by then. Originally, eight Chipmunks and two Airspeed Oxfords had been purchased from AST for

£14,000. The Chipmunks cost 1,600 each. Later, five more were bought from Airways Aero Associations for £1,800 each.

Previous flying experience among the cadets I've interviewed ranged from a young man who, when he was 13 years old on holiday with his parents, was airborne for a half-hour joyriding around Blackpool Tower to another who, having gained a PPL from Marshalls Aviation at Christchurch, virtually ran their joyride business flying around Bournemouth Pier for a whole summer. He joined Hamble as a cadet with 50 or so hours.

Although flying selection was an innovation when the College began and the earliest cadets attended for five days, by the late 1960s some cadets were being accepted without any flying selection whatsoever.

Notwithstanding this diverse background, the flying instructors were expected to train all their cadets to attain Commercial Pilots Licence and Instrument Rating standard before their graduation. To this end they had an

New cadets with Chief Flying Instructor George Webb, September 1960
Hamble pictures - BOAC

allocation of roughly 146 hours on the basic flight (Chipmunk) and a further 80 or so hours on the advanced flight (Apache).

Although instructors tended to remain with their cadets throughout their basic or advanced training, they alternated between the two flights during their career, spending periods of six months on basic followed by three months on the advanced flight.

For courses 601/2 their first six weeks were accompanied by the whir of training aircraft in the background, as the rump of ATS pupils finished their own training. There were ten flying instructors at that stage led by the

The CAT and the Hamsters

CFI George Webb (b.1908, ret. 1964). The other nine were Bill Anderson, Tony Farrell, Len 'Tubby' Fieldhouse, Ron Frost, Paddy Kinnin, Peter Duff-Mitchell, Cecil Pearce, Alan Smith and 'Taps' Tappin. Peter Duff-Mitchell (CFI from 01/09/64 @ £2,500 pa) and Cecil Pearce went on to become successive CFIs after the death of George Webb. Most of the others became flight managers during the next two decades, although Fieldhouse was the inimitable face of flying selection for many years. Farrell was very pleased with the transition from ATS to CAT and wrote: 'Our pay and conditions of service were vastly improved — not only a sizable salary increase but

CAT flying instructors circa 1970   *Liskutin*

fringe benefits such as health insurance, five-day week, more generous leave entitlement and a staff pension scheme. That really was a bonus; there had been nothing like that before.'

Subsequent instructor selection could be fairly informal: an interview with the CFI enquired about RAF experience with the accent on squadrons and postings; a quick review of the log book and that was often that. As I write this, more than 50 years after the college opened, not too many of the original instructors are still with us but here are the experiences of a small sample.

Cecil Pearce joined AST in September 1956 after flying Sunderlands in the RAF and instructing on Harvards. He left the service as a relatively lowly flight lieutenant but having got into the college on the ground floor, so to speak, found himself senior in longevity to group captains and squadron leaders who had joined behind him. Nevertheless he told me that previous RAF rank was not an issue in the flying instructors' common room at Hamble. He also said that each of the serving AST instructors was assessed as OK to

The CAT and the Hamsters

join the new college and they were joined by an ex-Airways Association instructor, Alan Smith.

Tony Liskutin was an RAF Squadron Leader with a distinguished war record who attended Hamble for interviews with his friend John Vickers. Both men had come to a point in their careers where desk flying was their most likely option. They were asked to start immediately but needed to finish their current service, so they joined in 1962.

Dave Lewry joined in November 1965 as he approached the eight-year optional retirement point of his RAF short-service commission. He remembers there were around 50 fellow instructors by that date. He told me that at 32 years old not only was he the youngest by five years or so (although the average age was over 40), but also his 3,000-odd flying hours experience was only about 60 per cent of what most of the others had acquired. However his interview panel, consisting of the Principal AV-M Bates and CFI Duff-Mitchell were suitably impressed with his A1 RAF rating to engage him.

Another instructor, Phil Nelson, who joined in the Seventies, was the CFI of the Southampton University Air Squadron based at Hamble. He was offered a job by Tommy Thompson, the College CFI at the time, on the basis that they frequently came into contact and so Tommy was familiar with Phil's ability. Just when the CFI needed more instructors, Phil's RAF career was winding down — so bingo!

From its modest beginnings the College output soon begun to increase, as did the need for additional instructors, so the following advert had appeared in Flight Magazine on October 28, 1960:

COLLEGE OF AIR TRAINING, HAMBLE
VACANCIES exist for Flying Instructors. Minimum qualifications are CPL with I/R and Instruct. endorsement. SALARY: £1,660-£1,960 with Contributory Pension Scheme. APPLICATIONS to: Bursar, College of Air Training, Hamble, Southampton. [1482].

Contrast the remuneration available above with the advert overleaf from the same magazine just two months earlier.

It's worthy of note that the airline salary scale jumped sharply after just two years experience to approach that earned by the instructors. In the course of researching this book it's become evident, from speaking to some ex-Hamble instructors, that their rates of remuneration became an issue. Who

The CAT and the Hamsters

> **BEA PILOTS**
> 20-27 with Commercial Pilot's Licence and Instrument Rating to start at £1,230-£1,410 (or at £500-£700 if well advanced to Instrument Rating). Applications are also being considered nowfrom pilots who expect to be so qualified and available late summer/autumn 1961. Send full details to Senior PersonnelOfficer (E & S), Flight Operations Department, BEA, Bealine House, Ruislip.

can blame them for being aggrieved when the salaries of former cadets outstripped their own within four years of graduating and became double or treble that figure within a decade?

Lewry says that his starting salary in 1965 was in the order of £2,200 to £2,400 a year, much more than his RAF emolument, and that figure reflected a recent pay rise negotiated on behalf of the Hamble instructors by BALPA. With 50 instructors on the staff, CAT was worthy of a Pilots Local Council within BALPA and this increased their negotiating power. Not all the instructors signed up to the association and Liskutin told me of disputes with Joe Douglas, who was an activist for BALPA.

College rules prevented CFIs from being BALPA members and precluded flight managers from taking part in negotiations but by June 30, 1979 *Flight* was printing the following advert:

> **COLLEGE OF AIR TRAINING, HAMBLE**
> College of Air Training Hamble, Southampton
> PERMANENT AND PENSIONABLE POSTS
> Due to expansion of our pilot training programme, applications from suitably qualified personnel are invited for the following vacancies. Salaries are comparative and are regularly reviewed.
> FLYING INSTRUCTORS
> High standards of instructional ability are required for the training of professionally selected students of high calibre who undertake a particularly exacting course. Any necessary supplementary training may be arranged for suitable candidates. For instructors already in possession of all required licences and ratings, emolument exclusive of certain fringe benefits may begin at about £8,500 p.a. on Annual Incremental Scale and with annual reviews.

Thus salaries had roughly quadrupled in the 20 years since the College had started, but pilots' pay within the newly formed British Airways had risen by a factor of five or six. It was hardly surprising that some instructors took to augmenting their earnings by working in the holidays.

Barry Byrne joined Hamble in November 1961 and after three or four

The CAT and the Hamsters

years he had some of ex-cadet pupils coming back to see him. He was not happy to find them earning more than he was. He was in his early forties by then and took his lead from another instructor Ted Kortens, who had contacts with Dan Air. Unlike some of the instructors, Barry was in possession of an ATPL. So after a brief check flight at Hurn he became a part-time captain on ex-BEA, Airspeed Ambassadors for Dan Air, during the weekends and college holidays.

During the August holidays of 1965 Barry operated many airline sectors but was taken to task by the college after a Ministry of Aviation audit discovered his 'other job'. He said that he felt the airline experience made his instruction on the advanced flight more relevant to real life but the MOA. didn't agree. Fed up with this attenuation of his earnings, he resigned in 1966.

These concerns were not communicated to the cadets and most of us remained largely unconcerned by anything other than struggling through the course towards graduation. Some instructors made the flying pleasurable and some made it purgatory. My own basic training tended towards the former and was with Bill Pash, lasting for eight months.

I can't remember much about him other than his extravagant moustache and the fact that he chided me for calling the mid-day meal dinner. At school we'd had dinner at mid-day and the women who doled out the overcooked cabbage and cadmium-yellow, lemon curd pudding were called dinner ladies. My parents referred to the meal as dinner; but as a cadet I should learn to call it lunch. If that's my most enduring memory of the chap I don't suppose he did me any harm but there was no warm, avuncular relationship. Readers of W E Johns novels would have been disappointed.

Nevertheless he did what all the instructors did for their Hamble pupils. He polished and refined whatever innate flying skill I possessed. He taught airmanship, precision, self-confidence and, above all, respect for the aerial environment. In dispersal was emblazoned a quotation I now know to be from Captain A G Lamplugh, British Aviation Insurance Group, London in the early Thirties. 'Aviation in itself is not inherently dangerous. But to an even greater degree than the sea, it is terribly unforgiving of any carelessness, incapacity or neglect'. After flying for 45 years of my life I can testify to its wisdom.

Overleaf is the page stuck into my log book showing the basic flying

The CAT and the Hamsters

```
              COLLEGE OF AIR TRAINING - FLYING EXERCISES
 1.   Air Experience
 2.   Effect of Controls
 3.   Straight and Level
 4.   Taxying
 5.   Climbing
 6.   Descending
 7.   M - Medium Turns    S - Steep Turns     C - Compass Turns
 8.   Stalling
 9.   Spinning
10.   Take-off   N - Normal    S - Short     C - Crosswind
11.   Circuit    N - Normal    C - Crosswind  B - Bad Weather
12.   Approach   G - Glide     P - Powered   H - 2000'
13.   Landing    T - Threepoint  W - Wheel   S - Short
                 C - Crosswind   F - Flapless R - Runway
14.   Action in event of fire
15.   Engine failure after take-off
16.   Missed Approach procedure
17.   Forced landing  G - without power    P - with power
18.   Instrument Flying  F - Full Panel   L - Limited panel   VDF
19.   Sideslipping
20.   Map Reading
```

exercises taught to cadets during first stage of training. After a day's flying, the cadet was expected to record, in the remarks column of their personal log books, which of the above exercises they had carried out. For me, the first flight in Chipmunk G-ARMG was undertaken on December 6, 1965 and lasted exactly one hour. In the aforementioned remarks column numbers 1-7, 10N, 11N, 8 and 22 are recorded.

Presumably the stalling exercise was carried out after the initial circuit but what I can remember are the aerobatics Bill demonstrated above the Isle of Wight. These culminated in me emptying the contents of my stomach over my new flying overalls. That perhaps explains why the list of exercises doesn't contain a No 13.

My first solo on the Chipmunk was after six hours, 25 minutes but I had the fortunate advantage of 36 hours previous experience. That was gained at the Hampshire Aero Club and the attendant Private Pilots Licence (PPL) course had been paid for by HM Government/RAF as a Special Flying Award.

Not everyone found their previous flying an asset. Bob was in our intake and had trained for his PPL at Biggin Hill on the Forney F-1 Ercoupe. This

The CAT and the Hamsters

The Air Products' Ercoup, the 'world's safest plane' which nevertheless cost one pilot his place.
Flight archive

was an American 'airplane' designed to be foolproof. Unfortunately the spin-proof Ercoupe taught Bob so many inaccurate techniques that he couldn't unlearn them in the time allocated. He was chopped!

The next big hurdle for us all was Progress Test 1 (PT1 to its friends, if it had any). Up until then we'd accomplished about 20 hours solo and 25 hours dual in the Chipmunk. Those hours encompassed the basic flying exercises shown in the table above, as well as cross-country flying exercises. Trips to the West Country — Exeter; Plymouth; Bristol (Lulsgate) and Gloucester (Staverton) — were favourites of mine because the south coast of Dorset and Devon unfolded as a beautiful panoply just under the left wing. Flying solo also meant the absence of a nagging instructor constantly chiding about height or heading and on one special occasion it allowed me to push back

The CAT and the Hamsters

the cockpit canopy above the orchards of Vale of Evesham in late April and luxuriate in the scent of apple blossom.

Flying cross-country 35 years (and nearly 20,000 hours later), albeit in a Chipmunk contemporary Cessna 170B, I was much less carefree and more conscious of other traffic, danger areas, geostrophic wind changes and Purple Airways. Ah well, that's experience – or old age. Although on the subject of not-so-carefree youth, I can recall my Chipmunk falling off the top of a badly executed loop above the Isle of Wight and thinking 'If this was 25 years ago I'd be trying to recover from this spin, while being shot at by a Messerschmitt 109.'

These relatively carefree days were leavened by others rendered less enjoyable by a visit up the steps to the control tower for a potential post-flight bollocking or worse. Sometimes two cadets were allocated to one aircraft, to engage in 'mutual'. The purpose of this was to build up the hours after the dreaded PT1 and also practise blind flying 'under the (canvas) hood'. This was rigged up in the front cockpit whilst the mutual pilot sat in the back ostensibly look out for other conflicting traffic. In reality though, he would spend most of the time taking the piss out of one's wretched attempts at flying straight and level 'without regard to external visual reference'.

During a mutual exercise with Malcolm in June 1966, he was taxying the aircraft – fully visual – or so he thought. From the front seat he failed to spot one of Hamble's airfield marker boards until I shouted an alarm. We stopped suddenly, so close to the large triangular red/orange marker that there was not enough room to manoeuvre around it. After a hurried discussion, which involved making sure that he had the brakes on, I climbed out of the aircraft and manhandled the marker away from where it stood less than ten feet from the propeller. He then taxied past and I replaced the marker before getting back into the Chipmunk. We then spent a nervous hour over the Isle of Wight wondering if anybody had seen our escapade.

Of course they had! Upon our return ATC commanded: 'Zulu Victor, report to the tower after shutdown.' However, it was not for a bollocking. The controller told us that he'd seen what was happening but before he could warn us of the obstruction, we'd dealt with the problem in our own way. Perhaps, before we stopped, he hadn't been watching us as closely as he should? In the event he congratulated us on our resourcefulness under pressure and we

The CAT and the Hamsters

breathed again. Unfortunately Malcolm must have transgressed in some other area because he was chopped during the next month. His record card is emblazoned with the chilling phrase 'Suspended on the grounds that he was unlikely to make a professional airline pilot'.

Hamble used three main grass strips as runways and marked the chosen one of the day with the boards mentioned above. These were designated by their orientation: one four; one eight and two zero. Naturally they had reciprocals: three two; three six and zero two. Because aeroplanes land and take off into

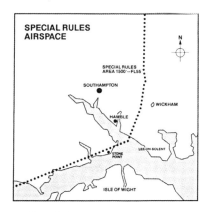 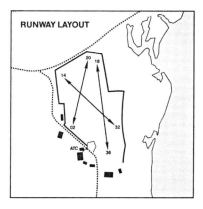

Hamble Airfield layout   Hamble pictures

wind whenever practicable, selection of the runway was determined by the surface wind. If the wind changed direction significantly so did the runway but it was an arduous process to move all the marker boards.

On the day in question a large anticyclone was dominating the British weather. Winds were light but had favoured the northerly runway 36 for many days. I took off from it for solo flying over the IoW and one hour later called ATC for joining instructions to return to the field. I was cleared for a 'straight in' approach to three six. The approach was going well and I was a mile or two from touchdown when the unmistakable voice of instructor John Vickers shouted over the R/T. 'All aircraft in the Hamble circuit for runway 18; there's an aircraft landing in the wrong direction.' It took me a microsecond to realise he was talking about me. It was a comprehension reinforced by lifting my gaze from my chosen landing spot to the other side of the airfield. Several Chipmunks hung in the sky, all on various stages of

The CAT and the Hamsters

Interior of the CAT control tower
Trevor Hughes

approach to runway 18 and all pointing at me. Runway one eight employed a left-hand circuit. Thus all the aircraft in that circuit were on my right, so I called ATC, identified myself as the errant aircraft and turned left towards the 'dead side' of the circuit pattern. From there I gained permission to join right — crosswind for 18, landed and taxied in for my interview with the CFI.

Peter Duff-Mitchell didn't appear to be a friendly man to us cadets, even when things were going well. So I entered his office, under the control tower, full of trepidation. He asked me to explain: 'What the hell I'd been thinking of approaching the airfield and trying to land in the wrong direction?' Respectfully I explained that was what I was cleared to do. 'We'll soon see about that!' he said and sent for the duty air traffic controller. There were no tape-recordings to back-up my assertion. So it was entirely due to the integrity of the controller that he admitted, after such a long period of time using three six, that he may have inadvertently cleared me straight-in on that runway; even though they had changed over to 18 a few minutes earlier.

'Furthermore!' he added, 'I think the cadet coped with the situation in a very professional manner.' I was in the clear but did I detect disappointment in the CFI's face?

Duff-Mitchell had not long been Chief Flying Instructor, having replaced George Webb who had retired in 1965. The deputy CFI to Duff-Mitchell was Vic Kinnin and I'm grateful to Dave Lewry for reminding me of that fact. Dave went on to say that the command structure of the instructors changed as the CAT expanded, with Tony Farrell and Bill Anderson as Flight Managers reporting to Duff-Mitchell. Later still, Deputy Flight Managers were

The CAT and the Hamsters

appointed. Each DFM was in charge of a given intake, rotating between basic and advanced flights as their intakes went through the system. When Cecil Pearce was appointed CFI in 1972, his title changed to Director of Flight Training. Later still there was also a Deputy Director of Flight Training and Dave was that DDFT to Tommy Thompson from 1980.

The two flying incidents mentioned above are insignificant hiccoughs within the complex process of training a professional pilot but they serve to illustrate how the college authorities imposed a mood of trepidation on cadets. It was a process which took the joy of flying away from some of us and replaced it with a fear of failure. For me the joy didn't return until I'd been in BEA for a couple of years and felt secure again. Despite that renaissance, an impending BA simulator check could often reawaken those old feelings of insecurity implanted by the College of Air Training.

Luckily the early problem of air-sickness was a transient one for me but for some cadets it proved to be a real challenge to graduation. For instance, in *The Chief Flying Instructor Report* written by G C Webb and dated October 26, 1962 he states: 'Apart from a tendency to air-sickness during the elementary phase of training Mr ******* had no difficulty in maintaining a very satisfactory rate of progress throughout.' At the risk of being slightly flippant; no doubt one of the purposes of flying selection, carried out over a period of four or five days during the first years of the college, was to bring up this problem. By 1970 that flying selection was a thing of the past, as were the Chipmunks.

Estimates before CAT was formed suggested that an annual Chipmunk utilisation of 800 hours would serve to cover the elementary training task. In reality it was nearer 660 hours and flying selection had not been included in the initial establishment of 18 Chipmunks.

An overall backlog of 1,200 hours had built up by September 1964 and the college was still expanding. The college Principal, AV-M E C Bates, told the governors that at least ten extra Chipmunks were needed urgently, as standards of training were being eroded. However he also pointed out that the Chipmunk was obsolescent and recommended Piper Cherokee 160s at a unit cost of £4,500. Some of the interim Chipmunks, in additional to the eight purchased from AST, had cost £2,750 from Dacier Ltd.

Setting a trend that would continue through the life of the college, the

The CAT and the Hamsters

governors and their airline paymasters fudged the issue and hired 12 more Chipmunks from the RAF for two years.

The Chipmunk's demise began in earnest on February 23, 1966 with a paper prepared for the governors by the Principal entitled *The Provision of Additional Basic Training Aircraft*. He reminded them that there were currently 31 Chipmunks in service with the college, 12 of which were hired from the Ministry of Defence. There was a perceived requirement for a further 22 more basic trainers, due to proposed expansion (Plan Golf). Flying training, he wrote, could be broken down into 70 hours *ab-initio* and 80 hours intermediate but each of these phases would need to use only one type of aircraft. He assessed the difficulties of obtaining more Chipmunks and concluded that 'there was very little hope of getting as many as 22 Chipmunks into service by September'.

On the other hand, Piper Aviation would provide 22 Cherokee 160s at a base price of £4,500 each and within the time frame mentioned above. The Principal cited the extra fuel endurance, two extra seats, tricycle undercarriage and higher avionics specification as reasons to buy the American aircraft.

The news that CAT was in the market for 22 aircraft produced a feeding frenzy of interest amongst the purveyors of single-engine aircraft. Letters arrived offering demonstrations and deals concerning the Cessna 150, Wassmer Super IV, Miles 'Student' (jet trainer), Beagle Pup, Sud-Aviation 'Horizon' and Bolkow-Siat 223 to name but a few.

All the while pressure mounted on the governors, due to Plan Golf, which aimed to reduce the course length to 18 months with an intake of 168 cadets per annum. A 20 per cent failure rate was factored in to produce 134 graduates a year. To achieve this increase in output it was proposed to fly training details seven days a week and reduce the annual holiday entitlement. On behalf of the flying instructors BALPA gave a big-thumbs-down, so the five-day week remained.

Additional complications were being caused by the Apache fleet and its perceived need for replacement. The CFI had already prepared a paper for the Principal on the possible candidates, as well as the additional need for two more Apaches *pro-tem* (P O M Duff-Mitchell, 6/05/1965). He listed Piper's obsolescent Apache 235 and its newer Aztec C, Beechcraft's B55 Baron and D95 'A' Travel Air as well as the new Beagle 206. Bates and

The CAT and the Hamsters

Beagle 206X and
Beagle Pup, from
company advert
*November 14, 1968,
Flight archive*

Duff-Mitchell had visited Shoreham on December 1, 1964 to look around the Beagle factory.

The British Executive & General Aviation Limited (trading as BEAGLE) was formed in 1960 when the Pressed Steel Company created an aircraft design office (to design the Beagle B206) and took over two separate aircraft manufacturers — Auster Aircraft Company of Rearsby, Leicestershire and F G Miles Limited of Shoreham, Sussex. Initially, production was split between Rearsby and Sussex but this did not last long because the three parts of the company were merged at Shoreham as Beagle Aircraft Limited in 1962.

In 1965 the parent company, Pressed Steel, was acquired by the British Motor Corporation. The company reviewed the involvement in light-aircraft manufacturing and requested financial help from the British Government, which nationalised Beagle in 1966 and provided the help needed. However, when the company needed more financial help in 1969, the Government put the company into receivership. The Receiver tried to revive and sell the company, now renamed Beagle Aircraft (1969) Limited, but failed and the company assets were sold and aircraft production ceased.

CAT's troubled involvement with the company dates back to 1964 when the College was considering the B121 Pup as a Chipmunk replacement. At that stage Beagle was developing a twin-engined Miles design which

The CAT and the Hamsters

became the Beagle 218. An all-plastic prototype first flew on August 19, 1962 but customers expressed a preference for an all-metal version. This became the Beagle B242, the concept of which interested CAT as an Apache replacement. However Beagle concentrated their limited resources on developing the B206 and the Pup to the detriment of the B242 and the project was shelved in 1966.

This left only the B206 in the race for the College's Apache replacement and in truth it was too big and too expensive for Hamble's modest infrastructure. The airfield and its attendant airspace also imposed limitations on the number of aircraft movements. So the governors proposed that the 80 hours of intermediate training be carried at satellite airfields such as Sandown and Goodwood. This made the provision of 12 intermediate trainers, with four seats and greater endurance than the Chipmunk, imperative. The fully-equipped Piper Cherokee 180C met the bill but would cost £7,680 each, ten per cent of which was import duty. To complete this modified Plan G a new study block would need to be built, bringing the total cost to £120,000. Four entries of 46 cadets a year, less 20 per cent wastage, would allow modified Plan G to output 147 graduates from a 68-week course.

Concern was expressed at the governors' meeting of May 19, 1966 concerning the lag in the training of 651/2/3, whose course had been scheduled to be shortened by nine weeks to facilitate college expansion (Plan G) and a new post-graduate intake. My intake, 654/5/6, was deemed to have suffered badly and was 25 hours per cadet under target. Our own 36-week course was due to be 30 weeks for the same reason but this reduction was deferred. None of this was explained to cadets, who were often made to carry the can of the extra pressure as they fell short of more stringent time constraints.

Despite the exigencies of the situation, nothing had changed by November

Cherokees at
Hamble Disp(
Trevor H(

The CAT and the Hamsters

10, 1966 and the CFI wrote to the Principal offering a solution (Duff-Mitchell, 1966). He advised a syllabus of 100 hours basic training on 30 Chipmunks, 56 intermediate hours on 12 newly-bought Cherokees and 69 advanced hours on 11 Apaches. By introducing the Cherokees, 12 hours of the erstwhile Apache training could be carried out during the intermediate phase and that segment at satellite airfields. He also drew attention to the three or four Chipmunks that were required for flying selection each day. Eventually all of the Chipmunks could be replaced if the new, aerobatic Beagle/Bolkow trainers that were on the drawing board were built and bought by CAT. These would become the new primary trainer.

Accordingly a board meeting to discuss the Chipmunk replacement was held at 10.30am on Wednesday December 21, 1966 in the board room on the second floor of the West London Air Terminal. Coffee and biscuits could be provided by phoning FROBISHER 4255, extension 2284 but that was the only thing that was certain, apart from the fact that they'd set up a committee to look at the procurement. Eventually it concluded: 'The Cherokee is basically a touring aeroplane which has been adapted to the training role. It does not possess the handling qualities desirable in a basic trainer and does not provide training in aerobatics or fully developed spins. It is nevertheless in extensive use as a basic trainer and will do the job provided its limitations are accepted.'

The Cherokee was first certified in America during 1960 and designated

Parameter	Chipmunk Mk 22	Cherokee 180C
MTOW	2,014lbs	2400lbs
Max payload	589lbs	1,090lbs
VNE	135 knots (155mph)	171mph
Normal maximum	120 knots (138mph)	152mph
Cruise	95 knots (110mph)	116 knots (134mph)
Stall speed (clean)	45 knots (52 mph)	50 knots (57mph)
Initial climb	840 ft/min	750 ft/min
Fuel consumption (cruise)	7.4 gallons/hour	5.5 -6 gallons/hour
...giving approx	12.8 n/miles per gall	19 n/miles per gall
Range (Mk 22A)	230 n/miles	655 n/miles

A table comparing performance data of the two basic/intermediate trainers (various sources).

The CAT and the Hamsters

the Piper PA-28 and first models were fitted with a 150hp Lycoming O-320-E2A, which was not really powerful enough for the four-passenger, full tanks configuration. So CAT purchased 22 of the 180hp model PA-28-180, which started to arrive in February 1967.

This new intermediate trainer was not aerobatic but the Cherokee's tricycle undercarriage made its ground handling far more straightforward than the Chipmunk and, like most American singles, its stall was pretty docile too. (*Flight* Team Test, 1973). Stalling speed with flaps extended was 57mph (50 knots) and with the aircraft 'clean', 10mph greater. As to spins, the following quote is from Piper's Cherokee 180 E owner's handbook: 'Intentional spins are prohibited in this aircraft' — hence the need for the retained Chipmunks.

Overlaying these factors, but germane to them, hung the spectre of total Chipmunk and Apache replacement. By April 1967, CAT were in possession of nine Cherokees but their calculations showed a requirement for 20 more aircraft for the basic flight. Their shortlist was more Cherokees, or the new, untried, untested Beagle 121-L Pup. CAT had paid £6,928 net for their first Cherokees (£798 import duty exemption and £1,070 discount deducted from the gross figure) but it was eminently possible that the availability of a newly-nationalised Beagle alternative might induce the Board of Trade to charge the import duty on any further Pipers. So once again the governors decision was clouded by external considerations.

A contemporary submission by the Department of Civil Aviation made it quite clear to the college Principal that 'aerobatic manoeuvres should (must) be included in the syllabus for commercial pilots training'. Accordingly, the Cherokee would not be suitable for teaching that part of the basic syllabus. So emphasis switched back to the Beagle Pup. The Principal wrote to P G Masefield, managing director of Beagle Aircraft Ltd, on April 26, 1967 asking for reassurances on costing, delivery dates and aircraft specifications. Masefield admitted that the desired Pup 180 could not be delivered within the CAT timescale but offered to lend/lease 12 of the Pup 150s *pro-tem* and then, when the 180s became available, 22 could be supplied by July 1968 at a price of £7,150 per aircraft.

Another option for CAT would be to order even more Cherokees, which would mean keeping a few Chipmunks to demonstrate and teach the specific aspect of aerobatics and spinning. The Chipmunk was not a cuddly, furry

The CAT and the Hamsters

Piper PA-23 at Hamble, 1967
Roger Guiver

North American squirrel of an aeroplane; it could bite if you treated it harshly but on the other hand the Cherokee wasn't the fierce warlike North American Indian either.

Before this was resolved, the Principal was forced to start another hare running. In a letter entitled *GB. 470 — Purchase of Additional Twin Engined Aircraft* he stated that due to lack of sufficient capacity in the advanced flight, intake 661/2/3 were all to be temporarily grounded to allow (my intake) 654/5/6 to finish on schedule.

Understandably I have no personal recollection of any of these momentous events because of the extreme workload and urge to succeed. Additionally the college ethos did not include mere cadets in the machinations of deciding which aircraft they might fly in the future. I have in my log book a list of the 56 exercises that my colleagues and I been undertaking while on the advanced flight. It's unlikely that they would change much even when the Apache replacement finally arrived.

At the commencement of advanced training, the cadet was in possession of a PPL and had at least 150 hours flying experience. Our own course joined the advanced flight in September 1966. After a couple of weeks we went solo on the Apache. This came about after six to eight hours of dual instruction. Mostly this was general handling but we also learned the delights of asymmetric flight.

In truth, the aircraft was easy enough to fly on two engines but the

The CAT and the Hamsters

instructors needed to be satisfied that the cadet could cope with the aircraft if one of its engines failed. Despite C M Lambert's assertion after his *Flight* air test, the Apache didn't have much in reserve when one of its engines was shut down. Perhaps this was because Piper had never designed the aeroplane to be a training workhorse and perhaps it was bought for the college b ecause it was reasonably priced in the late 1950s. Either way it was fast approaching its denouement.

The Apache was originally known as the Twin-Stinson and designated Piper PA-23. It flew for the first time on March 2 1952. The college ordered theirs in 1960 from Vigors Aviation Ltd at Oxford (Kidlington Airport). They were prepared to college standards at the same airfield by mechanics of the Air Services Division of Pressed Steel Co — who, ironically, would later become the owners of Beagle.

Prior to CAT, AST had operated pre-war Avro Ansons and Airspeed Oxfords. The latter were considered for purchase by the new establishment at a cost of £600 each but this didn't transpire. There was even a Douglas Dakota: all were aircraft designed in the 1930s and the field was a bit tight for the stately Dakota. So during the late 1950s AST had decided to purchase some Apaches. In choosing the American twin the college was eschewing British-built aircraft but because of the paucity it was not a difficult choice. They already had experience of the pre-war offering and although the De Havilland Dove first flew in February 1960 it was too big and too expensive. The Miles Gemini was also post-war but never a serious contender. Incidentally the Beagle 218 was its design replacement.

In 1954 *Flight* reported that the new Apache cost £11,600 in America ($32,500 was the launch price) and when C M Lambert did a flight test for them he commented: 'Altogether, for its size and price, the Apache is an excellent machine. It offers twin-engined operational safety and utility combined with a simplicity and ease of maintenance.' He found it pleasantly undemanding to fly and aerodynamically stable but not especially responsive to the controls. Single-engined performance was 'all that one could wish' although later chapters of this book may show otherwise. It was the lightest and cheapest of the American light-twins and the college had avionics fitted to full airways specification (ILS, VOR, ADF and VHF radio). It paid £12,676 for each basic airframe but ferry costs, import duty, radio and spares

The CAT and the Hamsters

Apache and cadets from 654: John Michie, Eric Tomlin behind nacelle and Roger Price on wing
Hamble pictures

pushed this up to £25,000.

During 1965 there had been an intake of university graduate cadets at Hamble. This left CAT needing two extra advanced trainers before the end of the year and three more to fulfil the erstwhile expansion scheme Echo in 1966. In addition they were still looking for an Apache replacement and considered Piper's Twin Comanche, Aztec as well as Beechcraft's Travel Air and Baron and mixed fleet of Beagle 206 and 242. Test flights and negotiations took place and the Beagle deal began to look possible.

However the Airline Chairmen's Committee let it be known through Captain J W G (Jimmy) James that the complexities of introducing an untried aircraft and the extra costs of the B206 were an obstacle to placing a contract with Beagle. Accordingly during November 1965 CAT purchased two second-hand Apache 160 aircraft from CSE Aviation for £15,000 each.

The decision elicited a furious response from Beagle MD Peter Masefield, who more or less accused CAT's board of being unpatriotic and visiting harm on the British aircraft industry. Beagle was itself nationalised by the UK Labour Government in 1966. Jimmy James reminded him the CAT had decided the B206 was not suitable and that was that. It didn't bode well for future expansion of the British plane maker.

The new Apaches were pressed into service and after completion of solo on type and because of Hamble airfield's propensity to wetness, the advanced flight often did its circuits and instrument approach training at nearby Hurn or Lee-on-Solent. The four seats in the Apache permitted the instructor to take three cadets for these away-days but more frequently two, especially

The CAT and the Hamsters

during the later exercises. In practise the airways flying and circuit work was divided equally but the non-handling cadet was expected to sit in the rear seats and learn from his buddy's mistakes.

Exercises eight to 16 consolidated the twin-engined and single-engined handling skills, as well as introducing various different landing techniques. Much of this work was solo with the stalls and steep turns being practised above the IoW and its long-suffering inhabitants. Then, after approximately 16 hours, the local bonds were relaxed and route flying began.

How cadets and instructors were paired up was never explained to the cadet. There were many shades of personality in each group. Sometimes they blended and sometimes they didn't and a personality clash could be seriously detrimental to a cadet's prospects. I was teamed with a second-generation, Polish buddy called Chris. I believe that his father had come to England during the Second World War. He may well have been a pilot with the RAF, for his son was slightly older than me. Our first instructor was called Pritchet. I don't believe I ever knew his Christian name.

By January 1967 we'd been transferred to a new chap called Stan Offer. Tragically we didn't get to know him either, because after just four details he was killed when our Apache crashed into the grounds of nearby Netley Hospital. The Air Investigations Board (AIB) report laid much of the blame at his door but there was more to the accident than his error. In chapter eight I'll go into more detail of that and the various other aircraft accidents which happened during the currency of CAT.

According to my logbook, after the accident the syllabus went by the board for a while as the college came to terms with the ramifications that the accident would have on the flying syllabus in general, the loss of a training aircraft, as well as the effect on Chris and me. Fortunately neither of us suffered severe injury but it was nearly three weeks before I flew again.

Unbeknown to us, the flight manager of the advanced flight 'Bill' Anderson felt constrained to write to the Principal on February 13, 1967. In a strongly-worded letter he earnestly recommended early replacement of the Apache fleet with a more modern and reliable aircraft. He cited a low serviceability factor of 55 per cent as being the root cause of the lowest-ever morale among instructors and cadets caused by shortage of aircraft. This in turn contributed to a deterioration of standards, due to the intermittent nature of the instruction.

The CAT and the Hamsters

On the header of his copy of Bill's letter Bates wrote peremptorily in red ink 'Dealt with — with CFI'. The letter didn't appear to be a welcome insight into real problems.

Stan's replacement was a Canadian called Bernie Batty. We began by doing my second detail of night flying and then, because of the break, some necessary consolidation. By then I had unwanted first-hand experience of how quickly a routine flight can turn into a catastrophe.

It was perhaps the most valuable lesson I learned at Hamble but also the most expensive in terms of human and collateral cost. In essence the lesson was: almost always, aircraft accidents occur as a result of a succession of untoward mistakes or circumstances and that the pilot's most important job is to prevent them linking up to form a chain of disaster.

So I had acquired over 20 hours on the Apache before we enacted an out-of-sequence exercise 31, at last joining the real commercial pilots on airways to Birmingham (Elmdon). It turned into an excruciating experience. Bernie was in a hurry to depart Hamble and chivvied us out to the Apache on the Tarmac. Chris was in the left-hand forward seat, traditionally where the aircraft commander sits, doing the take-off and joining the commercial airways system under ATC supervision.

In the back seat my function was to monitor, observe and learn by example but it didn't happen very much on that sector. I was increasingly aware that, in the rush to get airborne, I'd ignored my need to have a post-breakfast pee. By the time we were flying over Berkshire I was uncomfortable but by Oxford it had reached a new level of excruciation and I shamefacedly confessed my predicament to our instructor.

'You'll have to wait until we land,' he snapped over the intercom. 'Or go in a sick bag, if you can't wait.' My humiliation was intense but I hung on. Turbulence on the approach to Elmdon didn't help but Bernie must have had an outbreak of compassion after landing, because he asked the ATC ground controllers: 'Juliet Tango is it OK if we hold our position on taxyway alpha for 60 seconds?'. They approved this unusual request and he got Chris to stop the Apache and apply the parking brake.

'You've got 30 seconds' he said. 'Don't walk into the prop and don't face it either.' I was out of the aircraft in a flash — literally — but 30 seconds was barely enough time to relieve my distended bladder of what seemed

The CAT and the Hamsters

like hundreds of gallons of breakfast-time tea. Soon we continued taxiing towards the terminal, leaving a tell-tale puddle on the concrete. Nobody said anything else and ATC didn't enquire the reasons for our brief halt but I've often wondered what the plane spotters thought?

Of course the Apache training was concerned with much more than learning to control one's bladder. It was about learning to control a multi-engined aircraft without recourse to external visual reference; in other words, instrument-flying. That particular skill is well-documented elsewhere but, suffice to say, it involved interpreting what the aircraft's instruments were showing in terms of height, speed and direction. In turn the cadet was then expected to adhere to ATC instructions and follow his pre-planned route using ground-based radio facilities. Most of the exercises from then on practised the use of ADF, VOR and ILS.

To the radio buff these were modern, sophisticated, ground-based transmitters which should aid the experienced pilot to find his way in bad weather or at night. To the cadet pilot they were synonymous with thumbscrews, racks and ancient forms of torture. Once again I'll spare the details of how to fly an aircraft on instruments, guided solely by radio-nav, but I can reveal that a three-dimensional mental picture is essential. The spartan information displayed on two or three small round dials has to be interpreted accurately to construct that mental picture.

Imagine Henry Moore sculpting his *Reclining Figure* while the model describes himself to the artist over the telephone from several miles away. Then again, looking at the finished work of art, perhaps that's how he did it anyway! To help exercise the areas of grey matter involved in these feats, the basics of instrument flying had already been carried out within the comparative safety of a Link D4 Trainer.

This primitive simulator of flight was just an enclosed cockpit which stayed firmly bolted to the ground inside a classroom. CAT had six of them. At their inception they were called synthetic flying trainers.

Viewed from outside, the Link did rotate, roll and nod like a bear trying to escape from a swarm of angry bees but inside the 'sweat box' a trainee pilot was causing the gyrations and genuflections. This in an effort to imagine the imaginary information the machine created on its instruments at the behest of a Link instructor.

The CAT and the Hamsters

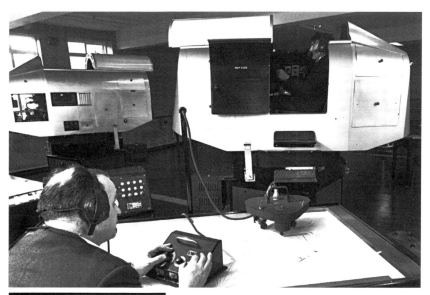

The Link Trainer and 'Crab'... imagine Henry Moore sculpting *Reclining Figure* via telephone.
Hamble Pictures & Fitzwilliam Museum, Cambridge

The baffling box was electronically linked to a thing called a crab. This consisted of a moving pen which traced the track of the imaginary aircraft by inching across a glass covered map-table. After the detail was finished the cadet could be shown the spidery lines tracing his progress over the map. One incarcerated cadet was surprised to have his thought train interrupted by the instructor saying 'Mike Victor if you don't make the turn towards the airfield soon the bloody crab's going to fall off the edge of my world'.

Those exercises had been accomplished during the intermediate phase of the course, in parallel with the Chipmunk, or better still the well- instrumented Cherokee. The advanced flight had two flight procedure trainers. They were sophisticated in comparison with the Link trainers. One simulator pretended to be in America and its twin chuntered around Europe and the UK. Or rather its instruments were supposed to create the mental picture of a four-engined jet aircraft wending its way from Heathrow to Frankfurt, for example. Cadets

The CAT and the Hamsters

Cadets from 655 operate the four-engine jet simulator
Hamble pictures - BOAC

got to practise airline-type procedures in an airliner-type cockpit without ever leaving the ground but there was no physical sensation of being inside the bee-stung bear. These simulators were static so the seat of your pants could tell you nothing, except that you were sweating profusely.

Perhaps because of that, the smell of fear inside those things was almost palpable but dread of tests and fear of failure served as a regular restraint on youthful male exuberance. Various hoops had to be jumped through during the advanced course, just as with the basic course. Most of these tests were conducted by the senior college flying instructors (CFI and his assistant or flight managers). Progress Test 1 and 2 again show up on the list of exercises. The former was normally done as the cadet approached 20 hours on the Apache and the latter about 50 hours after that.

Possibly my olfactory senses were sensitised to the said 'smell of fear' but I detected the odour at BOAC training centre Cranebank. Our intake was in mid-course but a day had been scheduled for the visit, presumably to show us what to expect after graduation to the airline.

At that stage most of us had expressed a preference to join BOAC in favour of BEA. We duly traipsed around Cranebank and arrived at the new Boeing 707 simulator, just as the training captain and his three 'victims' emerged. He was a small, officious, self-important little man with a Hitler moustache. The cowed victims emanated the powerful scent of trepidation mentioned above. I found the experience unsettling enough to visit the CAT Principal's secretary next morning and change my preference to BEA. On such flimsy tissue are lives mapped out.

Even though the flying instructors felt that their own remuneration compared unfavourably with airline rates of pay, the total cost to the college of fuel, staff salaries, aircraft maintenance, amortisation, insurance and spares was considerable. In a 1968 article *Flight* asserted that 'the direct costs of a light twin are around £20 per hour, but when everything is taken into account, the total mounts to between £30 and £35 per hour'. It's easy to see how those costs contributed to the constant pressure on CAT instructors to complete the flying syllabus within the flying hour constraints set by the accountants.

Other establishments such as AST at Perth, CSE at Kidlington and the London School of Flying at Elstree were charging £3,500 to £4,000 for a course culminating in a CPL/IR qualification. These applicants had to complete a course of 150 hours with at least 100 hours as pilot-in- command, including 20 hours of cross-country or overseas flying and ten hours of night flying. The remainder could be as pilot-in-command or co-pilot.

The solution to the aforementioned logjam was threefold: intake 664/5/6 were to complete their last 30 hours of twin-engined I/R on contract outside of Hamble; the flying instructors would be persuaded to adopt new working practices and CAT needed to purchase two Piper Aztec (PA-23-250) aircraft at £25,637 each.

The Hamble course was already longer than privately-run schools which stuck to a bare minimum and charged £1,000 to £1,500 less than the college. So the CAT ethos was very much 'can this cadet achieve our standard within the hours allowed? If not; then he must go', but this was occasionally tempered by the investment of time and effort put into his training thus far.

Ergo, the cadet might have reason to believe that having come this far (successful PT2 for example) they wouldn't chop him. How wrong could he be? Cadets were chopped right up to the brink of graduation and it was the airline's perceived need for pilots which caused the bar to be raised or lowered. This to achieve the number of graduates that the corporations felt they needed for the future.

History shows that they were spectacularly inept at this estimation but I

The CAT and the Hamsters

think they looked at it this way: it was cheaper to waste £5,000 or 6,000 of training costs than to payroll a pilot throughout a career where he was surplus to requirements. Anyway, the mid to late Sixties was when the corporations thought that they needed all the pilots they could lay their hands on.

As it noted in the list after exercise 49: 'Any time from now on the Ministry of Aviation (MOA) general flying test and instrument rating can be carried out subject to a satisfactory PT2'. So a type rating endorsement (general handling test) for the Piper PA-28 genre, sometimes called an 1179 test, due to the serial number on the MOA form which needed completing, was done in-house and included with the written/technical exams. However the MOA instrument rating test was carried out by the fearsome examiners from the official organisation that became Civil Aviation Flying Unit (CAFU).

During the first decade of CAT's existence the instructors would vary their final advice to their about-to-be-tested cadets dependent on which CAFU examiner was due to attend Hamble. Each of the CAFU people had his foibles. The lack of consistency didn't make an already exacting examination any easier for the cadet or his instructor.

Dave Lewry was later to accompany Cecil Pearce and Tommy Thompson (the three-man standardisation committee of CAT at that time) on regular visits to Stanstead and Gatwick to liaise with the new Civil Aviation Authority (CAA) from 1972. As the 'old guard' of CAFU retired, their replacements became more amenable to maintaining testing standards that were high but consistent as well.

As we've seen above, the Apache was coming to the end of its useful life and the crash of G-ASDH in January 1967 had served to highlight just how little the aircraft had in reserve when a critical situation developed. The Apache had been designed in the 1950s as a comfortable general aviation runabout in the USA which could cope on one engine if necessary. What was not foreseen was that any one would expect it to stand up to the regular rough and tumble of asymmetric flying by trainee pilots.

The loss of 'Delta Hotel' left a gap in the college fleet which was temporarily filled by acquisition of the two Piper Aztecs. This aircraft began life in 1958 as of the Apache, with 250hp Lycoming O-540 engines and a swept vertical tail (PA-23-250). In the longer term, serious limitations had

The CAT and the Hamsters

Piper PA23-250 Aztec
FlugKerl2 - Own work. Licensed under CC BY-SA 3.0 via Wikimedia Commons

been recognised with regard to the Apache, as the extract below from the Board of Trade accident report (CAP 306, page 11) shows.

The Apache had a hydraulic system operated by one hydraulic pump on the left engine. When that engine failed, operation of flaps and undercarriage reverted to a manual pump. It's obvious that the fleet could only be modified at great expense, so at a general meeting of instructors CFI Duff-Mitchell let it be known that he was looking for someone to evaluate the potential Apache replacements. At the Technical and Training meeting of May 30 he had received a paper from John Vickers detailing the desirable characteristics for the replacement aircraft. Later, Dave Lewry volunteered and was sent a letter by AV-M Bates authorising him to begin the process during July 1967.

He visited the Paris Air Show and the Biggin Hill Air Fair as well as

3. Recommendations

It is recommended that in twin engine aircraft which have a low rate of climb with one engine inoperative in certain conditions and which are used extensively for flying training, consideration should be given to the possibility of providing means to ensure:

(a) the aircraft instrumentation will give a ready indication of incorrect engine operation;

(b) the speed of retraction of flaps and landing gear is maintained regardless of which engine is rendered inoperative.

The CAT and the Hamsters

Beagle Aircraft Limited at Shoreham Airport, Rogers Aviation at Cranfield, who were agents for Cessna, Eagle Aircraft Services at Leavesden, who sold the Baron, and an option to buy further Aztecs from CSE at Oxford was also considered. People's ears pricked up when he said that he was looking to buy 12 aircraft. Eventually he settled on a shortlist of the Beagle 206 Series 1, the more powerful Series 2 and the American Beechcraft Baron 55. Both the B55 and more expensive D55 were evaluated but eventually the college and their airline sponsors settled for six of the Baron C55 with six seats and six with four seats. These were homogenised at Hamble to produce a five-seat version which could lift full fuel tanks with all seats filled.

In America the Baron's price was a little over $68,300 each in 1966 (about £24,350 but devaluation pushed that figure up by £4,000 by the end of the decade). On June 16, 1967, CAT had been quoted £22,436 each by CSE Aviation for 10 or more Aztecs and £4,524 each for the same number of Cherokee 140s. Import duty on each type was approximately 12 per cent of the total. More information arrived four days later based on a comparative evaluation of running costs by BOAC's flight operations accountant, Captain M R Aries. He assessed that the Beagle 206 would cost some £6,300 more to run than the Aztec, assuming a seven-year lifespan and concluded that the Beagle's initial purchase price needed to be lower by a commensurate amount.

A few days later, on June 21, a meeting was held in Room 241 at Shell Mex House between the Ministry of Technology, the Board of Trade, Beagle Aircraft Ltd, the Principal, CFI and chief engineer from CAT. With the British Government now established as the owner of Beagle, the political heat was being turned up and the B206 was back in the frame. Nevertheless, Dave Lewry produced a report on his deliberations regarding four contenders for Apache replacement. The report was seen and agreed by his fellow senior instructors, John Vickers and Les Craven. It came down firmly in favour of the Beechcraft Baron C55.

The Aztec mirrored the single hydraulic pump deficiency of the Apache and had additional pitch change problems when flap selections were made. The Baron B55 and the Beagle 206 were considered unsatisfactory in terms of single-engine performance when operating out of Hamble. So it seems some lessons had been learned from the accident to G-ASDH. In addition,

The CAT and the Hamsters

Parameter	Apache	Baron
MTOW	3,800 lbs	5,300 lbs
Max payload	1,600 lbs	2,225 lbs
Ceiling	11,000 feet	20,900 feet
Range	1,029 Nm	750 Nm
Cruise	166 knots	200 Kn
Stall speed (clean)	54 knots	67 Kn
Initial climb	1,260 ft/min	1,670 ft/min
Wing span	37 feet 1¾ inches	37ft 10in
Take off run	400 yards	200 yards
Landing run	220 yards	290 yards

Table comparing performance data of CAT's two advanced trainers (various sources).

the Beagle's field performance was not good enough for Hamble's short, grass runways.

That all seemed clearcut until J P W Mallalieu from the Board of Trade wrote an arm-twisting letter to Sir Giles Guthrie, the Chairman of BOAC on July 11. He was 'anxious that no decisions should be reached to buy foreign aircraft before I have had time to discuss it further with John Stonehouse and you.' John Stonehouse was the Labour Minister for Technology. Things were getting heavy!

(More than 20 years after his death in 1988, it was revealed that Stonehouse had been an agent for communist Czechoslovak Socialist Republic's military intelligence. In 1979 it was learned from a Czech defector that Stonehouse had been paid to spy for them since 1962. He provided secrets about Government plans as well as technical information about aircraft and received about £5,000. He was already in prison for fraud and the government decided there was insufficient evidence to bring him to trial, so no announcement or prosecution was made.

In contrast the proposed Beagle B206 was a larger, heavier aeroplane in its Series 2 format. Wingspan was about seven feet more than the Baron with a MTOW almost a ton more. After the 16 gallons per hour fuel consumption of the Apache, Dave Lewry said that the college was worried about the greater fuel consumption of the Beagle at 29 gallons per hour, while the Baron's

The CAT and the Hamsters

Barons on the Tarmac Trevor Hughes

was 22 gallons per hour. Beagle offered to build a lower weight version of the 206 but that still didn't improve the fuel consumption markedly. Anyway they had already cast adrift the B242 that the college had really wanted. When I interviewed Dave Lewry 45 years later he was still indignant about Beagle's perceived chicanery.

It's not the purpose of this book to unearth corporate deception but Dave Lewry is convinced that performance figures were deliberately misrepresented and the trial aircraft was under-fuelled to enhance the rather poor single-engined performance of the B206. The last thing that CAT wanted at that stage was another trainer which was a liability on one engine. Furthermore, one of the first Beagles to land at Hamble was flown by their test pilot. Unfortunately the biggest impression he made, was in the airfield boundary fence because on landing he failed to stop on the runway and had a whoopsie in what golfers call the rough.

The decision-making process culminated in an Airline Chairmen's Committee meeting on July 26, 1967. A proposal was considered: 'to purchase 21 Beagle Pup 150s to replace the 18 remaining Chipmunks and 12 Beechcraft Baron C55s to replace the 11 Apaches and two gash Aztecs'. The costs were to be shared between BEA and BOAC and stacked up as follows: Pups at £131,475 including import duty on engines and £6,000 worth of spares; Barons at £404,780 including £42,540 import duty and £20,000 worth of spares. The resultant bill of £536,255 would be ameliorated by an estimated £113,500 sale price for the college's existing aircraft.

The CAT and the Hamsters

BOAC chairman Sir Giles Guthrie had written to J P W Mallalieu at the Board of Trade on behalf of himself and BEA chairman Sir Anthony Millward two days before the crucial meeting mentioned above. In the letter he stated that not only was the Beagle 206 unsatisfactory from a safety point of view, it was also too expensive.

So CAT decided on the Baron, despite the ongoing sterling crisis and poor rate of exchange with the US dollar. The mighty Beechcraft duly arrived in March 1968 and training was initially carried out from the grass runways at Hamble. However problems began to manifest themselves in the form of noise complaints and soggy winter runways. The airfield had always been prone to waterlogging but Steve Leniston (694) remembers flying being severely curtailed during their basic training on Cherokees during the winter of 1969-70.

The heavier Barons fared even worse on the soft ground, so a decision was taken to move the advanced flight to Hurn. Purpose-built briefing rooms and simulator blocks were constructed and the whole advanced flight decamped, never to return to Hamble. This decision was to cause the college problems down the line, as angry residents under the circuit pattern complained vociferously to Bournemouth Corporation about the noise generated by regular night flying.

On April 1, 1969 Hurn had been purchased jointly by the Bournemouth Corporation and Dorset County Council and renamed 'Bournemouth Airport'. Its main runway 08/26 was pre-war concrete and 2,000 yards long. A secondary crossing runway 17/35 was 400 yards shorter.

Thirty-four cadets were accommodated in two commercial hotels from February 1971. The original intake of 48 was down to 36 after 12 cadets were suspended and two killed in a mid-air Cherokee collision over the Southampton suburb of Bursledon on February 27, 1970.

Cadets were billeted two to a room, unlike Hamble where each had his own study/bedroom. Nevertheless the young men appreciated the more relaxed atmosphere away from the quasi-military regime imposed during basic training. Cars had become something of a necessity, because the training day at Hurn was divided into early and late details and the six-mile journey was not particularly well-served by convenient public transport.

The hotels differed in character by virtue of their owners' personalities.

The CAT and the Hamsters

Cecil Pearce instructs on the Chipmunk   Hamble pictures — BOAC

The first, which no longer exists, also hosted 'normal' guests and the officious proprietor protected these members of the public by making certain areas of the hotel off-limits to cadets. The bar was especially 'verboten'. One evening Herr Fawlty admonished a group of cadets over their attire at dinner. He said they should maintain higher standards of dress, because of the presence of the general public. Accordingly the cadets turned up for their next meal in full evening dress. The issue was not mentioned again!

The other hotel began in a much more relaxed fashion, serving large portions of home-cooked food. However, after a few months it must have become obvious to the novice owners that 17 young men will consume very large quantities of victuals. So, over time, portion sizes and quality declined.

At the outset of Baron training the advanced flight devised a way of ameliorating flying costs. John Hall and Dave Lewry proposed a series of training flights to European destinations. The fuel bought overseas destinations was duty-free, thus making a saving of 30 per cent on UK loaded fuel. Fred Barnes, the head of liberal studies, was brought in to convince the Principal of the virtues of cadets experiencing proper 'airline style' nightstops.

Hurn had facilities for customs clearance so the 'international' trips expanded. Destinations included Jersey, Cherbourg, Dinard, Prestwick,

The CAT and the Hamsters

Shannon, Hamburg, Amsterdam, Dusseldorf, Frankfurt, Luxemburg, Brussels, Cologne, Nice, Rome, Cork and Geneva. Instructors and cadets stayed at the hotels used by BEA and in so doing took part in an informal 'knife and fork course' which was supposed to stand them in good stead when they became airline officers. Apparently the fuel tax savings more than covered the cost of the nightstops. It was all quite an innovation, because on the Apache I don't remember my instructor even taking me for a pint in the Bugle. The quieter, closer French airfields also served as a base to practise circuit training on asymmetric power and instrument approaches. However it was the more glamorous night-stop destinations which appear to have stuck in cadets' memories, even 45 years later.

Hamburg seems to have figured in more than one recollection and two Baron instructors contrived to arrive on the same night. Having served in Germany after the war they felt qualified to show their young charges the perils of the notorious Reeperbahn. Unfortunately their navigation skills on the ground could not match their airborne ones and by the time they did arrive in the area all the money had been spent on beer. We'll let the intervening years cast their mellowing mists over the rest of the story.

The Baron's long range and high performance made it well-suited for these educational forays but it had two specific problems of its own. The first was noise, most of which was caused by the variable pitch propellers. The change from fine to coarse pitch after take-off caused the residents of Ferndown quite a few disturbed nights and generated a consequent barrage of protest. The CFI at Hurn was Cecil Pearce and he had to field quite a few of the complaints.

One of my ex-cadet informants was in conversation with him one evening when the phone rang. Cecil answered it and said: 'Hang-on a minute, there's an aircraft going over I can't hear a word you're saying.' Unfortunately the caller turned out to be a local resident wanting to complain about the noise. It's also reported that a persistent complainer rang to say he was so fed-up that he would be setting up an anti-aircraft gun in his back garden. Cecil's reputed response was to say that CAT would retaliate by fitting bomb bays on the Barons. Quite what Airwork would have made of that light-hearted riposte it's impossible to say, for it was they who maintained the Hurn-based aircraft.

The CAT and the Hamsters

Cadets on Course 694 were the first to use the new set-up at Hurn, and among them was John Russell, who had two instructors: Slim Hardham and Ronnie Street. On April 14, 1971 Slim was on duty in dispersal while John carried out a night-flying detail on Baron G-AWAL. A few nights previously he'd suffered a malfunction of the undercarriage warning lights, so it may be that his sense of awareness of undercarriage foibles was heightened.

Whatever the cause, he reacted quickly and positively when he heard the electric motors retracting the landing gear just as he touched down. Full power enabled the aircraft to take to the air again without sustaining any damage but his faith in the undercarriage position indicators was now seriously undermined. However, a word with the tower and a low fly-past enabled Slim to visually confirm gear down and locked. The instructor also recommended a slower than normal approach speed and a long hold-off before the next touchdown.

John carried this out to the letter but as soon as the wheels touched the surface of Runway 35 the undercarriage retracted or collapsed, allowing the propellers to strike showers of sparks from the Tarmac. Once again the powerful Baron sprang into the air when full throttle was applied but the bent propellers delivered asymmetric thrust and the aircraft narrowly missed a hanger.

At this stage the tower pressed the crash button and every fire engine in Hampshire set out for Hurn. At least that's what it looked like to John, now circling to burn off fuel in the Hurn holding pattern. Thinking the situation through, he concluded that there must be a fault with the electric motors which operate the undercarriage, so he pulled out their circuit breaker and rendered the motors inoperative. He then had several minutes of contortions using the small manual winder to lower the gear into a locked position whilst still flying the damaged aircraft.

At last the decision to land was made and Alpha Lima touched down without incident, seemingly surrounded by more fire engines and ambulances than had been needed for the Blitz. John pre-empted the attempt to cut him out of the aircraft by the simple expedient of opening the door and climbing out unaided. What happened next was a prescient suggestion by John's instructor. 'You must sit down now, while everything is fresh in your mind and write a detailed resume of the sequence of events,' he suggested.

The CAT and the Hamsters

The might Baron's troublesome nose-gear   *Trevor Hughes*

Next morning a hastily convened board of inquiry (courts-martial) arrived from Hamble. It comprised Nick Hoy (head of ground studies), CFI Peter Duff-Mitchell and a senior instructor, Pat Farrell. John was summoned to appear before them at 10:00 hours prompt. He had no representative or advisor and for the next three hours these senior CAT men tried to browbeat him into admitting a mistake that he hadn't made. They even accused him of being colour blind and mistaking three red undercarriage-unlocked lights, for three greens. This quite overlooked the fact that the Hamble selection procedures screened out anyone with less than perfect eyesight. Throughout the process John reiterated the facts that he had written down the night before.

During this demeaning process HRH Princess Anne arrived at Hurn to fly off on official business somewhere. It had been arranged that she would pay a flying visit to the new CAT facility. G-AWAL needed to be part of the carefully choreographed display, so it was arranged for several of the larger cadets to stand in front of the aircraft's damaged propellers.

After she had departed, the chief engineer arranged for the aircraft to be towed to the hangers and set up on stands so that the undercarriage could be raised and lowered. Cadets, instructors and courts-martial board watched with interest. The undercarriage behaved normally until someone suggested

The CAT and the Hamsters

simulating a night-flying scenario and switching on the landing lights. Again the gear lowered normally but when the engineer kicked the tyres to simulate touchdown the undercarriage retracted spontaneously. Suddenly the courts-martial was congratulating John for saving the aircraft. Presumably his colour blindness was cured by the same miracle. The fault lay with a chafed wiring loom that energised the undercarriage retraction motors when a sudden jolt brought the bare wire into contact with the live part of the landing-light rheostat.

The Baron fleet suffered two further undercarriage faults during 1971. In one case the nosewheel failed to extend and lock down. The other was a belly landing when no part of the undercarriage lowered and damage to the aircraft was minimised by good airmanship. (G-AWAG landing at Hurn on December 9, 1971 with instructor Graham Jones, cadets Dennis Vaughan, Dave Summers and Jim Wilson on board).

The advanced flight moved to Hurn with course 694/5/6 but when they joined the CAT set-up at Hamble in 1969 the Chipmunk replacement problem had not been fully resolved. A governors' meeting on November 16, 1967 had heard from the Principal that there was little progress on the Beagle Pup 150. No specification had yet been received and he was 'most concerned with the general performance of the company'.

He even went so far as to emphasise the importance of recording every communication concerning the negotiations with Beagle. Jimmy James offered to send a suitable BEA project engineer to Shoreham to assess whether promised delivery dates would be met. Nevertheless on January 18, 1968 the Bursar noted that over the next nine to 12 months CAT would be disposing of 18 Chipmunks, 11 Apaches and two Aztecs, complete with spares. BEA Contracts were asked to secure the services of an aircraft broker.

In the spring, the governors considered a report on pilot training costs. The figures included a projection to complete the period until the college's tenth anniversary on August 31, 1970. In the current year the college had cost the corporations £703,000 to produce 145 graduated cadets. The average figure of £4,850 per man was about £800 more than the other flying schools and was largely accounted for by the extra flying time during the advanced phase.

It was drawn to the governors attention that the college and its assets had been purchased at an advantageous price. Capital appreciation over the

The CAT and the Hamsters

decade of operation might amount to as much as £1 million but a report from Captain F W Walton had assessed the average training costs over the decade to be even higher, at £5,286 per man.

Comparable costs at Oxford (£4,064), Perth (£3,767) and Carlisle (£3,927) made sobering reading. He drew the Board's attention to QFI utilisation and found that while instructors at Oxford averaged 567 hours per annum, the Hamble figure was 411 hours on single-engine types and 493 hours on twins.

In *Flight's* classified section on July 4, 1968 the following advert appeared within the auspices of a Shackleton Aviation Ltd – aircraft for sale.

> Ten De Havilland Chipmunks—Each aircraft has two seats and is fully aerobatic. Public Transport C of A. VHF 10 channel. Delivery starting October 1968. Deposits are being taken now against delivery. All the aircraft have been exceptionally well-maintained. £1,150 each. Spares available on all types. Deposits are being taken at our Head Office where full details may be obtained.

The college Chipmunks were being sold off as the Cherokees arrived. Contained within the same magazine was another reference to the college's aeroplanes.

> 'We have now sold all College of Air Training Apaches which were immediately available. However, deposits are now being taken for the remaining nine due for delivery in August. don't miss out! Deposits have been accepted on eight of the College of Air Training D.H. Chipmunks. 10 only remain. Details of aircraft available below: — aircraft from the College of Air Training, Hamble, available exclusively through this company.
> 'Nine Piper Apache 160s—All have four seats, Public Transport C of A and full airline radio stations. The aircraft are being sold with engines at half life. All the Apaches have had top-class maintenance. Two immediately available, the further nine from August 1968. £7,750.'

A prototype Beagle Pup had been loaned to CAT for four days from March 11, 1968 and appeared to be an excellent trainer but the loan was ten days shorter than promised and the prototype differed markedly from the draft specification issued by the college.

By the governors' meeting of July 18, 1968, CAT appeared to have burned its boats because the corporations had abandoned Plan G. That was devised to train 150 pilots per year. In its place a new requirement to follow course 682 (36 cadets joined on May 20, 1968) was only ten cadets in September that year. Thereafter, 144 cadets were anticipated in four intakes of 36 producing 115 graduates a year.

The CAT and the Hamsters

Current aircraft in operation were 12 Barons and 22 Cherokees and a rump of 18 college Chipmunks, although these had been offered for sale and six deposits had already been received. One Aztec and two Apaches had already been sold, the other Apaches had been offered for sale. Twelve hired Chipmunks had been returned to the RAF but no order had been placed for Pups. Four of the single-engined aircraft would be needed for flying selection, if that was continued. In addition, a Board of Trade working party was reviewing whether a requirement of 225 hours for the full course was still necessary. Indications were that the requirement might be cut to 210 hours and this could obviate the need to buy any new aircraft at all.

External events soon overtook the tortuous decision-making process, because in December 1969 the Government withdrew financial support for Beagle and the company was placed in receivership. Over 250 Pups were on order but production ceased with the 152nd aircraft. CAT took delivery of 15 additional Cherokees, beginning in March 1970 and by July the delivery was complete.

The following year an even more momentous event changed the college's prospects for ever. The Civil Aviation Act 1971 was enacted and that legislation formed the British Airways Board to control all the activities of BOAC and BEA. The airline corporations were joint-owners of CAT and the die was cast for the eventual rundown of the college nearly ten years later.

In its 22 years CAT trained almost 2,000 pilots, with more than 1,500 of them joining BEA, BOAC or latterly British Airways. It was the opinion of Captain Gill Gray, erstwhile Trident Flight Manager in BEA and Boeing 757/767 Chief Pilot in British Airways that 'The College of Air Training produced the best airline pilots in the world. No question!'

Many of the Hamble graduates went on to become training captains or flight managers themselves. One shining example is Peter Hunt from course 601, who rose through a series of management roles in British Airways to director level before joining the CAA in 1990 to become Head of Operating Standards Division within the Safety Regulation Group of the CAA and finally became Director of the UK Airprox Board. So on the face of it the College of Air training had fulfilled its role to supply high-quality civil airline pilots during the middle and latter half of the 20th century. In retrospect could it have done even better?

The CAT and the Hamsters

Aerial view of Hamble Airfield circa 1965   *Hamble pictures— BOAC*

From the distance of half a century, my overwhelming impression of the flying training set-up is of a good job done under unnecessarily trying circumstances. Many of those were self-inflicted by the muddle of politics. The CAT was a long time in labour during the 1950s and then, in common with many confinements, things happened all of a rush.

AST were happy to sell their operation at Hamble lock stock and barrel at a knockdown price and everyone must have congratulated themselves on a solution to a problem that had been rumbling on for the past decade. Unfortunately in commerce, if something looks too good to be true, then that's often because it is! In retrospect ATS were divesting themselves of several built-in problems, which would come back to bite CAT in the bum.

The first problem was the airfield. It was prone to waterlogging, had no hard runway or navigation aids and was situated close to Eastleigh, Hurn and underneath Red 1 Airway. In the early Sixties those were small considerations. However, as the industry it served came of age, the growth in air traffic and the sophistication of airliners showed Hamble to be a mid-20th century solution to a late-20th century problem.

In addition, as house-building burgeoned within the waterside parishes to the west of the Solent and likewise the south-eastern suburbs of Southampton of Netley, Bursledon and Warsash, so did the noise complaints. It mattered

The CAT and the Hamsters

not that Hamble was one of the oldest airfields in the country and predated a very large proportion of the new houses, the College authorities were bombarded with whinging protests about aircraft noise. The local MP even asked questions in the House.

Secondly, by saddling itself with ATS's choice of training aircraft CAT was storing up problems for the future. The dear old Chipmunk was obsolescent when the College opened but it was fine as an *ab-initio* trainer for teaching basic handling skills and for flying selection. Unfortunately those aspects of the 225-hour course could be covered in less than one third of the hours. What cadets needed after perfecting their handling skills was a modern instrument platform on which to learn the blind flying and radio navigation skills that they would need in their chosen career. What they got was another 65/70 hours marking time and learning little.

When the final phase of their training arrived on the advanced flight they had just the last third of their allotment to cram the learning multi-engined skills, in addition to getting to grips with instrument flying and radio-nav usage.

The common thread running through the whole life of CAT was ill-judged Government interference, either direct or indirect. During the Fifties, the Government vacillated over setting up the facility in the first instance then, because of the doctrinaire need to nationalise anything within reach, the flying training school was financially tied to its main clients, the State airlines. They were owned by the Government because of historic, state subsidisation. Ergo CAT needed permission from BEA and BOAC before it could make any major financial decision and the corporations needed permission from their paymaster, the Government, before they would sanction anything.

It was a sinecure for endless retired Air Vice-Marshalls, Lords and sycophant committee members, to whom the provision of coffee and biscuits at meeting was just as important as the provision of appropriate flying machines for the college. Indeed, once the Government had seen fit to nationalise Beagle it held in its hands the opportunity to re-equip the college with exactly the aircraft it needed and give the British aircraft industry a prestigious shot in the arm. Instead it kept the nascent company short of investment and allowed it to flounder.

Lack of money is why CAT didn't buy British and lack of money is why

The CAT and the Hamsters

The College library housed Liberal Studies   *Hamble pictures — BOAC*

the British aircraft builder didn't build commercially viable aircraft. Both the Pup and the B.206 were good basic designs. Even the B.242 could have met the college needs if sufficient funds had been available to develop it. All that was needed was a clear-headed, visionary leader to co-ordinate the various quangos and what did we get, a charlatan who spied for enemy countries.

Then their major clients, the airline corporations, were about as good as predicting their future requirements as the organisers of the 1985 International Conference of Clairvoyants, which was famously cancelled due to 'unforeseen circumstances'. All of this meant that the final adjustment of graduate numbers was done by raising and lowering the standards bar during the course. Consequently many young men who would have made perfectly adequate line pilots within the corporations were consigned to the scrap heap just to keep the bean counters happy.

Our intake had a particularly perverse example of the real-world effect of this, in BEA. When the time came to allocate the next tranche of training for promotions to captain from senior first officer (SFO), several of our cohort were missed out. Upon enquiry, the disappointed SFOs were told that the company had sufficient captains due to a recent take-over of the regional airlines Cambrian and Northeast. Their Trident captains were being taken

The CAT and the Hamsters

on at the substantive rank, even though a few were CAT failures who had completed their training at their own expense and then gone on to find work with air-taxi firms and finally the regional airlines. This convoluted route had short-circuited the slow promotional progress to command in BEA and they'd emerged from the midden of termination smelling of roses by being higher up the all-important seniority list.

In fairness it was not the fault of the regional captains, indeed some might say a reward for their persistence. However, the dreams of a large number of aspiring airline pilots crashed and burned after being chopped and that fact must weigh against the college. The governors were quite happy to preside over a wastage rate of 20 per cent of cadets with absolutely no hint of pastoral care for those who didn't make the grade pertaining at the time. This deficiency occurred despite the fact that, at times, senior flying instructors highlighted a diminution of standards and low instructor morale due to the shortage of available training aircraft: shortages which could be traced back directly to the vacillation shown at governor level over suitable aircraft procurement.

Furthermore, in an effort to produce gentlemen airline officers the college ran an extensive liberal studies curriculum. During my research I've been surprised just how much weight was carried by the views of that department. Nice to know how the Stock Exchange works but it is hardly relevant to pilot proficiency!

Then the productivity of the 'nationalised' college instructors, compared to their counterparts at the commercial establishments, was akin to the lower productivity of the other 'great nationalised industries' of the time. All these factors conspired to make the Hamble cadet more expensive to produce than his commercially-trained counterpart and that was a major factor in the demise of CAT.

Chapter 7

Ground-based training

WHEN the College of Air Training was established in 1960 it bought from AST much of their paraphernalia and training equipment. It also took on many of the ground and flying instructors. The college became a Board of Trade-approved flying training school which conducted 'Approved Courses' for Commercial Pilots licence(s) and instrument rating.

To that end CAT ground instructors taught a range of subjects, some of which were 'licence' subjects and three of which were 'college' subjects. In other words these last three: Electrical power and Electronics; Aerodynamics and Design plus Thermodynamics were in addition to the mandatory requirements for an airline transport pilot's licence (ATPL) laid out in CAP 54 (1961 edition). The pass-mark in the college subjects was 50 per cent. The licence subjects and their relevant pass marks were:

Navigation I (Plotting)	80%
Navigation II (Planning)	80%
Navigation III (Theory)	65%
Navigation IV	65%
Meteorology I (Theory)	65%
Meteorology II (Synoptic)	65%
Aircraft Instruments	65%
Radio and Radar Aids	65%
Aviation Law	70%
Signals	Pass/Fail
Oral & Practical Tests	Pass/Fail

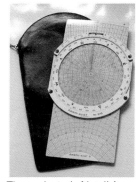

The navigator's friend! A Dalton computer—*Author*

In addition there were examinations to 'normal' Ministry standards in Airframes & Engines (Specific Type rating for PA 28 Apache or Baron) and Performance Group A and both those would be held prior to the graduation examinations.

Upon successful graduation, the cadets would typically have only sufficient

The CAT and the Hamsters

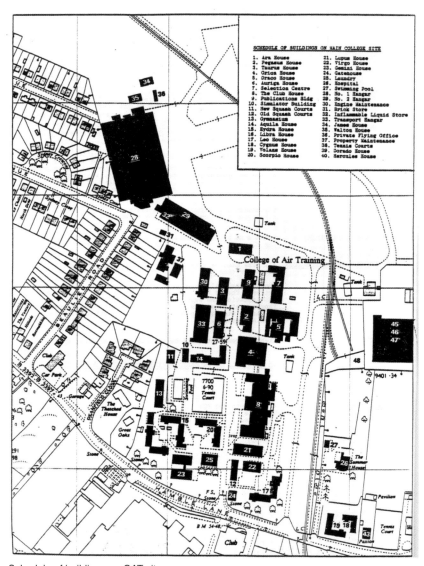

Schedule of buildings on CAT site

Hamble pictures

The CAT and the Hamsters

flying experience for the award of a commercial pilot's licence (CPL), despite their written exams being set to the higher ATPL standard. For a few years this deferred ATPL qualification counted for nothing because the Board of Trade insisted on BEA and BOAC first officers resitting the written exams after they had achieved the requisite flying hour experience during the course of their airline duties. Our resits were carried out in Wandsworth Town Hall, which had been hired for that express purpose.

As the first courses came up towards their finals in July 1962, a sub-committee on college standards recommended the following guidelines: to fail five or more subjects would be construed as a total failure and would result in suspension from training and loss of potential employment with the corporations; failure in four or less subjects (three of which were in the licence category) would result in less stringent sanctions. The cadet would be allowed three months further study at the college to be funded either by their LEA or, *in extremis*, the corporations.

Ground training was carried out in a number of college buildings, some of which were named after celestial constellations:

Name of House	Area (sq ft)	Built	Main purpose
Ara	6,340	1936	Admin and offices
Pegasus	7,000	1950	Classrooms, language lab and link trainers
Taurus	7,160	1938	Lecture rooms
Orion	9,093	1917	Classrooms and labs
Draco	8,890	1917	Classrooms and cinema
Auriga	8,600	1978	Lecture rooms
Selection centre	5,000	1917	Interview rooms etc
The Clubhouse	26,300	1937	Bar, lounge, library, mess hall, kitchens and billiards
Simulator Building	1,257	1950	Simulator training

Among the first technical lecturers in the period 1960-61, 'inherited' from AST, were the following: F A Garrad; D R Grant; R J Hilborne; C N Hoy; M C Johnson, A Palmer; S Richards; A G J Smith and R B Underdown. Maxie Johnson was a well-liked and popular character, which contrasted him with the head of ground training, Nick Hoy. I remember judging the latter as one of those men who are best avoided completely. Other former cadets I've interviewed speak of not wanting him to notice them because of his draconian mien. Roy Underdown lectured in meteorology and later rose

The CAT and the Hamsters

Hangar maintenance staff at work
Hamble pictures — BOAC

to become Principal of the college. His career progress was not untypical in that he served in the RAF during the Second World War. His role was as a navigation instructor at Cranwell but in 1946 he became a founder member of the instructional staff at AST. In the mid-Fifties he was elected Life Fellow of the Royal Meteorological Society and he was taken on by CAT in 1960. One of my favourite lecturers was Dennis Goodwin, who taught navigation and always sported Marks & Spencer checked shirts, perhaps because pattern reminded him of the graticule on his beloved maps.

Later on in the college's history there were 21 technical instructors, five liberal-studies tutors and six specialists in selection. These were part of a staff of more than 300 organised into six departments: flying; technical studies; liberal studies; engineering and administration, each with a head of department responsible to the Principal.

The first courses were scheduled to last 21 months and comprised 1,010 hours of technical lectures, 210 hours of liberal studies and 64 hours of compulsory PT. This latter activity was one of the first casualties of the quasi-military training regime. Technical instructors disliked getting up early in the morning to supervise PT and hard-worked cadets could always do with a few more minutes in bed. Although a cadet was appointed each month to ensure attendance of his fellows, my information is that cadets avoided this activity whenever and however they could. By the mid-Sixties it had been dropped, as had Saturday morning lectures.

The CAT and the Hamsters

Alan Smith
instructs cadets
from 701
*Hamble pictures
— BOAC*

It's difficult to summarise the syllabus of each of the 12 elements of the technical subjects because they were precisely that: technical subjects. Also the lectures given by the college didn't always correspond exactly to the Board of Trade exams because certain topics overlapped more than one written exam. Suffice to say that five decades have eroded my own command of these subjects to the point where they present an even more daunting body of learning than they did while I was at the college. The figures and analysis are based on the technical syllabus published in summer 1981 (Technical Subject Syllabuses, 1981).

Airframes consisted of 84 periods of study examining the components of an aircraft and its relationship to the fluid (air) in which it operated. To that end the physical forces on the aircraft and the effects of altitude, pressure and temperature were all explored. Cadets learned about aircraft controls, propellers and the principles of loading the machine.

What drove around the propellers — Engines, was the subject of 49 lectures. Internal combustion engines were covered in great detail, even though by 1981 modern airliners were almost exclusively jet-powered. Still it was useful stuff when we came to service our motor cars, especially the section on fault-finding. In Draco Room 1 were sectioned Spey, Conway, Derwent and Mamba engines. As the first two powered the Trident and VC 10 aircraft in commercial service with BEA and BOAC, they were much more relevant to a cadet's future career.

The CAT and the Hamsters

Twenty five Electrics periods were deemed necessary to learn about electricity and what it did in an aircraft. In common with most of the lectures only the most general study could be taught because manufacturers of airliners had different methods of generating, distributing and employing the power in their machines. However there was specific study of the college's advance trainer, be it the Apache or the Baron. Cadets had to learn and understand all the systems of the relevant aircraft because their Specific Type Rating would be appended to the CPL after successfully completing the two Ministry exams (1179 and Perf 'A'). All of that took up 74 periods.

Having learned how to build and power an aircraft, cadets were also initiated into the mysteries of Navigation/Planning. Standing at 192 lectures, it was the largest part of the syllabus. Much work was done on and with maps, all of which was valuable for the cadets appreciation of the world around which he was going to fly. Several periods focused on mental arithmetic and training the mind to remember long numbers. Although the basic elements of the lectures would have been familiar to a 19th century naval captain, the course eventually meshed with jet aircraft navigation. A great deal of the practical classroom work revolved around the drawing (and rubbing out) of long pencil lines on maps the size of tablecloths. Of course nowadays much of the radio/radar aids segment of 85 periods would overlap with navigation but in the mid-20th century GPS was yet to come, as was inertial navigation. Accordingly we learned about direction finding and Loran, Decca, Omega and Consol (CAP 59 was a particular treasure trove of obsolete knowledge). These were systems not dissimilar to the ones that had guided Lancasters to Berlin in 1944 but they were still on the syllabus and we learned their principles, never used them in anger, and consigned the knowledge to the large cranial wheelie bin. The brain was very much involved with interpreting Radio Magnetic Indicators (RMI), ADF, VOR, DME and ILS. Not least of which was remembering what all the acronyms stood for in the first place.

It took 55 periods to learn about instruments. Valuable stuff because the graduate pilot was likely to spend much of his professional life gazing into their limpid dials. Magnetism and compasses were important parts of this segment as well as the principles which drove the 'atmospheric' instruments. Despite interposing an 'air-data computer' in between the modern 'glass cockpit' displays, it's still important for the pilot to understand how height

The CAT and the Hamsters

and speed information is derived from the fluid surrounding his machine.

The part of the technical course that I enjoyed most is the one that still has the most relevance to my life nowadays: Meteorology. The composition of the atmosphere and its effects on our day-to-day lives are relevant to all human beings but to the airman they are especially germane. It took 72 lectures to acquire an insight into climate and weather and be told the difference between them.

We also learned a lesson in the unpredictability of the atmosphere when our tutor, a man called West-Jones, entered the classroom with the news that a line-squall was about to traverse the airfield. He was a newer instructor who also presented the local weather on the local ITV. At his behest the group of cadets trooped out onto the wet grass beside Orion House. There we waited for most of the hour-long period, in varying states of interest: sometimes looking at the sky; sometimes watching the vehicles driving into the adjacent coachbuilders. One completed vehicle drove outbound emblazoned with *Steel Parts Ltd* along its newly-panelled side. It was the highlight of the great line-squall lecture because the meteorological feature never appeared.

Initially, Aviation Law seemed of distant relevance to a Hamble cadet but Rules of the Air and Air Traffic Control Regulations (1966) and its contemporary companion, The Air Navigation Order (1966), soon came to their attention when they began cross-country flights. Additional delights were contained in 'The Air Pilot' and the Board of Trade issued another of its blue pamphlets through HMSO (CAP 85) as a précis of the knowledge needed to attain the PPL. The subject required 63 periods of study, much of it needed for the forthcoming Instrument Rating. Looking back through the syllabus it was naive not to realise that the tentacles of aviation law would reach into every aspect of operating an aircraft.

Aviation Medicine took up a mere eight lectures but was a welcome contrast to the dry world of maps and cut-away engines. As exceptionally fit young men we learned, in the classroom, of physical problems that might affect mere mortals. That was until we visited the decompression chamber at nearby Lee-on-Solent (RN). Here we sat inside a chamber playing snap while air was evacuated to simulate an unpressurised aircraft fuselage operating well in excess of 10,000 feet. Everyone was wearing equipment that allowed normal breathing but one poor soul (why is it always me?) had his oxygen

The CAT and the Hamsters

supply turned off. I remember it was my turn to put down a card but I didn't seem able to. In addition my inability seemed personally hilarious. Such were the practical lessons of detecting hypoxia in flight.

Communications was the series of 50 lectures in which the cadets went dotty over learning Morse code. It was essential to pass a test in which the candidate demonstrated familiarity with Morse sent at six words per minute. So if you've read the last sentence in less than three minutes you've done well. Small cubicles in the RTF Communications Lab each had a pair of headphones and a Morse transmission key. There was a useful HMSO pamphlet, CAP 46, which initiated the aspiring pilot into the covert and intricate world of R/T (Radiotelephony). Unfortunately nothing in the booklet prepared one for the staccato delivery of the ATC clearance at New York's John F Kennedy airport; or the mangled syllables and fractured syntax of most air traffic controllers east of Dover.

In 2013 I was talking to the son of a good friend. The young man was about to become a candidate on British Airways future pilot training scheme and wanted to know if I thought there was anything he could learn before he started the course. I suggested that it would do no harm to be familiar with the phonetic alphabet and the Morse code. He was agog at the latter idea. 'Surely we won't need to know that,' he said. So I told him to check for more up-to-date information with his older brother, who was already employed as a commercial pilot. His brother confirmed that, like my idea, Morse was a thing of the past. Perhaps that's the largest fault that one could find with the ground training at the CAT.

Fair enough, computers such as the BBC Model 'B' weren't on sale to the general public until the college was in fatal decline but the charge that Hamble ground instruction was backward-looking instead of the opposite is not altogether unfounded. Nevertheless, the instructors did their best to inculcate a huge body of knowledge into a cadet's mind in a relatively short period of time and given, the high pass marks in the final exams, they did a good job in a good humoured atmosphere.

Even the austere Head of Technical Studies could appreciate a joke, when the wind was in the right direction. He was teaching us the fundamentals of astro-navigation. To that end we had to learn to recognise and name stars, in the night sky but that was the point – the lectures were carried out in daylight

The CAT and the Hamsters

Maxie Johnson giving an instruments lecture. *Hamble pictures — BOAC*

using photographs and diagrams. It wasn't the most exciting subject and Nick Hoy picked up the general ennui. In an effort to reinvigorate interest he told us 'Just think how romantic it will seem to your girlfriends, when you're outside on a warm starlit night together and you can put a name to each of those stars'. Quick as a flash one brave, or foolhardy, cadet responded: 'Of course she'd be in a better position to see them, wouldn't she?' Luckily it brought the house down.

The CAT and the Hamsters

Chapter 8

Accidents and incidents

STARTING with the earliest flying machines, crashes have always been an integral part of aviation. In the beginning, pilots were inexperienced because flying was a new skill that had to be learned by trial and error (mostly error). Added to that, aircraft were also untried and untested: they malfunctioned and came apart in the sky because the pilots and designers hadn't appreciated the multitude of forces acting on the structure. Engines were equally unreliable and often contributed to crashes but as time went on and with the dubious help of two world wars, aircraft and their engines became more technically competent and pilots became better trained. Result: crashes declined in frequency.

However pilot inexperience remained a prime cause of crashes so you'd expect a flying school to have more than its fair share of accidents. In addition, Hamble itself was a modestly-sized grass airfield situated in crowded airspace with intensive circuit training and a restricted dispersal area. Each of these factors could be expected to cause problems. That there were relatively few accidents and incidents is a tribute to the skill and professionalism of those involved in running the airfield.

During the 1950s, prior to CAT, only a couple of civilian-registered Chipmunks from Hamble came to grief: one over the Isle of Wight and the other at Middle Wallop. The first recorded CAT accident, apart from a minor ground-handling incident caused by brake failure, involved cadet P G J and Chipmunk G-AOJY. On March 24, 1962 Juliet Yankee and Chipmunk WP800 (a military aircraft) were in the final phase of landing on R/W 06. The RAF Volunteer Reserve pilot appeared to have used a steeper approach angle and descended on top of Juliet Yankee before making visual contact at the last minute. An overshoot procedure by WP800 was accompanied by a hard bank to the left. During the course of this manoeuvre the left undercarriage leg of the RAF aircraft struck the tip of the CAT aircraft's main-plane. Both aircraft landed safely.

The CAT and the Hamsters

It was doubly unfortunate later in the year when two of CAT senior instructors were involved in mishaps. Chipmunk G-AOUP was being used for instrument take-off training on October 31 when cadet P J B allowed it to veer about five degrees to the right as the aircraft lifted off.

The starboard mainwheel clipped an airfield marker board. The marker flipped up and hit the leading edge of the tailplane. Luckily neither the impact nor the minor structural damage was sufficient to impede a safe return to the airfield. Capt W V (Paddy) Kinnin, the instructor, was adjudged to have suffered a 'temporary lapse' and the Principal E C Bates did 'not considered it necessary, or desirable, to award more than a reprimand'.

The second instructor, Bill Anderson, did not get off quite so lightly. What Bill did on October 26, was to taxi Apache G-ARJS northwards up the road behind Draco and the selection centre, to reposition it back to the hanger. The aircraft had originally been manhandled behind the cadet's clubhouse to facilitate a graduation photoshoot. It was supposed to be manhandled back but Mr W H Anderson 'on his own initiative' decided to start the engines and taxi back. Unfortunately Juliette Sierra's port wingtip came into contact with a brick ventilator, causing £112 worth of damage. The unfortunate man wrote as abject a letter of apology as I have ever seen, citing poor sleep patterns and a long visit to the dentist before starting a four-hour stint in the procedure trainer. He accepted full responsibility for an accident which he deemed 'stupid in the extreme'.

Bates agreed: 'I consider this accident to be entirely due to the negligence and bad airmanship by Mr Anderson,' he intoned. 'I have reprimanded him and forfeited his last increment of salary (£30) for the remaining six months

Apache G-ASDH
returned after
birdstrike
Hamble pictures

The CAT and the Hamsters

of his salary year. This means a loss of £15 in his gross salary over the next six months.' I doubt a cadet's feet would have touched the ground!

Things went quiet for the rest of the winter until May 7, 1963 when a two-pound Welsh seagull took a dislike to Apache G-ASDH flying overhead Rhoose NDB at 2,500 feet. The kamikaze gull embedded itself in the upper part of the aircraft's nose, leaving its vital fluids oozing out to impede visibility from the left-hand seat. Instructor D C Evans safely flew the aircraft to Hamble and was commended for his efforts by the Principal.

Six weeks later cadet W A M suffered a hydraulic failure on Delta Hotel and was forced to use the emergency CO_2 lowering system for the undercarriage. Was G-ASDH an unlucky ship?

The rest of the year almost passed without major incident but on November 28, cadet R N-S managed to get Chipmunk G-RME 'low and slow' on finals for R/W 17. He carried out a bit of light hedge trimming on the airfield boundary using the port elevator and was admonished.

On May 25 1964 cadet V F N did a similar thing with Apache G-ASDI on a night-flying detail. On this occasion the Apache's nosewheel struck a portable threshold marker light. This cadet was also admonished. However two nights later Apache G-ARJT made a wheels-up landing whilst in the hands of a cadet from course 624. Cadet E P Le-G was not alone in the cockpit, because instructor-in-charge D G Evans was riding passenger to make a first-hand assessment of the local weather.

Three circuits were completed but the undercarriage was not lowered on the third. Late in the flare the passenger/instructor noticed an absence of three greens and called overshoot, at the same time applying full throttle. It was all too late because the aircraft struck the ground in a landing attitude. In all £1,200 worth of damage was caused. CAT had paid just over £12,600 for the basic aircraft four years previously.

The cadet testified that during the day he had completed a two-hour period in the flight procedure trainer before lunch and two Apache sorties during the afternoon. In all he completed 15 take-offs and landings prior to his night flying. He was adjudged to be blameworthy but at this distance in time, surely he had every right to be fatigued and somewhat distracted by an instructor chirruping away on the second radio trying to get Met data while downwind. Both cadet and instructor were admonished.

The CAT and the Hamsters

July 14 saw a heavy landing by Chipmunk G-ARMC. Cadet A E S and his instructor Joe Douglas were refreshing for the cadet's Progress Test 2, which was due next day. The instructor closed the throttle just after take-off (100 feet) to simulate an engine failure and the cadet responded appropriately but the engine was then slow to respond when power was applied for the climb-out. Accordingly the aircraft struck the ground tail first and damaged the tailwheel assembly. Neither pilot was assessed as blameworthy but the minimum height for this training manoeuvre was raised to 250 feet.

G-ASDH was in the wars again on September 23 when, during night taxying, the starboard prop came into contact with a portable ground light, which may not have been illuminated at the time. On November 10 another night-flying, propeller/airfield light interaction occurred. This time a Chipmunk G-ARMF was involved and unlike the Apache incident the cadet was severely admonished by the CFI.

A couple of heavy landing incidents marred the beginning of 1965 and in late January instructor Les Craven was commended by the Principal for dealing successfully with a partial engine failure at Lee-on-Solent involving Apache G-ARJW. No sooner had February started than Delta Hotel was in the news again. This time cadet R C S was somewhat distracted by low oil-pressure readings on his port engine and forgot to lower the Apache's undercarriage. Luckily the Hamble airfield senior air traffic controller spotted the aircraft on short finals and ordered an overshoot.

The cadet was found to be at fault and reprimanded but the Apache undercarriage operation was beginning to cause concern. In operation three green lights indicated wheels down and locked, just as in all British aircraft, but a single red light was fitted to the Apache system and this indicated undercarriage locked up. In addition there was a warning horn which was supposed to sound if the flaps were down and the throttles closed without the wheels down. The latter mechanism was tested and found to operate too late to prevent disaster.

Applications were made to the Air Registration Board for modifications to be made. It has to be remembered that the Apache was never designed as a training workhorse and accordingly the ARB would not allow modifications to its undercarriage indicator lights.

1966 began with a forced landing incident involving Chipmunk G-AOUN.

The CAT and the Hamsters

On January 11 the aircraft made a precautionary landing at Elmsworth Farm, Porchfield on the Isle of Wight in a field owned by Farmer Ablitt. One unfortunate sheep was spooked and had to be destroyed later but no other injuries occurred. The aircraft was partly dismantled and returned to Hamble with the participation of Farmer Ablitt's tractor, a CAT lorry and the Isle of Wight ferry.

Cadet R J H and his instructor J D Beech were plucked from the field soon after landing by an air/sea rescue helicopter which had been scrambled after RAF Thorney Island intercepted the Chipmunk's distress call. The detail prior to the forced landing was routine: simulated engine failure after T/O; eight stalls; two spins and a practice forced landing using Farmer Ablitt's field. However the practice exercise turned into a real one when the engine failed to respond normally. Farmer Ablitt was paid £45 for the dead sheep and his help during the aircraft recovery.

More Apache undercarriage problems occurred at Cranfield on March 21 when the port leg collapsed. G-ASDI sustained minor damage to wing-tip, propeller and flap. Cadets E R S and M A W were onboard the aircraft.

CAT documents do not offer much further definitive detail on the Cranfield incident, even though tests were carried out. However the documents do indicate a natural preoccupation with the fatal crash of Chipmunk G-ARME near to Sandown on the Isle of Wight on March 29. Cadet G G S, who was flying solo, was killed in the crash and the aircraft completely destroyed. A Board of Trade investigation was conducted and a yellow-covered report published as CAP 274. It concluded that the 19-year-old cadet had about 150 hours experience on the Chipmunk but had been given a 'special flight test' by the CFI on the morning of the crash due to concerns about his lack of progress.

After the flight, which did not go well, the CFI told him that 'unless he made a positive effort to improve his standards, he would have very little chance of continuing with the advanced stage of his course'. During the afternoon the cadet was authorised by 'Taps' Tappin, his own instructor, to complete a forty-minute detail of touch-and go landings at nearby Lee-on-Solent. He was specifically instructed to return to Hamble by 13.45. Mike Echo took off from Hamble at 13.05 and flew to 'Lee' where three of the prescribed landings were executed. It then left the circuit and flew across the Solent to the eastern side of the Isle of Wight.

The CAT and the Hamsters

Chipmunk G-ARME after its crash on the IOW
Hamble pictures

Testimony from a pilot of a Seahawk in the vicinity and witnesses on the ground established that at a height of around 3,000 feet the Chipmunk entered a right-hand spin from which it failed to recover. No one can know for sure why the cadet failed to return to Hamble at the prescribed time or why he entered the fatal spin. Intentional spinning below 6,000 feet was prohibited by CAT standing orders.

The next Chipmunk accident occurred at Bristol Lulsgate on June 24. Cadet R J W was taxying G-AOJY towards the apron along R/W 03 after his landing on R/W 28. The cadet had been to Lulsgate previously and had just over 100 hours at the time of the accident. The surface wind after landing was 270-280/20-23 knots and he reported that a gust caught Oscar Yankee, causing it to veer sharply to the left. His corrective action failed to prevent the port main wheel from entering a shallow trench hole dug by workmen earlier in the day. The Chipmunk spun sharply left around the axis of the undercarriage leg and made a hard impact with a roadroller which was parked adjacent to the hole.

Shortcomings were highlighted during the accident investigation by the CFI He told the Principal that CAT was not scheduled to receive Class I NOTAMS (Notices to Airmen published by the Board of Trade) only the Class II NOTAM by post. It was within the Class I group that details of the work in progress (WIP) were promulgated.

The Principal was not happy and had formed the opinion that the accident was caused by 'carelessness and poor airmanship'. He demanded that the

The CAT and the Hamsters

cadet be brought to his office by the CFI on July 8 at 10.30 hours. But he also confused Class I and Class II NOTAMS in his letter and accordingly considered that the cadet's instructor Captain G H Farley was deserving of censure for not briefing R J W about the WIP before departure.

Bates's letter was appended to the cadet's file, from where it came to the attention of his flying instructor. The latter wrote a furious letter to the Principal accusing him of 'very questionable ethics...without having first checked with the instructor the accuracy of the facts concerning the case. He concluded: 'It occurs to me that before I take any action on this matter that you may wish to offer some explanation.' At the instigation of the Principal the CFI investigated further and in a memo was: 'unable to agree to a suggestion the Capt Farley should be deserving of censure'.

I reproduce the Principal's reply of August 5 in full: 'I have considered your memorandum of 5th August. Under the circumstances, I accept that there was no oversight on the part of Captain Farley, and that he is not, therefore, deserving of censure. Please inform Captain Farley.'

Who said sorry seems to be the hardest word? Cadet R J W, who was part of my own intake was suspended on the same day.

Thus far the year had been an unhappy one for the Chipmunk flight and it didn't improve when, on November 21, G-ATDE suffered a fractured cylinder head on No 2 pot while over the Isle of Wight. As a result the aircraft force-landed in a field near Godshill, owned by Farmer Brown, but Capt B D Buswell and cadet J G K did a great job of putting Delta Echo down gently. So much so that, after a new cylinder head was fitted in the field, the aircraft was flown back to Hamble by Capt R N Frost. This all made happier reading for the Principal, who issued congratulations all round and also fired off a letter of thanks to Farmer Brown. The wry farmer responded that he was pleased to have had a field available in the right place at the right time.

All humour disappeared on December 7, when a mid-air collision occurred between Chipmunks G-ATEA and WZ 864 of the RAF University Air Squadron (UAS). The aircraft were on finals for R/W 35 about 100ft to 150ft above the ground when the collision occurred. Capt 'Tubby' L A Fieldhouse was assessing PHP on a selection flight when the RAF aircraft descended into his right wing. Although it suffered considerable structural damage it still provided enough lift for Tubby to land Echo Alpha safely.

The CAT and the Hamsters

G-ASDH crash at Netley Hospital
Author

The RAF aircraft was not so lucky. It crashed into the garden of a house in School Lane, which is part of Hamble village. Mercifully, although the University Air Squadron pilot N J R D sustained serious injuries they were not life-threatening. A Board of Trade investigation was conducted and a yellow-covered report published as CAP 293. It concluded that 'sun and haze made observation of other aircraft difficult at low altitudes'. The inexperienced UAS pilot 'did not follow the standard practice for rejoining the circuit'. He'd realised he was late and opted for a straight-in approach from the Isle of Wight via Calshot. Consequently he overtook Echo Alpha on the approach and collided with it. The report also pointed out that the 'minimal' R/T procedures in force on the day may have been a contributory cause.

Any hopes that 1967 would prove to be less accident-prone were dashed on January 10. Captain 'Stan' Offer was instructing cadets S L and M C K on aspects of asymmetric flying in the Hamble circuit using Apache G-ASDH when it crashed. M C K was observing from the rear of the aircraft and S L was in the left-hand seat under instruction. I suppose I should admit at this juncture that S L was me. However to maintain consistency I will write this account in the same manner as employed for the incidents earlier in the chapter, only making personal comments at the end if they might enhance the reader's understanding of the situation.

It was originally Capt Offer's intention to fly to Hurn with three cadets but that airfield was congested and the plan was changed. Cadet

The CAT and the Hamsters

Delta Hotel pancaked to the left of this picture
Author

M C K operated the aircraft during a period of general asymmetric handling practise over the Isle of Wight. The aircraft returned to the Hamble circuit and cadet R C G was allowed to leave the aircraft because he was suffering from a head cold. At this point cadet S L moved to the left-hand seat and carried out a normal right hand circuit on R/W 32. Just before the aircraft entered the flare, S L was instructed to overshoot and once the aircraft was climbing away Capt Offer closed the right throttle at about 500 feet to simulate an engine failure. Cadet S L carried out the correct shut down procedure, part of which involved moving the engine's mixture control to 'idle-cut-off'. This action cut off fuel feed to the right engine.

The detail continued to practise a single-engined circuit but during the latter downwind phase Capt Offer took control of the 'dead' engine and after opening the mixture control to 'full-rich-on' he restarted it. However to carry on with the asymmetric exercise, he had set what was called 'zero-thrust' by unfeathering the propeller and adding just enough throttle/power to overcome the drag created by the rotating propeller. Ostensibly the aircraft behaved as if it was flying on one engine but the second engine was available to give power when it was needed.

Cadet S L carried out a successful circuit and approach to the point of the flare, 10 or so feet above the runway. At this point Capt Offer instructed another overshoot. This was achieved on two engines because of the 'zero-thrust' artifice. Once again at about 500 feet a throttle was retarded to simulate another engine failure. This time it was the port engine but the circuit apparently continued in just the same manner as the previous one, until the low 'overshoot' call. At this point the configuration of the aircraft

138

The CAT and the Hamsters

was gear down, flaps fully down at 40 degrees.

Instead of climbing away as on the previous occasion, the aircraft swung strongly to port. Witnesses saw the aircraft climbing slowly in a left turn until 30 degrees off the R/W heading. The port engine appeared to be rotating slowly. Delta Hotel hit some tree tops on the western boundary of the airfield before disappearing behind them. Soon afterwards black smoke was seen.

On board the aircraft Captain Offer had taken hold of the controls without the customary call of 'I have control'. Cadet S L, relieved of the unequal struggle to keep the aircraft straight, climb it above the impending treetops and preserve the speed, asked if the undercarriage should be raised. Airspeed was 65 to 70 knots and decreasing at this stage, meaning that insufficient airflow over the rudder was compromising directional control as well. The gear had to be manually assisted by S L pumping it, a subtle sign that the only hydraulic pump was not functioning fully. It was fitted to the left engine on the Apache. S L then asked to raise the flaps and received an affirmative from his instructor but the cadet selected only 20 degrees because he didn't want to affect the lift of the stricken aircraft.

The collision with the treetops was slight but the aircraft descended sharply after this and pancaked into a sports field in the grounds of Netley Hospital. Its forward momentum carried it across the field where its wings impacted with two trees, slowing it down somewhat but the remainder of the mainplanes and still-attached fuselage continued onwards before crashing into a brick wall. The starboard engine was still operating at full power as the aircraft crashed. The starboard wing was severely damaged by the impact with the trees and most likely its integral fuel tank ruptured. The single exit door was on the starboard side and would only open to one third of its normal aperture.

Both cadets were aware that Capt Offer was unconscious in the right-hand seat and after undoing their seatbelts and his, tried to pull and push him from the machine. Fire started under the hot starboard engine and M C K jumped clear. This allowed S L to exit onto the burning starboard wing and try to drag his instructor clear. This too was unsuccessful because the fire had set light to the cadet's clothing and he was forced to jump clear as well. After beating out the flames S L tried to return for a further rescue attempt but was beaten back by the inferno. Capt Offer emerged unaided but all ablaze. His flames were extinguished and as soon as the ambulance arrived he was taken

The CAT and the Hamsters

to the serious burns unit at Odstock Hospital Salisbury. Tragically he died of his injuries ten weeks later.

A Board of Trade investigation was conducted and a yellow-covered report published as CAP 306. It concluded that at the end of the final downwind leg Capt Offer failed to move the port mixture control from its 'idle-cut-off' to the 'full-rich-on' position, as required for the engine to function normally so although the engine instruments showed boost and RPM; the engine was in reality shut down. Accordingly the overshoot was carried out from ground level, at low speed, with flaps and gear in the landing position where they caused maximum drag on one functioning engine. The windmilling port engine added to the aerodynamic drag. It was standard CAT procedure to use 'carb heat' in potential carburettor icing conditions. This also reduced the power from the operating starboard engine.

A Board of Trade inspector visited the college and carried out performance tests on a similar Apache but at a safe altitude. He discovered that the Apache could not climb in that configuration except when a pilot traded speed for height. When the aircraft was 'cleaned up' it climbed at just over 60 feet per minute. The Board of Trade recommended that 'in twin engined aircraft which have a low rate of climb with one engine inoperative in certain conditions and which are used extensively for flying training, consideration should be given to the possibility of providing some means to ensure:

'The aircraft instrumentation will give a ready indication of incorrect engine operation (all Apaches were later fitted with cylinder head temperature gauges) and the speed of retraction of flaps and landing gear is maintained regardless of which engine is rendered inoperative. In other words fit two hydraulic pumps to such aircraft'.

My personal view is that the Apache was never designed by Pipers to fulfil the role asked of it by CAT. However, while researching this book I conducted an interview with Capt Tony Liskutin who, as a CAT senior instructor, was appointed Flight Safety Officer.

In that role he was asked by the Principal to prepare a preliminary report on the accident. A major finding in his report was that Hamble ATC had called Delta Hotel while we were downwind. Stan Offer answered their request for information on the weather conditions over the Solent. Tony asserted that this request and trying to answer it disturbed Stan's concentration and that's

The CAT and the Hamsters

The aftermath of the fire
Author

why he omitted to move the mixture control back to its correct position.

It's possible that immediate recognition of the absence of power on the port engine and closing of its starboard companion might have facilitated a return to earth within the airfield. W J Durrant, who was an ATC assistant, made an official report to the inspector of accidents on January 11, 1967. He was attending to centre-line marker boards for R/W 32 at the time of the accident and attests that when he first noticed Delta Hotel it was midway down the runway and about 30 feet above it.

I suppose the mindset of a trainee to any untoward behaviour of his aircraft is that most often he has caused it by some mistake. I surmised that the initial yaw was probably my fault until I saw my instructor struggling just as much as I had been. Then it quickly dawned on me something extraneous had happened. In attempting to reduce the drag on our stricken machine I'd focused my attention inside the cockpit. When I looked out we were close to and a little below the tops of some large leafless trees. I knew we must hit them but instead of terror I thought 'We're really going to get into trouble (with the college) for this.' It's a bizarre insight, that the CAT inspired more fear than crashing!

After hitting the tops of the trees the aircraft stalled steeply nose down. Capt Offer made no input to the controls. Instinctively I pulled back on the control column with all my might and there must have been just enough airflow over the elevators to pitch the nose up before impact. That was lucky, as was the conveniently-placed sports pitch and the suitably spaced trees. They slowed us up so that we survived hitting the wall. Stan Offer had told us previously that he had a bad back and that he needed to ease himself up out

The CAT and the Hamsters

of his seat in case of a firm landing. To that end he kept his seatbelts looser than we did and banged his head on impact and was knocked unconscious.

The unfortunate man was only alone in the aircraft for a few seconds longer than his cadets but in that time the fire burned him horribly. I beat out his flames with my bare hands after rugby-tackling him. It was the only way to arrest his agonised, flaming progress but I will always regret that I was unable to rescue him earlier, and save his life. M C K and I were treated in a Southampton hospital and taken back to Hamble, where Bill Anderson scooped us up into another Apache and flew off over the Isle of Wight. My burned and cut hands were bandaged and stitched up but M C K was encouraged to fly the machine. I don't know if it was 'hair of the dog' or an exercise to see if we freaked out.

Meanwhile my poor mother had been shopping in Southampton and passed a streetseller of the *Southern Evening Echo* yelling out 'Plane crash – three dead' over and over again, as is their wont. She was only placated when I appeared at the door, having been kindly taken to my parents' home by college transport. We cadets spent the night in the college hospital and slept badly.

The initial interviews of witnesses began the next day but the Principal's demeanour could not have been improved by a letter he received from a Mr I R W from Newport on the Isle of Wight. He was 'Hon. Sec. I W Aircraft Control Committee and he wrote: 'I am writing to the Board of Trade to enquire how many aircraft from Hamble have been involved in mishaps during the past year. Should the figures be disturbing, as I suspect they may be, I intend to ask the Board to hold an inquiry into the administration of the college.' It was probably an attempt to make political capital out of the accident by a group opposed to the college and its noisy aeroplanes. There were an awful lot of likeminded people in the Solent/Isle of Wight area and they were very vociferous.

On October 25, 1968 an inquest was held at Salisbury. It was attended by me, C K and the CFI. All were cross-examined by legal counsel Mr Phillips representing the interests of Stan Offer's widow. It was suggested to the CFI that the 'low overshoot' procedure with one engine at 'zero-thrust' was inherently dangerous. Capt Duff-Mitchell agreed but stated that it was not an authorised procedure at Hamble, although under cross examination

The CAT and the Hamsters

The collision in Hangar 49   *Hamble pictures*

he agreed that the operations manual had been altered on this aspect since the accident but he had no knowledge of any instructors using the procedure before the accident. In my interviews carried out with Hamble instructors and cadets I've relayed that assertion and it has been greeted with incredulity.

There was always pressure on Hamble instructors to save time and the 'low overshoot' procedure did just that. To make a fullstop landing from an approach meant brake and undercarriage wear. It meant carrying out all the after-landing and pre-take off checks and it meant taxying back to the holding point on a very busy, congested airfield. So that's obviously what you'd do if you were pressed for time. Evan Davis & Co. solicitors representing Capt Offer's widow, wrote to the college secretary on January 8, 1969 alleging negligence by CAT Properties Ltd.

If the Board was concerned about I R W's letter, more ammunition was provided on May 31 when nine of the new Cherokees were parked for the night in Hanger 49. At 19.30 a licensed aircraft engineer Abdul Jalil Chowdhry was working on G-AVBD and in the course of his checks, swung the propeller. Unfortunately, the mixture control was in the 'rich' position with ignition on and the engine started. Because the aircraft brakes were not on it leapt forward and collided with G-AVBI, G-AVBC and finally embedded itself into the rear fuselage of G-AVAY. An internal enquiry found A J C responsible and he resigned from the college. Bravo India sustained moderate damage, while the other three Cherokees had major damage and were out of action for some time.

The CAT was now facing a serious shortage of training aircraft as the result of the two accidents outlined above.

Some light relief occurred on August 26, although E C Bates didn't view

The CAT and the Hamsters

it as such. Piper Twin-Comanche G-AVFW made an unauthorised visit to the field to pick up four passengers. Hamble was prior permission only (PPO) and the four passengers were trespassing foreign journalists who wanted a gander at an International Power Boat Race being held in the Solent. Even though the college security guard raced to the scene on his pushbike, he could not stop the aircraft departing. It had been chartered by Fairey Marine, who had part-owned the site during the First World War. Later on G-AVFW returned and was confronted by an enraged Principal riding not on a bicycle but on a very high horse. Fairey were being cheeky but Bates snitched on them to the Board of Trade, who referred the matter to the DPP. It appeared, eventually that the pilot was a PPL holder not a CPL holder so he was breaking the law in several ways.

A year had passed since Delta Hotel had crashed and CAT had purchased two Aztecs to cover the hiatus in advanced trainers. Then on the morning of January 29, 1968 a nosewheel yoke casting failed as G-AVNL completed its landing run on R/W 18 at Hamble. The aircraft had flown 422 hours from new. Cadets R P H and A K B were returning from a cross-country trip and the latter was the handling pilot. Tony Liskutin investigated and cited the increasingly undulating airfield surface as a contributory factor. The CFI wrote to the Principal confirming the poor surface state of the airfield and saying that although the Aztec was 1,500lbs heavier than the Apache, Pipers had not beefed up the nosewheel yoke casting. The yoke was bench-inspected and the fracture assessed as caused by stress not fatigue.

Poor A K B was affected by the incident and was sleeping badly and feeling nauseous. He was sent off flying on February 2 in Apache G-ATMU to practise night solo circuits at Hamble. He completed two without incident but on the third he forgot to lower the undercarriage. The aircraft was damaged by landing without the gear down. However, despite the 'medical' evidence the Principal held A K B fully culpable for the accident but decided not to discipline him.

A further report by Capt N V Todd of BOAC highlighted shortcomings in the operations manual and the shortfalls in the Apache's suitability, especially the undercarriage warning system.

On March 15 Chipmunk G-AOTZ ripped open the canvas underside of the

The CAT and the Hamsters

starboard wing at Bembridge during a flapless approach/landing. The aircraft had drifted off the centreline of R/W 31 and hit a marker pole but neither Capt P Kennett nor the cadet under instruction, K S F, noticed anything untoward. The aircraft continued flying for most of the afternoon with a two-foot tear in the fabric and minor damage to the starboard flap. As a result, Bembridge airfield was asked to shorten the marker poles so that they would pass under a Chipmunk's wing.

More untoward ground contact occurred on May 21 when Cherokee 180 G-AVBH was found to have a bent propeller tip. This mark of PA-28 with the heavier engine was prone to this type of damage especially where uneven runway surfaces (Hamble) caused porpoising.

Another Cherokee G-AVBB was in trouble on November 12 when it suffered carburettor icing in the circuit at Lee-on-Solent. The solo cadet H was not censured because he force-landed in a field adjacent to the RN aerodrome without damaging the aircraft. Indeed when the CFI attended the scene he was able to start up and taxi out of the field onto a convenient road, whilst the police stopped the traffic. Proceeding in an easterly direction and within the speed limit, he turned off the carriageway into the airfield proper and returned to Hamble by air. Ops manual procedures regarding 'carb-heat' were modified.

By March 21, 1969 the new Barons had arrived with a bang. Unfortunately the bang on G-AWAI was caused by a nosewheel eye-bolt fracturing on take-off from Eastleigh. The aircraft returned to Hamble but notwithstanding the best efforts of Capt R J Noyes, including deployment of the emergency lowering mechanism, the nose-gear collapsed during the landing. Technical issues surrounding the Baron undercarriage operating system were highlighted

Bravo Juliet on the wrong side of the tracks
Hamble pictures

The CAT and the Hamsters

but the accident was attributed to stress, initiated during a skittish landing at Jersey on the March 7.

In the previous month a NOTAM 88/1969 had been received. It stated that sometime after March 25 Concorde 002 would be taking its maiden flight from Filton to Fairford. Maps of a restricted area were enclosed along with information that a further Class I NOTAM would be issued on the exact day of the flight. The chosen day was April 9 and the flight managers briefed cadets and instructors about the restricted area early in the morning but did not know exactly at what time the restricted area would be activated — because Hamble still did not receive Class I NOTAMS.

Later in the morning Cherokee flying instructor L J Otley briefed three cadets for their first solo cross-country flights. They were to take three separate Cherokee aircraft on a route Hamble-Grove-Blackbushe-Hamble. Unfortunately the disused airfield at Grove was inside the restricted area and the last Cherokee G-AVNT, flown by cadet D A L, was overhead as Concorde banked around him 1.5 miles to the east. The incident was witnessed by RAF Brize Norton Radar, Concorde test pilot Captain Brian Trubshaw was advised and he effected a minor course change just to be on the safe side.

Hamble's Senior ATC Officer Mr R T Hunt protested that the exact time of Concorde's flight was not known because the Class I NOTAM had not reached them. Nor would he accept any Hamble ATC responsibility for pointing out that the third and last Cherokee would infringe the restricted area whilst it was active. Later CAT internal correspondence pointed out that NOTAMS arrived by post and bemoaned the lack of a teleprinter. As this was the second incident related to Class I NOTAMS perhaps it was a false economy that Hamble ATC was not linked to the national AIS teleprinter service?

The press had jumped to the conclusion that the 'air miss' was the fault of an inexperienced cadet. Bates let them believe that but privately blamed Capt Otley. Unfortunately if he was dismissed the CAT might be let out of the bag. So the instructor was persuaded to resign and the cadets were given a 'gypsy's warning'. Although the Minister of State expressed his concern, the Board of Trade accepted the Principal's handling of the matter.

There had been a previous air miss incident between a BAC 111 and Baron G-AWAO on August 2, 1968. Capt Peddell was outbound in the Mayfield

The CAT and the Hamsters

holding pattern at 2,500 feet when the 111 descended rapidly to its cleared altitude of 3,000 feet. The Baron had called 'out of' 3,000 but had descended slowly, so the large twin-jet must have looked close but ATC sent written reassurance that 500 feet separation must have existed.

Back on the ground, an accident on May 9, 1969 to Cherokee G-AVBJ elicited yet another report from the hard-working F E Stokes, CAT's chief engineer. His task was to assess the damage to the college's increasingly long list of battered aeroplanes, then allocate a job number and decide how to bring the machine back on the line.

This accident involved a landing on R/W 24 during which Bravo Juliet skidded onto the railway tracks running along the south-western side of the aerodrome. The line was a 1926 legacy of a Shell Mex and BP petrol and oil depot to the south of Hamble Lane. Despite the track's age it was still strong enough to wipe off the nose wheel and starboard main gear, as well as inflicting considerable damage to both wings and the propeller.

Shortly before landing, a heavy thunderstorm had hit Hamble. Capt A Jackson had taken control from cadet M I R because of heavy rain on the downwind leg but the weather had cleared by the time the instructor made a normal landing. Unfortunately the braking action was very poor, due to standing water hidden by the long grass, and this caused aquaplaning. An investigation by Capt. John Vickers, Flight Safety Officer, concluded that Hamble's two shortest runways 06/24 and 12/30 were marginal and precise operating limits needed to be promulgated for both. In addition it was recommended that Hamble ATC were more proactive when advising pilots of surface conditions.

February 27, 1970 saw a horrible accident when two Cherokees collided about one mile north of Hamble. Cadet A J P in G-AVBD had just taken off from the northerly runway to engage in solo circuit training. Cadet J M S was in G-AVBI and had been solo to Lee-on Solent. He joined the 'dead' side of the right-hand circuit and should have insinuated himself into the traffic pattern by crossing the upwind end of the runway at 1,000 feet before turning right downwind. At that height any aircraft taking off would be at least 500 feet below him. Tragically he pushed his crosswind leg further north and this put him on a collision course with Bravo Delta.

The collision occurred about 14.05 and both aircraft plunged to earth in south Bursledon, destroying the aircraft and killing their young

The CAT and the Hamsters

Alpha Golf is
brought home
Hamble pictures

pilots. Bravo India caught fire after crashing. Once again 'limited R/T' was in force in the circuit. Both cadets were sons of BEA personnel and A J P's father was a very popular captain on the Trident fleet. Many people in the college and the airline were saddened by the death of the two young men. N S Head investigated the accident and his report was published in April 1972. He apportioned blame onto the cadets for not keeping an adequate lookout and cited the relative inexperience of the cadets as causal.

In an effort to avoid a repetition it was proposed to halve the limit on circuit traffic to five aircraft, to take steps to improve the all-round visibility from the Cherokee cockpit, to make the aircraft easier to spot and to discontinue 'limited R/T'. Captain J P refused to accept these findings concerning his son and exercised his right for a review. The CAT governors were informed of this at a meeting on May 18, 1972.

Two more Cherokees collided on March 20, 1970, this time over the Isle of Wight. The aircraft involved were G-AYAW, which force-landed at Lambslease Farm, Porchfield on the island and G-AVNS, which made it back to Hamble. Two weeks later, on April 14, cadet J W F R experienced the electrical fault on Baron G-AWAL which is referred to at length in Chapter 6. Cherokee G-AYAT made a bad month worse when cadet A G S overcorrected a ballooned solo landing on R/W 36 at Hamble and relanded on his nosewheel. The propeller and nosewheel were badly damaged.

The preliminary assessment of the undercarriage fault on Baron G-AWAL concluded that it was probably a one-off. It wasn't! G-AWAO suffered a nosewheel fault on May 4 at Hurn and landed on R/W 17 employing just the two main wheels. The flight originated in Cherbourg and was carrying

The CAT and the Hamsters

Capt A W Peddel and cadets J and C as passengers. Cadet C R was under instruction from Capt. A Smith, who eventually carried out the emergency landing. The fault was a fatigue fracture of an undercarriage operating arm. There had been previous incidents with Barons, so all CAT examples were grounded pending replacement of the offending part.

The rest of 1970 saw no further accidents and the lull continued until July 6 the following year when an alert ground engineer noticed that Cherokee G-AXZC had a nosewheel out of alignment. Interrogation of cadets who had carried out the previous 24 landings found one who admitted a 'marginal' event. He did not feel it was necessary to report it. It was emphasised to him by Capt A W Farrell, the Flight Safety Officer, how important it was to err on the side of caution when reporting 'marginal events'. Farrell was involved in an investigation six days later when Cherokee G-AVNF was found to have a line of scoring on the underside of the port wing which continued across the chord of the wing and continued under the port aileron. Cadets R G T and G K wrote reports affirming that nothing untoward had happened during their pilotage. Seeing as the deputy CFI was carrying out a check on one cadet, his testimony could not be faulted. Indeed the other account was backed up by Portsmouth ATC who had been observing G-AVNP during its exercises. The Flight Safety Officer admitted: 'This one has got me baffled.'

On 22nd October Cadet P A L was carrying out his first solo. During the landing flare he says that he believed that a bird, startled by his approach, took off and was going to strike the windscreen. Instinctively he ducked and

Air Vice-Marshall Bates with cadets in the early days of the College
Hamble pictures

149

The CAT and the Hamsters

in so doing pushed forward on the control column, thus affecting a heavy, nosewheel-first landing. Considerable damage resulted as with G-AYAT in the spring.

Nor was the Baron fleet immune to this spate of landing accidents. Following the failure of the nosewheel on G-AWAO, its sister ship G-AWAG went one better on December 9 when the whole undercarriage failed to lower. F E Stokes found the gearbox of the retracting/lowering mechanism to be partly seized. The instructor Capt G W Jones received a written commendation from F W Walton, chairman of governors CAT citing a 'high standard of airmanship' in landing safely and minimising damage to Alpha Golf.

More undercarriage problems occurred on February 14, 1972 but this time with a Cherokee G-AYAB. Cadet N J G was landing on R/W 32 at Hamble when the right main-gear leg collapsed during the roll-out. A torque link bolt had sheared at some point. The investigating Flight Safety Officer, Capt P I H. Courtney, highlighted several deficiencies in the CAT safety procedures: the crash alarm was not sounded immediately; the aircraft was moved before a search for the broken bolt could be carried out on the grass runway and ATC did not have a clear view of the threshold of R/W 32 due to reflections on the glass in the control tower.

That these accidents were expensive is borne out by the Chief Engineer's estimate for repairing Baron G-AWAE. The total damage to propellers, engines and undercarriage was around £1,900 on April 6, 1972, over £21,000 at 2014 prices. The accident occurred when Capt J G Neale was giving initial taxying tuition to Cadet R J M at Hurn. The cadet attempted to use asymmetric power to tighten a turn but opened up the wrong engine. Even though the instructor took control, the nosewheel left the taxiway and collapsed. It has to be said that the nosewheel didn't seem to be the strongest part of the Baron D55!

A report by Capt P I H Courtney found that the grass immediately adjacent to the taxiway was undermined by burrowing animals and that the nosewheel had penetrated the turf by almost two feet. This was contrary to the requirements of CAP 168 par 31/2 p.35, which stated 'there should be no holes or ditches within 35 feet of the edge of the taxiway'. The deputy CFI Capt W V Kinnin accepted the report and moderated the blame on the crew, blaming instead the airfield owners.

The CAT and the Hamsters

Firemen recover the Cherokees from the River Hamble estuary.
Hamble pictures

Luckily no costs or damage occurred when solo cadet S D B experienced a complete brake failure in Cherokee G-AVNR on June 1 1972. After ATC failed to locate any instructors on the ground who might offer advice, Capt E E Kortens offered help from G-AXAR. Indeed he landed on R/W 20 without applying his brakes, thus demonstrating empirically that S D B had nothing to fear. The brake failure was due to a failed 'O' ring and ATC were mildly admonished for not setting off the crash alarm.

Over the dozen years since CAT opened, very few air-miss reports had been generated, apart from the spectacular involving Concorde 002. However British United Air Ferries (BUAF) operated ATL 98 Carvairs out of Lydd and Southend carrying passengers and their cars to the Continent. Sometimes these aircraft cancelled their flight plans and proceeded VFR outside of controlled airspace. It was in this manner that Cherokee G-AVNM, being operated on a solo cross-country by cadet R M P, came to the attention of a Carvair crew who were overtaking him on the same track at the same height. They filed an air miss, despite the 'Rules of the Air' requiring them to take avoiding action. Acting Flight Safety Officer Capt N L D Kemp made a spirited defence of the cadet, which was nice. But then he was a brave man; in receipt of a DFC for flying Hurricanes during the Battle of Britain.

On April 8 1971 *Flight* magazine had carried a very short paragraph on page 477. 'Group Capt R Scott is to become Principal of the College of Air Training at Hamble on the retirement of AV-M E Bates in June'. So an era ended and I'm not sure if, after reading through hundreds of pages of

The CAT and the Hamsters

documents while researching this chapter, I've detected a softening in Bates' attitude. Early on one gains the impression of a 'shoot first and ask questions afterwards' approach to any cadet or instructor involved in an incident. Latterly when flight safety officers and instructors seemed to be trying to ameliorate the censure of the cadet, did he show a increasing tendency to give the benefit of the doubt? For example: Capt W V Kinnin was reprimanded in 1962 for a 'temporary lapse' but ten years later he was deputy CFI. As I say, I'm not sure and readers must make their own judgement.

The training of pilots carried on at Hamble for more than a dozen years but course 744 was the last destined for British Airways. CAT bought no more new aircraft types and attempts made during the late 1970s to keep the establishment going meant that various external clients sponsored cadets into the training establishment. Because of the fragmented nature of the last decade of its existence, certain accidents and incidents occurred which did not fit into the pattern we have been examining thus far. Accordingly the retirement of Bates might be a convenient time to wind up this chapter.

Nevertheless there were still loose ends from the double Cherokee collision from February 1970. Although N S Head had submitted his report in April 1972, the fathers of the two cadets, most notably Capt Jimmy Proctor, disagreed with the findings, which laid the blame on their sons. Accordingly the Department of Trade and Industry (formed in October 1970 to replace the Board of Trade) commissioned a review before Capt R R Critchley and R M Yorke QC.

This was published in April 1973 and its findings were less censorious of the cadets, although the inspector stated: 'I am in substantial agreement with, and confirm, most of Mr Head's careful report.' However the Hamble circuit and ATC procedures came in for a certain amount of comment as well, even though the proceedings were not adversarial. Both of the reviewing officers commented on the 'spirit of inquiry and investigation' and felt that this was 'a tribute to all who took part.'

Right-hand circuits were felt to be a contributory factor and 'at aerodromes where basic flying training is carried on' the criteria for using them should be reviewed'. The climbing turn onto the crosswind leg was also criticised and a recommendation was made for a straight climb-out to circuit height. Extra transparent panels had already been fitted into the cockpit roof of the

The CAT and the Hamsters

Cherokee to improve external visibility. Strobe lights and more conspicuous paint schemes were being considered along with mandatory recording of ATC traffic.

In an awful postscript to the accident examined above, two more Cherokees, G-AVJB & G-AXZC, crashed after a mid-air collision on April 30 1981. The two cadets killed in this accident were Libyans in their early 20s because by now the college, in an effort to stay afloat financially, had loosened its ties with British Airways and was training foreign nationals. The Department of Trade investigator L S H Shaddick wrote a report No. 5/82 which was published on September 6, 1982.

Unfortunately his conclusions were similar to N S Head's report from a decade earlier. The collision occurred on finals and the aircraft crashed onto the muddy shore of the Hamble River estuary and once again the right-hand circuit was cited as a major causative factor. Additionally, the relative inexperience of the solo cadets and the poor external visibility of the Cherokees both featured once more as contributing to the crash. Plus ça change, plus c'est la même chose!

What conclusions can be drawn from the accidents described in this chapter?

Firstly the airfield itself was inadequate for the tasks required of it. The surface was undulating, prone to waterlogging and even the longest runways were of marginal length for Baron operations. It's fairly obvious that the Baron had a congenital weakness in its undercarriage and several of the accidents can be attributed to that but on the smooth, hard-surface runways of its native USA these faults were slower to manifest themselves.

Exactly the same comment could be made about the Cherokee 180. Propeller tip damage and nosegear oleo weakness were both exacerbated by bouncy student landings and 'porpoising' caused by Hamble's undulating surface. When CAT took issue with Beechcraft about the third nosewheel eyebolt failure, the manufacturer and its agents wrote that 'the failures were probably due to harsh use of an aircraft not originally designed for training'. I bet Beechcraft didn't mention that limitation when the College were looking to buy the Barons in the first place!

So should the CAT have bought more robust aircraft? Well in the Chipmunk they did but it was obsolescent when the college opened. Furthermore it had

The CAT and the Hamsters

no capacity for radio/nav training. Given better and more decisive strategy by the Government and the college governors Beagle aircraft could have provided CAT with much of what they needed: a strong basic trainer based on the Beagle B121 Pup and a twin engined instrument trainer based on the Beagle B242.

If necessary the Cherokee could have provided an intermediate trainer between the two Beagles. Incidentally, a much more adventurous investment policy by the Government and more forward-thinking by CAT could have been instrumental in providing the college with purpose-built aircraft and GB Ltd. with a nucleus of orders for a burgeoning light aircraft industry. Instead it was a case of caution and penny-pinching from both parties.

Unfortunately that's the theme that threads its way through most of these accidents. The very site of the College was bound to lead to an increasing risk of air misses as the nearby airports at Hurn and Eastleigh became busier. This, combined with the growing urbanisation of greater Southampton and the both banks of the Solent, lead to more and more vociferous complaints by residents about aircraft noise. The two factors forced the college into a cramped right-hand circuit operation which was inherently unsafe.

It is something of a tribute to the professionalism of the college instructors that so few fatal accidents took place but one can only conclude that they were a body of men under pressure. That pressure was often caused by a shortage of aircraft, either caused by the losses due to accidents and incidents mentioned above or by expansion of the training programme without a necessary procurement of extra aircraft. In a way it was a self fulfilling prophecy: a shortage of aircraft led to pressure; pressure led to accidents; accidents led to fewer aircraft.

I have discovered no evidence that the accident record of CAT weighed in the balance when the final future of the college was decided but there's plenty of evidence that the financial pressures did weigh heavily, as will be shown in the next chapter.

Chapter 9

The denouement

O N FEBRUARY 1 1967 *Flight* published the following: 'Sir Giles Guthrie, chairman of BOAC, presented diplomas to 76 graduates of the College of Air Training who have recently completed their courses at Hamble and are now on further training and/or flying as second officers with BOAC and BEA. The graduates entered Hamble between August 1964 and July 1965. Since the first cadets entered the College in September 1960, 284 have successfully graduated. The facilities are being expanded to permit 168 cadets a year (twice the present number) to be trained so as to meet the growing demand for pilots.'

In the first year 41 candidates entered, rising to 64 in the second and third years. The intakes were split into several courses, numbered sequentially and preceded by the year. For example, 1960 gave rise to three courses in that series: 601, 602 and 603. There were often 15 cadets in a course but numbers varied considerably from as few as seven but never more than 16. By 1963, numbers had risen to 84 cadets in seven courses split between two intakes. Appendix 1 and its tables give fuller details. My own course was 655 and after that year course numbering changed. The year of joining still formed the first two numbers but the third number was the intake, which was further subdivided into courses by the addition of a capital letter suffix, for example 661A, 661B, 661C. Then 662A, 662B and so on. In that year, 1966, the total intake reached 150 cadets.

Flight was alluding to four intakes of 40 in the future, some of whom would be university graduates on a shortened course. Much of this expansion can be attributed to Plan Golf but this was subsequently cast aside in late 1968. Its successor anticipated 144 cadets in four intakes of 36 producing 115 graduates per annum.

A week after the article reproduced above, *Flight* had more to say: 'Revised contracts worth £3 million are to be placed with the Oxford Air Training School by BEA to train 90 university graduates and 60 'A' level

The CAT and the Hamsters

654/5/6 with Southampton Council dignitaries and head of Liberal studies Colin Barnes —*Author*

school-leavers every year. The graduates will take a 12-month course and the school leavers an 18-month course. Both groups will qualify with the CPL and instrument rating.

'The increase in training requirements has become necessary because of the operating limits placed on Hamble, because of its closeness to Southampton. By the end of this year Hamble will reach it maximum training capacity of 168 cadets each year doing 18-month courses. Training costs are in the region of £5,000 per cadet. A total of 1,500 students will be given BEA-sponsored training in the next five years at Hamble, Oxford and Perth. At the moment 60 university graduates are being trained at Oxford under the BEA/BOAC scheme which began last year.'

By the end of 1969, 616 pilots had graduated from CAT and their training had been jointly sponsored by BEA, BOAC and the BoT. In another landmark the very first of them to be promoted to captain in BEA, in April 1970, was Viv Gunton. During that time the Government had paid £1.2 million to the college.

Two months previously Roy Mason, President of the Board of Trade, announced in the House of Commons on February 6 that the Board of Trade would reduce its financial support for CAT from £175,000 to £100,000 a year

The CAT and the Hamsters

from April 1. The Board had also been contributing 25 per cent of the cost of training airline sponsored students at Perth, Oxford and Carlisle and had spent about £450,000 since 1965/66. Under this training scheme 373 pilots had graduated and a further 80 were still under training — all for BEA and BOAC.

During the next year the magazine had more to say. *Flight*, dated August 12, 1971, was headlining a BOAC pilot problem. It stated that up to 100 graduates would be surplus to requirements in 1972. BOAC blamed a pilots' strike, weak finances and failure to take on extra Boeing 747 options. BEA indicated that it could be in a position to offer some of the graduates employment. The first course to be affected would see 11 of their number go to BEA and 25 would be 'deferred'. Cadets at the CSE Oxford training establishment were also affected. Many learned of their career hiccough by reading of the decision in a local newspaper. Wonderful!

Flight continued: 'The College at Hamble is definitely going to be training cadets (at a cost of £7,000 each) until January 1973. Although at the moment it appears that they will be in decreasing numbers. The July and October intakes for this year have already been cancelled. Prediction of air traffic growth and thus indirectly pilot requirements has always proved difficult. Coupled with the requirement for nearly two years lead time to train pilots, this has resulted in notorious fluctuations in the intakes at Hamble, somewhat erratic contracts set by BEA/BOAC with the commercial schools at Oxford and Perth and the offer of employment earlier this year to 80 RAF pilots who resigned their commissions on the basis of the offer which was then withdrawn. The corollary to this was an increased chop rate at Hamble. Of the 95 who joined in 1971, 22 failed to graduate; or as the Principal put it, a 'wastage rate' of more than 23 percent.

Despite this assessment early in the decade, BEA and BOAC apparently still believed that there would be a severe shortage of pilots, peaking during 1976/77. The airlines predicted a retirement bulge of 500-600 senior crew in 1979 and foresaw the need for 200 new pilots a year until then.

Then only six months later, in November 1974, *Flight* was reporting the opposite: 'British Airways has told the 38 students who will graduate from the College of Air Training, Hamble, on November 29 that they will not be needed by the airline for 12 months. The students have been given a retainer

The CAT and the Hamsters

HS121 Trident 1C - G-ARPO was a 3 crew aircraft.
Author

of £600 and promised employment at the end of 1975. At present there are some 275 students at Hamble and 30-40 graduates every three months. British Airways is to review the situation every three months; no decision has yet been taken about the employment of the next batch of graduates. Meanwhile, no new cadets will start at Hamble for the next year.' What was going on? In fact there was a complete hiatus between October 14, 1974 and February 13, 1978. What the hell was going on?

Expansion; then laying people off — how could they get it so wrong? To understand the answers we need to delve into a bit of Civil Aviation history. In 1967 the government established a committee of inquiry into civil aviation under Sir Ronald Edwards. The Edwards Committee reported in 1969 and one of its recommendations was the formation of a National Air Holding Board to control finances and policies of the two corporations.

The recommendation was enacted in 1971 with the passing of the Civil Aviation Act 1971. That legislation formed the British Airways Board to control all the activities of BOAC and BEA, including the newly-formed BEA Airtours subsidiary and in 1972 the BOAC and BEA managements were combined.

The operations of the separate airlines were merged into British Airways on April 1, 1974. At the time it was the biggest merger in the aviation industry, creating the world's largest network route network. Three-crew aircraft such as the VC-10 and Vanguard were retired and although the new Lockheed Tri-

The CAT and the Hamsters

Star had a three-crew configuration it would soon join the Boeing 707 and Hawker Siddeley Trident on the scrapheap.

Their replacements, the new Boeing 737, 757 and 767, needed just two operating pilots in the cockpit. Eventually even the longhaul Jumbo Boeing 747-400 was a two-crew aircraft. British Airways was still owned by the Government but 13 years after its formation it was privatised in February 1987. During that period over 23,000 jobs were cut and the pilot shortage was cut with them. As for CAT, it was in the hands of the receiver by then.

Other factors such as the 1973 oil crisis also had an effect on passenger numbers and proposed airline expansion. The crisis had started in October, when the members of Organisation of Arab Petroleum Exporting Countries, or later OPEC, proclaimed an oil embargo. A year later the oil price had quadrupled to nearly $12 per barrel.

It would be easy to attribute all the fluctuations of CAT's output requirements on the factors listed above but within the airline I remember that the pilot force was sometimes exhorted to work harder due to a shortage, only to be warned of lay-offs a few months later.

The *Flight* article had mentioned the 'notorious fluctuations in intakes'. This didn't just manifest itself in graduates being laid off and potential cadets who had passed selection being sent off on indefinite furlough. It was a commonly-held belief among cadets that the exam standards bar was raised or lowered dependant on the airline's perceived short-term requirements. If that was the case, then it shows a dreadful callousness towards young men who had committed two years of their lives to pilot training only to be chopped and cast into the wilderness just because some anonymous BA bean-counter had calculated a new total for pilot recruitment.

Many of those chopped by CAT persisted and went on to have successful careers as pilots but many also took a blow to their self-esteem and turned their back on the industry. Given the very high standards demanded by the selection procedure, every cadet who didn't graduate was a failure of the CAT system and a squandering of a valuable human resource. Yet as late as November 1973 the college was still placing full-page adverts inviting prospective cadets to apply.

The hiatus and uncertainty continued throughout the early years of the 1970's until on June 12, 1975 *Flight* ran an article 'Uncertain Future for

The CAT and the Hamsters

Hamble'.

'The graduation of course 744 in 1976 will be the end of an era for the College of Air Training at Hamble. For more than 15 years BEA, BOAC and now British Airways have sponsored their own cadet pilot training scheme at the college. The requirement for the proposed courses in 1975 and 1976 has disappeared. Over 200 cadets are still to be absorbed by the airline and of these 100 or more have already graduated. A three-year wait for a flying job is very likely for many of these. Why should there be such a great surplus? The mass retirement of wartime pilots which the corporations anticipated over the past five years never materialised. Many have indeed left, but not in such a way as to create vacancies at the bottom of the ladder. It appears that British Airways lacks awareness as far as pilot requirements are concerned.'

Eventually in 1977 BA were minded to respond to agonised letters in the correspondence columns of *Flight* and wrote: 'We would like to say immediately that British Airways has every sympathy with these young Hamble-trained pilots who have not yet been invited to join the airline. The reason for this is simple. To produce a pilot ready for entry into airline service takes a great deal of time. When these young men were recruited for Hamble, the airline's expectations were of expansion. Then, as everyone knows, we were hit by the oil crisis, closely followed by the general economic decline.

'This double setback stifled the expansion and also created a small pilot surplus. But our forward planning now indicates that we should be able to invite Hamble-trained pilots who have not yet joined to take up flying positions with British Airways. This will of course be a gradual absorption, but we expect it to be completed by mid-1979. We have investigated the pilot surplus likely to exist in the 1980s, and the indications are that it will not meet our requirements. Our plans, which are reviewed virtually from month to month, show that after the current Hamble surplus has been taken in we will need a further 32 Hamble pilots in 1980.

'Because of the stringent selection procedures and length of the Hamble course, we must act now to meet this requirement. Selected candidates will be offered a place at Hamble — the date has yet to be settled — but each will be told from the outset that there will be no automatic entry into British Airways at the end of the course. If, however, our general economic recovery is swift and we can continue with our expansion plans, they will be able to

The CAT and the Hamsters

FOR SALE
by direction of The College of Air Training (Properties) Ltd
a wholly owned subsidiary of

A Flying Training Establishment
together with subsidiary let industrial investment properties
and 11 residential properties at **Hamble, Southampton, Hants**

AS A WHOLE or in lots

complete with licensed freehold airfield, hangars, educational and
residential buildings on approximately 189 acres of freehold land

A Fleet of 48 Training Aircraft
spares, engineering equipment, a variety of road and other vehicles,
training and maintenance equipment, etc.

with POSSESSION on May 1st, 1982, or earlier by arrangement

Surveyor L.F. Walters FRICS
Property Services Department British Airways PO Box 10
Heathrow Airport Hounslow Middlesex TW6 2JA
Tel: 01-750 5564 Attention: Frank Wyatt Bsc ARICS

Solicitor D.M. Scott
Legal Department British Airways Speedbird House
Heathrow Airport Hounslow Middlesex TW6 2JA
Tel: 01-759 5511 ext. 3244

Consultant G. Edwards FRICS
402 Drake House Dolphin Square London SW1
Tel: 01-834 9929

Cover of Sales Brochure *Author*

The CAT and the Hamsters

join us as soon as they have completed the course.'

At time of publication CAT had 22 Cherokees, 12 Barons and seven Chipmunks on strength. It was being run as a private company and educational institute, jointly owned by BEA and BOAC, under partial control of the DoTI, which contributed a small percentage of the necessary finance. Some people assert that it was this private status which led to its final downfall, because in the run-up to privatisation BA could find no place for CAT on its books.

BA sold The College of Air training to Hamble Airfield Properties for £5.2million in the summer of 1982 and in February 1984 it went into receivership and closed for good.

Epilogue

THE College of Air Training ceased to exist as a commercial entity in February 1984 when it went into receivership. However the last pilots who were trained, ostensibly for British Airways, graduated on June 9, 1981. Whilst the college was fighting for its life some training activity still took place.

Overall, CAT trained about 700 foreign nationals in two tranches. The first during the second half of the 1970s and the second after BA's sale of the facility in 1982. From late in 1976 to February 1978 there was a hiatus in training pilots for BA and during that time young men, predominately from Iran, but also Libya, Sudan and other Middle Eastern countries were trained as pilots or technicians. The second tranche carried on from 1983 well into the following year and included Cypriots, Zambians, Libyans, Ivorians and one chap from Malawi. In addition courses CP(H)1-6 trained a few helicopter pilots during the late Seventies.

These attempts at diversification indicate the increasing alarm reflected in comments recorded by the governors at their regular board meetings. Firstly, Government funding had been withdrawn. Secondly, CAT's unit cost of training a pilot to 'line-standard' was not competitive, being about 25 percent more expensive than the Oxford Air Training School. Consequently the demand for CAT-trained pilots by British Airways was tailing off because it was being largely fulfilled by the training schools at Kidlington and Perth.

About this time, faced with the threat of closure, an 'Employees Action Group' was formed. They produced a comprehensive report which was submitted to H.M. Government. In it they state: 'When British Airways announced their swingeing economic cuts, the closure of the College was part of that package. The Board of Governors and senior college management are required to follow a policy of sale or closure.' The group submitted that 'notwithstanding the serious economic difficulties surrounding the situation, sufficient evidence has been adduced to show that to allow the College to

The CAT and the Hamsters

close will be irresponsible.

The 35-page report produced no discernible response, and College of Air Training (Properties) Ltd was advertised for 'sale as a whole or in lots' in February 1982. The then Principal, Harry Hirst, told the *Southern Evening Echo:* 'I think someone will buy it, sell off some of the peripherals, and keep the remainder as a flying school and other aviation activities' (sic).

The peripherals included 11 residential buildings, some of which were student blocks but several of which were (potentially) private houses, on approximately 189 acres of freehold land with attendant hangers (some let for industrial use).

In addition, 48 aircraft complete with spares, training and maintenance equipment comprised the largest collection of aviation-related paraphernalia to be sold in one place since Pontius gave up flying.

The 13 Beechcraft Baron, 34 Piper PA28-180C Cherokee and two DH Chipmunk T22A's were just the tip of the iceberg. Simulators, six Link trainers, a wind tunnel, sectioned aero-engines, an Ohm's Law demonstration model, Glim lamps in red/white/amber and green are all mentioned in a 60-page catalogue of astonishing diversity and complexity. If I'd known that they had all that stuff stashed away I might have paid more attention to ground-school lectures.

The sale was to Hamble Airfield Properties and netted British Airways £5.2 million. The new company proposed to train civilian pilots from all of the countries mentioned above but would also offer some military options through its associate Specialist Flying Training. Use of turbo-prop aircraft from Hamble's grass runways was contemplated but reckoned without the local anti-noise lobby, a vociferous bunch in their own right.

In the event it all came to naught, because on January 3, 1984 Paul Oakley-White and Alan Barrett of Deloitte, Haskins & Sells were appointed joint-receivers and managers to the company. The 32 remaining aircraft were sold by tender on May 2 by Edward Rushton Son and Kenyon of Manchester (ERS&K), and the other assets by auction on May 16. The site was purchased by Southern Ideal Homes Ltd but the price was not disclosed.

Tony Sedgewick hosts a web page called Hamble's Airfields and he notes that 'Ron Souch of the Antique Aircraft Company and Carill Aviation used

The CAT and the Hamsters

Beginning of the end for CAT as the demolition gang move in

the airfield while Southern Ideal Homes produced their development plans and worked towards gaining planning permission: meaning that the last aircraft to fly out of Hamble was flown by Ron Souch on April 6, 1986 in Piper Cub G-AMPF'. However a little bird tells me that on Christmas day 1995 a DH86A Tiger Moth, G-ANEN, made a brief touch-and-go. Could it have been Santa on his way home?

The housing developer entered into a protracted tussle with Eastleigh Council, local residents and Hamble Parish Council, led by Roy Underdown, the erstwhile lecturer in meteorology and Principal of the college. Large-scale development was turned down but that's a story outside the scope of this book.

At the time of writing this —July 2015 — the bulk of the airfield surface is undeveloped but proposals to dig for gravel still hang like a pall over the area. Previous development plans for a golf course, marina and large housing estate have all come to nothing. The area which was under bricks and mortar already (classrooms, admin-buildings, accommodation blocks and hangers) was all razed to the ground and replaced by residential housing. Some of the new roads bear the names of previous features of the site.

The CAT and the Hamsters

On Friday May 15, 2015 more than 100 ex-employees, ex-cadets and ex-instructors assembled for a Hamble reunion at the Follands Sports and Social Club on the outskirts of Hamble-le-Rice, as the village now calls itself. Organised by the redoubtable Phil Nelson (erstwhile flying instructor), it was advertised as the last of its kind, partly due to the venue itself being redeveloped and partly because of the amount of time and effort needed to organise such an event.

So that's it then. This particular perspective is at an end – unless you know otherwise!

Appendix 1

The CAT courses

Visitors to The College of Air Training entered the site beside the gatehouse just off Hamble Lane. In front of them stretched the main drive with Ara House at its far end. Inside this imposing three story building much of the day to day administration of the establishment was carried out.

What visitors could not hope to see, on a shelf within the office of the Principal's secretary, was an olive-green, metal card index with two lockable drawers. It was only 20 inches long and eight inches wide, yet it carried the names of a large proportion of Britain's post-war commercial pilots. It now sits beside me as I write this.

Each card measures five inches by three inches and carries the following typed information in black ink: name; date of entry; course number; date of leaving. About one sixth of the cards carry typing in red ink. You have to hope that one of them is not yours, because following on from the date of leaving is this chilling phrase: Suspended on the grounds that he is unlikely to make a satisfactory professional pilot.

Sometimes the cards carry other typed information such as: resigned for medical reasons; training terminated or even graduated but it's not until the latter years of the CAT that one set actually carries the Christian names of the cadets and they're written as an afterthought in ball-point pen. It's as if the rigid quasi-military brio briefly relaxed into Biro during senescence.

On the reverse of the cards dating from the first five years are sets of densely-typed figures in six columns, headed Test 'A' to 'E' and Finals. All the college ground-school subjects are in the columns along with the achieved mark to one decimal place. Each column has an average for the subjects taken in the test, never less than six subjects, never more than ten. The exception is Finals which has 11: Aero; Th; Elec; Inst; Radio; Met; Plot; Law; Plan; Theory and N.Gen.

The CAT and the Hamsters

Marks generally range from the mid-sixties to the mid-eighties but an occasional 90% and above creeps in, especially in law. Marks below 50 per cent are rare but can be found on cards emblazoned with that chilling phrase in red on the obverse. Sometimes the red ink creeps onto the reverse side, when a final exam has been failed, but next to it is usually the reassuring black of a pass mark. What you don't want is red in on both sides of your card!

There are 1,794 cards for BA fixed-wing pilots, starting with DW Acton and ending in the second drawer with FA Zubiel. Sprinkled among them but not included in the list, are a few from the late-Seventies which comprise the helicopter trainees. Also in the drawers are 700 or so foreign cadets who studied flying and aeronautical subjects from 1976 until the end. For the purposes of this book I have not listed either category.

Originally I proposed to type the details from the obverse of the cards into a computer database to reproduce as complete a list as possible, although I decided not to include any of the information typed in red ink. However, you know what computers are like— they encourage you to play around with stuff, crunch the numbers, analyse the trends and things like that.

So it was a simple matter to find out how many days each cadet spent at the college, by subtracting the date of leaving from the date of starting. This threw up some surprising results as two men stuck it out for only one day before resigning. As I mentioned earlier, the induction talk was anything but welcoming but perhaps that's being a bit too sensitive. The record of 2,106 days before resignation must have a story behind it but I'm not privy to what that story is. Pete C however is more understandable and typical. He joined 661A in December 1965 had an accident which severed a finger and was temporarily suspended for medical reasons. After recuperation and a check-up with the CAA he resumed his studies with 672B and graduated in November 1968 after 1,335 days.

The first 'two-year' courses with their generous sprinkling of liberal studies and compulsorily PT took a prescient 757 days, but this was exceeded by the 1974 intake who achieved 767 days. Who'd have thought Boeing would pay such attention to detail? Gradually a few days were shaved off courses in the early 1960s bringing them down to around 700 days but it wasn't until the middle of that decade that the 18-month duration course was introduced. The

The CAT and the Hamsters

65 and 66 series were allowed 588 days with the nadir of 522 days reached by the intake of 1968. From then on the attendance period began to increase again as the realisation began to dawn on the governors that they were asking too much of the limited resources available to the college staff.

Just over 19 per cent of the 134 courses achieved a 100 per cent graduation rate and the bulk of them date from just three years out of the establishment's 22 years of operation — 1968, 1972 and 1978 were years that gave cadets the best chance of avoiding the chop. Indeed when I was interviewing one cadet from the mid-Seventies he was amazed to learn that having a member of one's course suspended, or resigning, was the norm and not the exception. At that 'other end of the spectrum' some courses in the early to mid-Sixties lost 50 per cent (and in one case a shocking 56 per cent) of their members. The average failure rate amongst the 1794 cadets was 17.32 per cent.

I've postulated earlier in the book that somehow the pass/fail standards were adjusted to produce the number of cadets required by the corporations. Perhaps when they felt there was a line-pilot surplus, more people got chopped than when the airlines thought that they wanted every man they could lay their hands on. If that's true it's a cynical and disturbing waste of talent. Given free rein and no time pressure, over 95 per cent of the cadets graduated successfully from the 1974 intake of 149 (there were two medically-induced resignations). The governors knew that there was unlikely to be an intake in 1975 and with time pressures removed, 743C had a leisurely 767 days from induction to graduation. All of them graduated! BA offered them non-flying jobs and eventually released them from their obligations. Britannia, Emirates and Cathay were pleased to employ them.

The College of Air Training used several delineations when numbering cadet groups but in every case the last two digits of the entry year formed a prefix to the cohort. For example; in the first year of operation 1960, each of the courses was preceded by 60 and then in the subsequent year by 61 and so on.

The fundamental teaching unit was the course, so in that first year 601 was the first course and 602 the second. There were 10 members in each but as CAT got into full swing 15 was a more usual starting number and several courses were inducted on the same date as an intake of around 45 individuals. What the Principal euphemistically referred to as 'wastage'

The CAT and the Hamsters

sometimes depleted course numbers to such an extent that the remaining cadets were re-coursed, or in extreme years, courses were amalgamated. On the following pages is every individual course, its starting date and the names of the cadets, along with the date that they left the college. Also shown is the percentage who graduated and the number of days spent at Hamble.

Course 601
Joined on the **15th September 1960** and **80%** of them graduated 757 days later.
D.M. Biltcliffe . . . . 12 October 1962
J. Harris . . . . .01 March 1962
E.M.H. Johnson . . . . 12 October 1962
W.P.D. Lawrence . . . . . . 12 October 1962
G.W. Prichard . . . . .1 March 1962
P.D. Roberts . . . . 12 October 1962
P.W. Stanwell . . . . 12 October 1962
R.J.A. Stephens . . . . 12 October 1962
D.W.L. Wright . . . . 12 October 1962
H.E.W. Young . . . . 12 October 1962

Course 602
Joined on the **15th September 1960** and **80%** of them graduated 757 days later.
G.R. Barker. . . . . 12 October 1962
A.J. Battson . . . . .31 March 1961
E.J.M. Davys . . . . 12 October 1962
T.O. Drake . . . . 12 October 1962
R.J. Dunning. . . . . 12 October 1962
M.P. Glegg . . . . 12 October 1962
P.A.F. Hogge. . . . . 12 October 1962
P.J. Hunt . . . . 12 October 1962
J.A. Johnson. . . . . 12 October 1962
C.E. Preece . . . . 8 December 1961

Course 603
Joined on the **15th September 1960** and **80%** of them graduated 757 days later.
V. Gunton . . . . 12 October 1962
E.J. Hatfield . . . . 12 October 1962
J.C.S. Jackson . . . . 26 October 1962
A.I. Johnson . . . . 13 April 1962
M.A. Riley . . . . 12 October 1962
B.L.G. Squirrell . . . . 12 October 1962
D.R. Stafford. . . . . 12 October 1962
P.J. Stanton. . . . . 12 October 1962
K. Warburton . . . . 12 October 1962
T.T. Weller . . . . 12 October 1962

Course 604
Joined on the **15th September 1960** and **81.82%** of them graduated 757 days later.
D.P.A. Dundas . . . . .31 March 1961
D.S. Gilson . . . . 12 October 1962

P. Grenet . . . . 12 October 1962
P.A. Gutteridge . . . . . . .30 November 1962
P.J.B. Hope . . . . 12 October 1962
E.G.D. Jones . . . . 12 October 1962
N.J.R. Minchin . . . . 12 October 1962
C.E.R Phillips. . . . . 12 October 1962
J.R. Reayer . . . . 12 October 1962
A.W. Robinson . . . . 12 October 1962
J.M. Westgate . . . . 03 March 1961

Course 611
Joined on the **1st September 1960** and **62.5%** of them graduated 700 days later.
J.D. Aldington . . . . .26 July 1963
K. Allen . . . . .19 February 1962
P.J.V. Benest . . . . 02 August 1963
P.H. Bennett. . . . . .08 May 1962
A.A. Campbell. . . . . 02 August 1963
R.F. Cooper . . . . 02 August 1963
P.G. Jameson . . . . 02 August 1963
P.J. King. . . . . 02 August 1963
D. Leah . . . . 02 August 1963
C.L.R. Martin . . . . 02 August 1963
D.D. McAngus. . . . . 02 August 1963
L. Richards . . . . .08 May 1962
C.A.G. Schofield . . . . 02 August 1963
R.B. Sillett . . . . 02 August 1963
R.S.I. Smith . . . . 02 August 1963
B.R. Westbury . . . . 09 October 1962

Course 612
Joined on the **15th September 1961** and **60%** of them graduated between 728 & 756 days later.
C.J. Barrows . . . . .31 May 1962
A.B. Blake . . . . 27 September 1963
R.F. Collins. . . . . 27 September 1963
R.W. Gorton. . . . . 10 April 1963
J.R. Hanauer . . . . 27 September 1963
R.H. Holt . . . . 27 September 1963
P.P. Icke . . . . 27 September 1963
W.E. Jones. . . . . 27 September 1963
D.A. Martin . . . . 27 September 1963
N.O. Nnachi. . . . . 27 September 1963
D. Porteous . . . . 27 September 1963
D.B. Price . . . . 27 September 1963
J. Reed . . . . 14 October 1963

The CAT and the Hamsters

J. Reeves . . . . 13 April 1962
A.W.S. Taylor. . . . . 25 October 1963

Course 613
Joined on the **27th October 1961** and **50%** of them graduated 728 days later.
D.D.A. Baker . . . . 25 October 1963
C.R. Barber . . . . 13 April 1962
J.G. Capey . . . . 07 September 1962
I.A. Cochrane . . . . 25 October 1963
E.J. Haddon . . . . 25 October 1963
J.A. Heaven . . . . 20 August 1962
W.D. Hellewell. . . . . 11 June 1963
D.J. Hoddy . . . . 13 April 1962
W.A. Morris . . . . 25 October 1963
D.E. Phillips . . . . 25 October 1963
G. Pratt . . . . 25 October 1963
K.P. Thomas . . . . 24 June 1963
R.S. Voice . . . . 13 July 1962
C.C. Whapshare . . . . 25 October 1963
R.L. Williams . . . . 25 October 1963
D.M. Wood . . . . 25 October 1963

Course 614
Joined on the **24th November 1961** and **47.06%** of them graduated 728 days later. . . . .
A.J.R. Allen . . . . 22 November 1963
J.M. Banks . . . . 22 November 1963
K.P. Barton . . . . 22 November 1963
P.L. Bugge . . . . 22 November 1963
H.R. Fair . . . . 14 December 1961
N.P. Higginbotham . . . 22 November 1963
A.S. Johnstone . . . . 13 April 1962
A.J. Laidler . . . . 16 November 1962
R.E.J. Lovegrove . . . . 13 March 1962
C.L.R. Mills . . . . 22 November 1963
R.B. Munro . . . . 15 November 1962
R. Sales . . . . 22 November 1963
I.F. Scott . . . . 14 March 1962
C.S. Shard . . . . 16 November 1962
J.W. Spicer . . . . 22 November 1963
R.G. Steele . . . . 09 October 1962

Course 621
Joined on the **5th January 1962** and **50%** of them graduated 714 days later.
P. Adlington . . . . 20 December 1963
W. Archer . . . . 20 December 1963
K. Connor . . . . 20 December 1963
P.D. Cook . . . . 13 April 1962
D.A. Debell . . . . 25 July 1963
R.J. Howard-Alpe . . . . 20 December 1963
J.D. Landymore . . . . . 16 September 1962
D.O. Lilley . . . . 25 July 1963
R.R. Livingstone . . . . . 20 December 1963

T.J. Malone . . . . 27 May 1963
D. Pascall . . . . 20 December 1963
A.P. Peebles . . . . 27 June 1962
D.M. Pool . . . . 20 December 1963
R.R. Scullion . . . . 27 May 1963
M. Smith . . . . 25 July 1963
S.D. Wand . . . . 20 December 1963

Course 622
Joined on the **26th January 1962** and **50%** of them graduated between 693 & 917 days later after extensive recoursing.
M.R. Beatty . . . . 20 December 1963
J.G. Cook . . . . 18 September 1962
J.A. Passmore . . . . 31 July 1964
B.E. Randall . . . . 15 November 1962
W.R. Stammers . . . . . 18 September 1962
P.G. Waterfall . . . . 20 December 1963

Course 623
Joined on the **31st August 1962** and **90.91%** of them graduated 700 days later.
P.H. Atkinson . . . . 31 July 1964
M.J. Austin . . . . 31 July 1964
D.P.H. Belam . . . . 31 July 1964
R.W. Benham . . . . 31 July 1964
J.H.K. Clark . . . . 31 July 1964
P.A.D. Clarke . . . . 31 July 1964
C. Edgell . . . . 31 July 1964
C.V. Fairbrother . . . . 31 July 1964
D.C. Ford . . . . 31 July 1964
B.R. Gibbs . . . . 10 October 1963
B.W. Smith . . . . 31 July 1964

Course 624
Joined on the **31st August 1962** and **78.57%** of them graduated 700 days later.
G.J. Blackman . . . . 31 July 1964
R.G. Green . . . . 31 July 1964
D.A. Harker . . . . 31 July 1964
T. Henderson . . . . 31 July 1964
C.B. Hutchings . . . . 07 May 1963
A.F. Lee . . . . 31 July 1964
E.P. Legresley . . . . 31 July 1964
D.G. Lusher . . . . 31 July 1964
K.P. Malone . . . . 10 April 1963
R.J.C. Neal-Smith . . . . 31 July 1964
S.R. Newman . . . . 31 July 1964
V.F. Nicholas . . . . 31 July 1964
P.J. Stradling . . . . 31 July 1964
D.J. White . . . . 31 July 1964

The CAT and the Hamsters

Course 625
Joined on the **31st August 1962** and **44.44%** of them graduated 700 days later..
C.R. Ayres .... 31 July 1964
G..M. Paddon .... 19 August 1963
M.J. Philpott .... 31 July 1964
R.J. Prowse. .... 10 October 1963
S.J. Quinn. .... 10 October 1963
R.J. Rumbold .... 17 May 1963
J.M. Scott .... 01 May 1963
D. Simmons .... 31 July 1964
C.B. Stephens .... 31 July 1964

Course 626
Joined on the **31st August 1962** and **85.71%** of them graduated 700 days later.
A.G. Bailey .... 31 July 1964
A.D. Butcher.............. 31 July 1964
R.A. Glass .... 31 July 1964
D.H.W. Turner .... 10 October 1963
R.M. Warnock............. 31 July 1964
P.A. Woodburn .... 31 July 1964
N.J. Wright .... 31 July 1964

Course 631
Joined on the **1st February 1963** and **75%** of them graduated 686 days later.
D.E. Browning. .... 18 December 1964
C. Duthie .... .22 March 1965
T.D. Howe........... 18 December 1964
A.R. Jenkins .... 18 December 1964
H.J.C. MacLean ..... 18 December 1964
E.G.D. McCready.... 18 December 1964
T.K. Pearce.......... 18 December 1964
J.P. Snelling ....25 September 1964
R.J. Taylor........... 18 December 1964
D.R. Watson .... 18 December 1964
J.M. Woodhouse..... 18 December 1964
J.E. Wright .... 06 May 1964

Course 632
Joined on the **1st February 1963** and **70%** of them graduated 686 days later.
S.M. Barnicott....... 18 December 1964
S. Bell.............. 13 September 1963
J.D. Bratt .... 18 December 1964
R. Carter........... 18 December 1964
N.R. Collins......... 18 December 1964
D. Green........... 18 December 1964
L.B. Hattam .... 18 December 1964
E.M.H. Lindsay-Jones 13 December 1963
I.C. McNeilly........ 13 December 1963
D.G. Sanders .... 16 September 1963

Course 633
Joined on the **1st February 1963** and **84.62%** of them graduated 686 days later.
J. Britton .... 18 December 1964
P. Brown........... 18 December 1964
M.D. Cumming ......08 November 1963
G.J. Currie.......... 18 December 1964
Q.W. Harris .... 18 December 1964
D.J. Heathcote...... 18 December 1964
D.A. Kersey .... 18 December 1964
R.N. Kershaw....... 18 December 1964
C.G. Richardson .... 18 December 1964
P.G. Sheard .... 18 December 1964
M.D. Waldron....... 18 December 1964
R.J. Walker ....12 November 1963
W. Wilson.......... 18 December 1964

Course 634
Joined on the **1st February 1963** and **50%** of them graduated 686 days later.
J.A. Crew............... 06 April 1965
C.B. McMahon...... 18 December 1964
R.P. Minards .... 13 December 1963
P.W.O. Skinner...... 18 December 1964
K.R. Squires......... .04 November 1963
C. Wren .... 18 December 1964

Course 635
Joined on the **30th August 1963** and **86.67%** of them graduated 700 days later.
P.G. Ball................ .30 July 1965
I. D'A. Bean .... .30 July 1965
R.A. Burroughs .... .30 July 1965
G.G.F. Flatt............. .30 July 1965
I.S. Gardiner .... .30 July 1965
N.J. Goff .... .30 July 1965
J.R. Green .... .30 July 1965
J.L. Hampson .... .30 July 1965
C.P. Head .... .30 July 1965
I.F. Kew .... 26 June 1964
P.G. Madgett .... .30 July 1965
J. McIlwham .... .30 July 1965
F.G.B. Smith........... .30 July 1965
A.E. Stenhouse .... .30 July 1965
E.S.N. Thomas........... 26 June 1964

Course 636
Joined on the **30th August 196**3 and **86.67%** of them graduated 700 days later.
D.W. Acton......... 23 September 1964
A.J. Beatty............. .30 July 1965
A.G. Burdess............ .30 July 1965
P.J.V. Dibble. .... .30 July 1965
T.T. Duhig............. .30 July 1965
P.M. Foreman........... .30 July 1965
J.W. Holl............... .30 July 1965

The CAT and the Hamsters

S.R. Last................ 30 July 1965
D.R. Mauleverer........... 30 July 1965
A.R. May................30 March 1965
E.H.J. Moody............. 30 July 1965
R.G. Mulligan............. 30 July 1965
R. Stewart................ 30 July 1965
P.F. Strange.............. 30 July 1965
J.W. Warburton........... 30 July 1965

Course 637
Joined on the **30th August 1963** and **78.57%** of them graduated 700 days later.
P.C.B. Brooks............. 30 July 1965
J.S. Clark................ 30 July 1965
T.R. Cooper .... 30 July 1965
J. Fox .... 03 February 1965
J. MacKelden............. 30 July 1965
G. Martin-Dye............. 30 July 1965
J.M. McLannahan.... 09 November 1964
A.R. Radford.............. 30 July 1965
R.C. Sawyer .... 30 July 1965
R.L.W. Skeet.............. 30 July 1965
J.L. Taylor................ 30 July 1965
M. Turner................ 30 July 1965
K. Wilson ....02 March 1964
D.J. Woodward........... 30 July 1965

Course 641
Joined on the **31st January 1964** and **83.33%** of them graduated 686 days later.
R.H. Atkinson .... 17 December 1965
S. Deakin.......... 17 December 1965
J.R. Dearnaly .... 17 December 1965
R.M.J. Graham....... 17 December 1965
P.R. Henderson....... 17 December 1965
P.T. Jenkinson....... 17 December 1965
G.F. Mussett .... 17 December 1965
J.H. Richards .... 17 December 1965
A.J. Smith............ 20 January 1965
J.R. Stewart .... 17 December 1965
C.A. Swan............. 20 January 1965
C.A.G.J. Warriner .... 17 December 1965

Course 642
Joined on the **31st January 1964** and **83.33%** of them graduated 686 days later.
P.J. Bryant .... 17 December 1965
C.D. Creak .... 17 December 1965
I.K. Croft............ 17 December 1965
R.H. Cuthbert .... 17 December 1965
M.H.R. Elliott....... 17 December 1965
I.M.S. Finlay .... 16 February 1965
D. Goodyear........ 17 December 1965
R.F. Grubb .... 03 November 1964
R. Lockyer .... 17 December 1965
A. Marshall .... 17 December 1965
R.A. Mills .... 17 December 1965

R.H. Watson......... 17 December 1965

Course 643
Joined on the **31st January 1964** and **90.91%** of them graduated 686 days later.
J.A. Hill .... 17 December 1965
R.D. Martin .... 17 December 1965
P.J.E. Ormonroyd..... 17 December 1965
R.J. Pascoe .... 17 December 1965
M.R. Peirce .... 17 December 1965
J.W. Pitcher .... 17 December 1965
P.J. Roles............. 21 October 1964
I.H. Shepherd .... 17 December 1965
K.H. Tyrrell.......... 17 December 1965
A. Watson .... 13 July 1964
S.J. Wheeler .... 17 December 1965

Course 644
Joined on the **31st August 1964** and **66.67%** of them graduated 694 days later.
R.J.L. Blanden............ 26 July 1966
J.R. Craggs.......... 03 February 1966
P.R. Dyson............... 26 July 1966
D.J. Ebert .... 10 March 1965
R.J. Garvin............... 26 July 1966
D.J. Guy................. 10 May 1965
D.C. Hughes .... 02 March 1966
G.A. Latham .... 26 July 1966
A.K. Lovering............ 26 July 1966
P.T. Lumb............... 26 July 1966
E.G. Murray.............. 26 July 1966
M.F. Oliver............... 26 July 1966
J.M. Preston............. 26 July 1966
P.R. Sparkes............. 26 July 1966
D.J. Walker .... 08 February 1966

Course 645
Joined on the **31st August 1964** and **66.67%** of them graduated **694** days later.
I.D. Bardrick .... 19 February 1965
I. Davies................. 26 July 1966
R.J. Holland..............26 April 1965
L.C. Mullett .... 26 July 1966
A.M. Partridge............ 26 July 1966
I.R. Price .... 28 May 1965
M. Read................. 26 July 1966
G. Shepherd .... 26 July 1966
E.R. Smith .... 26 July 1966
B.E. Sweet .... 26 July 1966
T. Szolnoki .... 06 July 1965
I.F. Todd............. 16 February 1966
S.A. White .... 26 July 1966
M.A. Williams............. 26 July 1966
G.V. Wright............... 26 July 1966

173

The CAT and the Hamsters

Course 646
Joined on the **31st August 1964** and **66.67%** of them graduated 694 days later.
B. Dedman . . . . 26 March 1965
R.A. Flavell . . . . 26 July 1966
R.M.J. Frampton . . . . 09 April 1965
R.M.J. Haydon . . . . 14 April 1967
S. Hill . . . . 26 July 1966
I.J. Lemanski . . . . 26 July 1966
R. McDonnell . . . . 14 April 1967
R. Nicholson . . . . 26 July 1966
J.T. Penwill . . . . 14 April 1967
D. Pollard . . . . 23 May 1965
P.C.W. Raine . . . . 19 October 1965
B.K. Wedrychowski . . . . 26 July 1966
P.H. Winks . . . . 26 July 1966
C.N. Wright . . . . 26 July 1966
C.J. Wythers . . . . 26 July 1966

Course 651
Joined on the **1st January 1965** and **73.33%** of them graduated 721 days later.
J.T. Fomes . . . . 23 December 1966
B.S. Gamet . . . . 29 July 1966
G. Golder . . . . 13 July 1965
A. Holmes . . . . 23 December 1966
G.L. Jennings . . . . 23 December 1966
M.J. Ker . . . . 23 December 1966
P.R. Kite . . . . 23 December 1966
I.C. Lemon . . . . 23 December 1966
I.J.E. Lintner . . . . 23 December 1966
W.J. Rettie . . . . 28 July 1965
J.W.D. Robertson . . . . 23 December 1966
P.D. Selley . . . . 23 December 1966
P.A. Somerville . . . . . . 23 December 1966
G.G. Stewart . . . . 29 March 1966
W.F.S. Thompson . . . . 23 December 1966

Course 652
Joined on the **1st January 1965** and **81.25%** of them graduated 721 days later.
P.D. Adams . . . . 23 December 1966
C. Ashman . . . . 20 January 1966
R.W.O. Bull . . . . 23 December 1966
R.K. Burfoot . . . . 23 December 1966
I. Chancellor . . . . 23 December 1966
P.F. Chilcott . . . . 23 December 1966
A. Gille . . . . 17 January 1966
R.A. Hall . . . . 23 December 1966
T.J. Halsey . . . . 23 December 1966
P.A. Lambert . . . . 19 February 1965
J.P. Russell . . . . 23 December 1966
R.F. Selby . . . . 23 December 1966
S.M. Sisnett . . . . 23 December 1966
M.S. Smith . . . . 23 December 1966
S.P. Threlfall . . . . 23 December 1966

R.O. Whitefield . . . . 23 December 1966

Course 653
Joined on the **1st January 1965** and **100%** of them graduated 721 days later.
A. Bayley . . . . 23 December 1966
M.J. Clews . . . . 23 December 1966
R.J. Harris . . . . 23 December 1966
D.R. Ince . . . . 23 December 1966
J.M. McCormick . . . . . 23 December 1966
D.J.O. Morris . . . . 23 December 1966
R.J. Paine . . . . 23 December 1966
P.F. Rawson . . . . 23 December 1966
H.A. Rose . . . . 23 December 1966
R.A. Skillington . . . . . . 23 December 1966
A.J. Speakman . . . . . . 23 December 1966
D.R. Stephenson . . . . . 23 December 1966
M.J. Tarry . . . . 23 December 1966
P.I. Terrington . . . . 23 December 1966
A.F. Thomas . . . . 23 December 1966

Course 654
Joined on the **3rd September 1965** and **64.29%** of them graduated 588 days later.
S.J. Clapson . . . . 14 April 1967
M.R. Coleman . . . . 02 June 1966
B.R. Garner . . . . 14 April 1967
J.M. Hodgkins . . . . 14 April 1967
C. James . . . . 05 August 1966
J.D. Michie . . . . 14 April 1967
M.R. Miller . . . . 14 April 1967
R.R. Morrison . . . . 14 April 1967
J.C.S. Pettit . . . . 14 April 1967
R.L. Price . . . . 14 April 1967
J.E. Steward . . . . 03 March 1966
N.E. Tomlin . . . . 14 April 1967
R.J. Whiley . . . . 05 August 1966
K.J. Whitehead . . . . 14 April 1967

Course 655
Joined on the **3rd September 1965** and **86.67%** of them graduated 588 days later.
M.J. Aries . . . . 14 April 1967
R.F. Bond . . . . 14 April 1967
P.R. Chipperfield . . . . 14 April 1967
P.R. Clough . . . . 14 April 1967
J.D. Cotterill . . . . 14 April 1967
N.C. Kolasznski . . . . 14 April 1967
P.J. Lawless . . . . 14 April 1967
S. Logan . . . . 14 April 1967
I.A. Pullin . . . . 14 April 1967
J.S. Radcliffe . . . . 14 April 1967
D.M. Robinson . . . . 14 April 1967
W.H. Scrivens . . . . 11 October 1966
R.J.N. Turnbull . . . . 14 April 1967
E.W.B. Winter . . . . 14 April 1967
R.W.G. Young . . . . 14 July 1966

Course 656
Joined on the **3rd September 1965** and **77.78%** of them graduated 588 days later.
R.J. Barbour . . . . 14 April 1967
C.D. Breward . . . . 14 April 1967
B.M. Bristow . . . . 14 April 1967
J.M. Brookes. . . . . 14 April 1967
M.T. Fitzpatrick-Nash . . . . . . 14 April 1967
G.A. Raven . . . . 25 April 1966
D.J. Rust . . . . 14 April 1967
D.A. Stephen . . . . 14 April 1967
C.F. White . . . . 17 September 1965

Course 661A
Joined on the **31st December 1965** and **71.43%** of them graduated 574 days later.
B.P. Adams. . . . . 28 July 1967
J.M. Ambrose . . . . 27 May 1966
R.J. Bickerstaff . . . . 28 July 1967
A. Bowden . . . . 28 July 1967
R.J. Brennan. . . . . 28 July 1967
G.B. Brousson . . . . 28 July 1967
K.M. Carter. . . . . 19 May 1966
J.A. Challen . . . . 28 July 1967
P.J. Clements . . . . 15 November 1968
L.M. Dutton. . . . . 20 May 1966
P.B. Godfrey . . . . 28 July 1967
R.C. Guiver. . . . . 28 July 1967
C.J. Heal. . . . . 28 July 1967
R.W.A. Holland . . . . 28 July 1967

Course 661B
Joined on the **31st December 1965** and **80%** of them graduated 574 days later.
J.G. Kiernan . . . . 28 July 1967
R.J. King. . . . . 16 June 1966
D.J. May. . . . . 27 April 1967
J.C.S. Milward . . . . 28 July 1967
D.J. Powell . . . . 28 July 1967
G.J.A. Regan . . . . 28 July 1967
C. Rule . . . . 28 July 1967
B.J. Salmon . . . . 28 July 1967
J.A. Sheffield . . . . 28 July 1967
N.D.H. Stokes. . . . . 28 July 1967
P.S. Swan . . . . 28 July 1967
M.J. Tarling. . . . . 28 July 1967
M.R. Toller. . . . . 28 July 1967
R. Wyldbore . . . . 28 July 1967
P.C. Youngs . 20 October 1966

Course 661C
Joined on the **31st December 1965** and **57.14%** of them graduated 574 days later.
A.D. Anderson . . . . 28 April 1967
P.J. Dobson . . . . 28 July 1967
A. Jewsbury . . . . 08 July 1966
A.B. Lough . . . . 28 July 1967

R.W.D. Noon . . . . 28 July 1967
J.B.J. Porteous . . . . 28 July 1967
I.D.E. Timms . . . . 12 May 1966

Course 662A
Joined on the **22nd April 1966** and **100%** of them graduated 662 days later.
C.R. Arkle . . . . 18 December 1967
I.S. Broadfoot. . . . . 18 December 1967
J.R. Cooper . . . . 18 December 1967
B.W. Croot . . . . 18 December 1967
N.E. Eames . . . . 18 December 1967
P.D. Gates . . . . 18 December 1967
B. Jordan. . . . . 18 December 1967
B.J. Kaye . . . . 18 December 1967
M.I. Kelly . . . . 18 December 1967
R.A. Ketteringham . . . 18 December 1967
D.F. Leatherdale . . . . 18 December 1967
C.C. Manning . . . . 18 December 1967

Course 662B
Joined on the **22nd April 1966** and **100%** of them graduated 662 days later.
J. Miller . . . . 18 December 1967
C. Pointon-Taylor . . . . 18 December 1967
J.D. Quick . . . . 18 December 1967
J.E. Rhodes . . . . 18 December 1967
R.E.J. Salisbury . . . . . 18 December 1967
P.A. Smith . . . . 18 December 1967
B. Stephens. . . . . 18 December 1967
T.P.J. Tomalin . . . . 18 December 1967
D.B. Townsend . . . . . 18 December 1967
J. Vella-Grech . . . . 18 December 1967
J.R. Weddell . . . . 18 December 1967
I. Whittaker. . . . . 18 December 1967

Course 662C
Joined on the **22nd April 1966** and **92.86%** of them graduated 662 days later.
R.I. Auty . . . . 18 December 1967
G.S. Edwards . . . . 18 December 1967
R.A. Harben. . . . . 18 December 1967
R. Hoare . . . . 18 December 1967
J.W. Knight . . . . 18 December 1967
G.S. McDavid . . . . 18 December 1967
K.A. Morris. . . . . 18 December 1967
R.D. Morris. . . . . 02 May 1966
P.D. Shufflebottom . . . 18 December 1967
L.D. Thomas . . . . 18 December 1967
R. Tickner . . . . 18 December 1967
H.A. Webbon . . . . 18 December 1967
P.G. White . . . . 18 December 1967

The CAT and the Hamsters

Course 662B
Joined on the **22nd April 1966** and **100%** of them graduated 662 days later.
J. Miller . . . . 18 December 1967
C. Pointon-Taylor . . . 18 December 1967 a
J.D. Quick . . . . 18 December 1967
J.E. Rhodes . . . . 18 December 1967
R.E.J. Salisbury . . . . . . 18 December 1967
P.A. Smith . . . . 18 December 1967
B. Stephens . . . . 18 December 1967
T.P.J. Tomalin . . . . 18 December 1967
D.B. Townsend . . . . 18 December 1967
J. Vella-Grech . . . . 18 December 1967
J.R. Weddell . . . . 18 December 1967
I. Whittaker . . . . 18 December 1967

Course 662C
Joined on the **22nd April 1966** and **92.86%** of them graduated 662 days later.
R.I. Auty . . . . 18 December 1967
G.S. Edwards . . . . 18 December 1967
R.A. Harben . . . . 18 December 1967
R. Hoare . . . . 18 December 1967
J.W. Knight . . . . 18 December 1967
G.S. McDavid . . . . 18 December 1967
K.A. Morris . . . . 18 December 1967
R.D. Morris . . . . 02 May 1966
P.D. Shufflebottom . . . . 18 December 1967
L.D. Thomas . . . . 18 December 1967
R. Tickner . . . . 18 December 1967
H.A. Webbon . . . . 18 December 1967
P.G. White . . . . 18 December 1967

Course 663A
Joined on the **2nd September 1966** and **92.87%** of them graduated 587 days later.
M.B. Apperly . . . . 11 April 1968
A.K. Baker . . . . 11 April 1968
T.C. Bayliss . . . . 15 May 1967
R.J.S. Calcutt . . . . 11 April 1968
K.R. Collyer . . . . 11 April 1968
A.E. Everett . . . . 11 April 1968
I. Finlay . . . . 11 April 1968
B.A. Hardy . . . . 11 April 1968
R.P. Helyar . . . . 11 April 1968
N.A.E. Jones . . . . 11 April 1968
A.J. Perry . . . . 11 April 1968
A.J. Simpson . . . . 11 April 1968
A.P. Summers . . . . 11 April 1968
A.H. Telford . . . . 11 April 1968

Course 663B
Joined on the **2nd September 1966** and **85.71%** of them graduated 587 days later.
M. Callaway . . . . 11 April 1968
R.A.D. Eyre . . . . 11 April 1968
R.G. Glover . . . . 11 April 1968
P. Hopper . . . . 11 April 1968
G.J.W. Lee . . . . 11 April 1968
M.A. Mogford . . . . 11 April 1968
C.G. Morffew . . . . 13 November 1967
D.L. Ord . . . . 11 April 1968
A.R. Slater . . . . 11 April 1968
A.K. Smee . . . . 11 April 1968
A.H. Townsend . . . . 11 April 1968
M.P. Whelan . . . . 13 January 1967
R.H. Wilkinson . . . . 11 April 1968
D.C. Woodley . . . . 11 April 1968

Course 663C
Joined on the **2nd September** 1966 and **64.29%** of them graduated 587 days later.
I. Anderson . . . . 20 November 1967
G.S. Brown . . . . 11 April 1968
N.J.E. Case . . . . 11 April 1968
A.R. Cox . . . . 11 April 1968
M. Hewish . . . . 18 January 1967
W.P.D. Jefferies . . . . 11 April 1968
R.G. Landon . . . . 11 April 1968
R.C. Owen . . . . 10 May 1968
J.S. Page . . . . 17 March 1967
C.L.R. Pollock . . . . 11 April 1968
J.M. Preston . . . . 11 April 1968
P.F. Shipperlee . . . . 20 January 1967
R.R. Stacey . . . . 12 January 1968
B.M.H. White . . . . 10 May 1968

Course 664A
Joined on the **25th November 1966** and **91.67%** of them graduated 532 days later.
M.S. Beevers . . . . 10 May 1968
V.C. Berry . . . . 10 May 1968
C. Cowpe . . . . 10 May 1968
R.C. Dawe . . . . 10 May 1968
R.A. Dredge . . . . 10 May 1968
D.R. Griffiths . . . . 10 May 1968
I.G. Hebdidge . . . . 10 May 1968
A. Henderson . . . . 10 May 1968
D. Plumb . . . . 10 May 1968
M. Robertson . . . . 10 May 1968
R.S.I. Slater . . . . 23 March 1967
G.P. White . . . . 10 May 1968

Course 664B
Joined on the **25th November 1966** and **81.82%** of them graduated 532 days later.
R.F. Aldous . . . . 10 May 1968
M.S. Beresford . . . . 10 May 1968
I.H. Jago . . . . 10 May 1968
K.H. Murray . . . . 10 May 1968
J.H. Nicholson . . . . 10 May 1968
C.G. Pocock . . . . 10 May 1968
M.J. Robb . . . . 10 May 1968

A. Scrowston . . . . 10 May 1968
M.J.H. Tate . . . . 10 May 1968
P.R. Tyrrell. . . . . 10 May 1968
J.N. West . . . . 10 May 1968

Course 664C
Joined on the **25th November 1966** and **72.73%** of them graduated 532 days later.
P.D. Ball . . . . ?
S.T. Bates . . . . 10 May 1968
P. Coomber. . . . . 10 May 1968
R.C. Greaves . . . . 10 May 1968
I.W.D. James . . . . 10 May 1968
D. Johnson . . . . 10 May 1968
E.P. Minost . . . . 19 September 1967
P.S.E. Robbins . . . . 10 May 1968
D.W.V. Stubbs. . . . . 30 May 1967
J. Turner . . . . 05 October 1968
M.J. Williamson . . . . 10 May 1968

Course 671A
Joined on the **24th February 1967** and **87.50%** of them graduated 525 days later.
C.J. Brockman . . . . 02 August 1968
P.E. Cannon . . . . 02 August 1968
N.G. Charlton . . . . 02 August 1968
C.J. Dale. . . . . 02 August 1968
B.O. Dickinson . . . . 02 August 1968
J.R. Edwards . . . . 02 August 1968
D.A. Hodges. . . . . 02 August 1968
C.R.M. Holdaway . . . . 02 August 1968
P.T. Hughes . . . . 02 August 1968
S.D. Hull . . . . 02 August 1968
V.T. Hunt . . . . 02 August 1968
R.E.J. Long. . . . . 02 August 1968
G. MacDonald . . . . 14 December 1967
D.J. Mitchell . . . . 02 August 1968
A.R. Varco . . . . 02 August 1968
C.F. Wilkins . . . . 19 December 1967

Course 671B
Joined on the **24th February 1967** and **66.67%** of them graduated 525 days later.
M.D. Cox . . . . 09 February 1968
P.A.W. Hackman. . . . . 02 August 1968
C.H.K. Hood . . . . 02 August 1968
I.A. MacDonald . . . . 31 July 1967
R.A.N. Marchant. . . . . 02 August 1968
J.B.J. McLaughlin. . . . . . . 02 August 1968
C.J. Plowman . . . . 25 January 1968
P.A. Richards . . . . 02 August 1968
J. Rudd. . . . . 02 August 1968
S.J. Sessions . . . . 15 May 1967
R.A. Smith. . . . . 02 August 1968
P.J. Talbot . . . . 30 November 1972
D.A. Warren . . . . 02 August 1968
G. Williams . . . . 02 August 1968

P.G. Wolstenhome . . . . 02 August 1968

Course 671C
Joined on the **24th February 1967** and **53.33%** of them graduated 525 days later.
J.S. Allott . . . . 12 March 1968
P.R. Cozens . . . . 26 January 1968
A.G. Foggon . . . . 01 June 1967
C.J. Gaffney. . . . . 02 August 1968
J.R.V. Green. . . . . 02 August 1968
J. Howe . . . . 02 August 1968
J.R. Leahy . . . . 02 August 1968
N.C.L. Lee . . . . 21 November 1968
P.M. Neave . . . . 02 August 1968
N.R. Ogilvie-Robb . . . . 02 August 1968
R.Q. Poldon. . . . . 30 July 1968
M. Pratt . . . . 24 May 1967
F. Robertson . . . . 02 August 1968
M.H. Smith . . . . 02 August 1968
K.A. Wilson . . . . 01 June 1967

Course 672A
Joined on the **19th May 1967** and **92.86**% of them graduated 546 days later.
R.C. Andrews . . . . 15 November 1968
A.J. Balfour . . . . 15 November 1968
G.V. Bromage . . . . 15 November 1968
M.J. D'Alton . . . . 15 November 1968
J.I. Davies . . . . 15 November 1968
M.A. Fleckney . . . . 15 November 1968
K.J. Fleming. . . . . 01 September 1967
G.K. Gilbey . . . . 15 November 1968
D.W. Grace . . . . 15 November 1968
D.J. Hanks . . . . 15 November 1968
D.C. Jack. . . . . 15 November 1968
J.M. Lawrence . . . . 24 September 1968
N.G. Ley . . . . 15 November 1968
M.W. Morren . . . . 15 November 1968

Course 672B
Joined on the **19th May 1967** and **100.00%** of them graduated 546 days later.
J.M. Bennett . . . . 15 November 1968
P. Burnett . . . . 15 November 1968
L.E. Davies . . . . 15 November 1968
B.R. Oliver . . . . 15 November 1968
R.A.H. Owen . . . . 15 November 1968
A.W. Potter . . . . 15 November 1968
C.A. Raincock . . . . 15 November 1968
A.P. St John . . . . 15 November 1968
C.J. Stothart . . . . 15 November 1968
A.J.E. Tiley . . . . 15 November 1968
A.J.A. Weal . . . . 15 November 1968
T.J. Westcott . . . . 15 November 1968
T.A. Wiffen . . . . 15 November 1968
M.A. Woolley . . . . 15 November 1968

The CAT and the Hamsters

Course 672C
Joined on the **19th May 1967** and 86.67% of them graduated 546 days later.
N.C.C. Barritt . . . . 15 November 1968
P. Burton . . . . 16 October 1968
M. Glinski . . . . 15 November 1968
C.C. Hammond . . . . . . 15 November 1968
D.B. Hankinson . . . . . . 15 November 1968
P. Hawkins . . . . 02 December 1968
R.L. Horsnell . . . . 15 November 1968
A.F. Jordens . . . . 15 November 1968
M.H. Kennedy . . . . 15 November 1968
R.S.C. MacLeod . . . . . . 15 November 1968
J.E. Puddle . . . . 15 November 1968
R.I. Ramsey . . . . 15 November 1968
N.G.R. Shaw . . . . 15 November 1968
P.D. Withers . . . . 15 November 1968
F.D. Wright . . . . 15 November 1968

Course 673A
Joined on the **1st September 1967** and **93.75%** of them graduated 541 days later.
R.P. Barker . . . . 23 February 1969
R.S. Brooking . . . . 23 February 1969
R.A. Burgess . . . . 23 February 1969
R.J. Burns . . . . 23 February 1969
S.T. Garner . . . . 06 February 1969
C. Gray . . . . 23 February 1969
D.V. Hymers . . . . 23 February 1969
G.A. Jackson . . . . 23 February 1969
D.C. Lean . . . . 23 February 1969
C.J.D. Orlebar . . . . 23 February 1969
N.J. Parks . . . . 23 February 1969
R.S.I. Pontin . . . . 23 February 1969
P.N.A. South . . . . 23 February 1969
A.R. Thompson . . . . 23 February 1969
R.A. Wilson . . . . 23 February 1969
T. Wright . . . . 23 February 1969

Course 673B
Joined on the **1st September 1967** and **100%** of them graduated 541 days later.
R.D. Barnes . . . . 23 February 1969
J.R. Bellamy . . . . 23 February 1969
M.W. Bryant . . . . 23 February 1969
S.J. Cubbage . . . . 23 February 1969
J.R. Frohnsdorff . . . . . . 23 February 1969
B.E. Helm . . . . 23 February 1969
J.M. Hopkins . . . . 23 February 1969
K. Hull . . . . 23 February 1969
A.M. Luscombe . . . . 23 February 1969
D. Martin . . . . 23 February 1969
D.E. Plante . . . . 23 February 1969
R.A. Ranscombe . . . . . . 23 February 1969
I.L. Shearer . . . . 23 February 1969
M.H. Thompson . . . . . . 23 February 1969

F.C.C. Wicks-Bagot . . . . . 23 February 1969

Course 673C
Joined on the **1st September 1967** and **86.67%** of them graduated 541 days later.
G.P.H. Booth . . . . 30 October 1968
P.J. Brown . . . . 23 February 1969
C.J.DE G. Delmege . . . . 23 February 1969
D.A. Dickson . . . . 23 February 1969
J.E. Few . . . . ?
P.W. Horton . . . . 23 February 1969
R.L. Jenkins . . . . 23 February 1969
J.B.J. Leggatt . . . . 23 February 1969
N.P. MacHon . . . . 23 February 1969
S.P. Masey . . . . 23 February 1969
D.C. Mountain . . . . 23 February 1969
W.C. Mullins . . . . 23 February 1969
T.J. Rawlins . . . . 23 February 1969
P. Redman . . . . 23 February 1969
R.J. Sharp . . . . 23 February 1969

Course 674A
Joined on the **27th November 1967** and **75%** of them graduated 529 days later.
G.C. Bell . . . . 09 May 1969
P.J. Chalmers . . . . 09 May 1969
I.A. Davies . . . . 09 May 1969
P.E. Duckworth . . . . 21 April 1969
A.R. Fawkes . . . . 09 May 1969
J.E. Grout . . . . 08 October 1968
P.G. Gutteridge . . . . 09 May 1969
J.M. Jack . . . . 08 February 1968
T.D.G. Lancaster . . . . 09 May 1969
J.D. Manning . . . . 20 February 1968
C.A. Robey . . . . 09 May 1969
A.G. Smith . . . . 09 May 1969
R.N. Taylor . . . . 09 May 1969
S.L. Vaughan . . . . 09 May 1969
A.I. Wood . . . . 09 May 1969
T.P.J. Wright . . . . 09 May 1969

Course 674B
Joined on the **27th November 1967** and **60%** of them graduated 529 days later.
A.D. Bell . . . . 25 March 1969
M.J. Churms . . . . 09 May 1969
M.J. Easley . . . . 30 September 1968
S.J. Fisher . . . . 09 May 1969
K.S. Forrest . . . . 10 May 1969
R.J. Hart . . . . 18 July 1968
R.P. Hewitt . . . . 09 May 1969
S. Hollingsworth . . . . 09 May 1969
P.R. Larratt . . . . 09 May 1969
P. Lewis . . . . 09 May 1969
M.N. McKeown . . . . 09 May 1969
A.H. McKibbin . . . . 09 May 1969
J.H. Richmond . . . . 09 May 1969

The CAT and the Hamsters

R.C. Smith . . . . .26 June 1968
D.B. Tomlinson . . . . 19 April 1968

Course 674C
Joined on the **27th November 1967** and **86.67%** of them graduated 529 days later.
P.J.V. Allison . . . . 02 April 1968
M. Bannister . . . . 09 May 1969
R.G.J. Cavendish . . . . 09 May 1969
J.M. Charnley . . . . 09 May 1969
R.M.J. Ewart . . . . 09 May 1969
R.J.W. Gallop . . . . 09 May 1969
C.E.R Hay . . . . 09 May 1969
M.R. Holliday . . . . 09 May 1969
A.J. Hunter . . . . 09 May 1969
A.P. Mathews . . . . 24 September 1968
M.G. Oliver . . . . 25 April 1968
D.F. Roberts . . . . 09 May 1969
R.H. Smith . . . . 09 May 1969
W.T. Spearing . . . . 09 May 1969
A.S. Trickett . . . . 09 May 1969

Course 681A
Joined on the **26th February 1968** and **100%** of them graduated 530 days later.
C.S. Barradale . . . . 01 August 1969
L.J.S. Castle . . . . 01 August 1969
A.C. Crossley . . . . 01 August 1969
D.I.R. Graham . . . . 01 August 1969
P. Higton . . . . 01 August 1969
J.E. Keates . . . . 01 August 1969
C.A. Lankey . . . . 01 August 1969
B.C. Morris . . . . 01 August 1969
R.F. Parker . . . . 01 August 1969
B. Sams . . . . 01 August 1969
D.A. Small . . . . 01 August 1969
R.M. Underhill . . . . 01 August 1969

Course 681B
Joined on the **26th February 1968** and **100%** of them graduated 530 days later.
N.P. Broad . . . . 01 August 1969
I.G. Campbell . . . . 01 August 1969
P.F. Clark . . . . 01 August 1969
K.T. Dean . . . . 01 August 1969
N.J. Duncan . . . . 01 August 1969
A.J. Mills . . . . 01 August 1969
D.J. Munson . . . . 01 August 1969
M.C. Redrupp . . . . 01 August 1969
M.H. Severns . . . . 01 August 1969
A.H. Thomas . . . . 01 August 1969

Course 681C
Joined on the **26th February 1968** and **100%** of them graduated 530 days later.
R.J. Carey-Hughes . . . . 01 August 1969
H.C.F. Deck . . . . 01 August 1969

I.F. Herve . . . . 01 August 1969
D.G. Hughes . . . . 01 August 1969
P.J. Larner . . . . 01 August 1969
S.J. Osborne . . . . 01 August 1969
M.P. Sambrook . . . . 01 August 1969
C.C. Shields . . . . 01 August 1969
R.A. Small . . . . 01 August 1969

Course 682A
Joined on the **19th May 1968** and **90%** of them graduated 530 days later.
R.A. Batchelor . . . . 31 October 1969
G.B. Beer . . . . 08 August 1969
C. Flooks . . . . 31 October 1969
P.L. Foster . . . . 31 October 1969
K.H. Hicks . . . . 31 October 1969
D. Hopkinson . . . . 31 October 1969
T.M. Jailler . . . . 31 October 1969
D. McF. Mitchell . . . . 31 October 1969
C.E.R Norris . . . . 31 October 1969
M.J. Oldham . . . . 31 October 1969

Course 682B
Joined on the **19th May 1968** and **100%** of them graduated 530 days later.
R.J.S. Burchall . . . . 31 October 1969
B.D. Jones . . . . 31 October 1969
I. Osborne . . . . 31 October 1969
R.M. Otto . . . . 31 October 1969
J.M. Ralph . . . . 31 October 1969
S.M. Rendall . . . . 31 October 1969

Course 682C
Joined on the **19th May 1968** and **100%** of them graduated 530 days later.
J. Brassington . . . . 31 October 1969
G. Carfoot . . . . 31 October 1969
A.C. Hughes . . . . 31 October 1969
M. Smalley . . . . 31 October 1969
R.W. Stephens . . . . 31 October 1969
W.H.V. Steynor . . . . 31 October 1969
I.M. Tait . . . . 31 October 1969
T.G. Wiltshire . . . . 31 October 1969

Course 683
Joined on the **2nd September 1968** and **100%** of them graduated 515 days later.
D.J. Allen . . . . .30 January 1970
C.S. Claxton . . . . .30 January 1970
M.P. Grace . . . . .30 January 1970
D.J. Lowson . . . . .30 January 1970
S.I. Pamment . . . . .30 January 1970
D.N. Robins . . . . .30 January 1970

The CAT and the Hamsters

Course 691A
Joined on the **17th February 1969** and **100%** of them graduated 529 days later.
J.W. Biggs . . . . 31 July 1970
J.R.F. Bristow . . . . 31 July 1970
D.I. Buckley . . . . 31 July 1970
C.E. Challenger . . . . 31 July 1970
R.E.J. Dennis . . . . 31 July 1970
J.R. Downey . . . . 31 July 1970
D.A. Evans . . . . 31 July 1970
D. Hawkins . . . . 31 July 1970
M.M. Robarts . . . . 31 July 1970
A.H. Stewart . . . . 31 July 1970
J.R. White . . . . 31 July 1970

Course 691B
Joined on the **17th February 1969** and **69.23%** of them graduated 529 days later.
A.J. Barralet . . . . 03 November 1969
F.G. Brejcha . . . . 14 April 1970
J.A. Broadley . . . . 31 July 1970
R.V. Carter . . . . 31 July 1970
D.A. Day . . . . 31 July 1970
M.J. Dobson . . . . 31 July 1970
J.A. Duke . . . . 19 December 1969
A.J. Hawkins . . . . 31 July 1970
G.R. Hendry . . . . 31 July 1970
B.R. Holland . . . . 31 July 1970
M.I. Robinson . . . . 31 July 1970
T. Tierney . . . . 31 July 1970
M.A.J. Woodcock . . . . 18 December 1969

Course 691C
Joined on the **17th February 1969** and **100%** of them graduated 529 days later.
C.E. Coulson . . . . 31 July 1970
N.H. Dover . . . . 31 July 1970
F.A. Dudley . . . . 31 July 1970
A.R.L. Hewison . . . . 31 July 1970
P. Howard . . . . 31 July 1970
P.W. Jefferies . . . . 31 July 1970
P.S.E. Oglesby . . . . 31 July 1970
D. Mac.F. Pattison . . . . 31 July 1970
W.G.D. Watt . . . . 31 July 1970

Course 692A
Joined on the 1**6th May 1969** and **81.82%** of them graduated 546 days later.
R.P. Babbe . . . . 13 November 1970
W.A. Buffin . . . . 13 November 1970
P.D. DuPre . . . . 13 November 1970
N.M. Haig-Brown . . . . 03 November 1969
R.V.J. Howell. . . . . 13 November 1970
J.A. Kendal . . . . 13 November 1970
G.G.J.B. Layton . . . . . 13 November 1970
N.S.M. Rendall . . . . . . 13 November 1970
M.H. Rushbrooke . . . . 08 October 1969
M.A. Surowiak . . . . 13 November 1970
M.G. Waters . . . . 13 November 1970

Course 692B
Joined on the 1**6th May 1969** and **72.73%** of them graduated 546 days later.
C.J. Barnard . . . . 13 November 1970
M.J. Dudley-Cave . . . . 13 November 1970
J.K. Hanlon . . . . 13 November 1970
C.R. Hawkins . . . . 13 November 1970
R.R. Johnstone . . . . . 18 December 1969
B.I. Kuflik . . . . 13 November 1970
D.S. Moore . . . . 13 November 1970
P. Robinson . . . . 13 November 1970
D.F. Shaw . . . . 05 January 1970
R.G.P. Taylor . . . . 13 November 1970
P.D. Winder . . . . 06 August 1970

Course 692C
Joined on the **16th May 1969** and **81.82%** of them graduated 546 days later.
J.F. Ahern . . . . 13 November 1970
J.M. Codd . . . . 13 November 1970
R. J. Grimstead . . . . . . 13 November 1970
C.M.J. Hooper . . . . 20 April 1970
P.J. Howard . . . . 13 November 1970
D.R.L. Jack . . . . 13 November 1970
C.R. Jackman . . . . 31 August 1969
D. McCulloch . . . . 13 November 1970
D.S. Phillips . . . . 13 November 1970
C.G. Robinson . . . . 13 November 1970
C.S. Treadwell . . . . 13 November 1969

Course 693A
Joined on the **2nd September 1969** and **72.73%** of them graduated 528 days later.
W.G. Andrews . . . . 12 February 1971
P.B. Barnes . . . . 17 April 1970
A.J. Buchanan . . . . 12 February 1971
G.R. Custard . . . . 07 May 1970
J.F. Darycott . . . . 12 February 1971
R.C. Dukoff-Gorden . . . . 12 February 1971
S.D. Edwards . . . . 12 February 1971
D.S. Evans . . . . 19 November 1970
D.I. Fidler . . . . 12 February 1971
I.P.S. Gurney . . . . 12 February 1971
R.A. Wallis . . . . 12 February 1971

Course 693B
Joined on the **2nd September 1969** and **90.91%** of them graduated 528 days later.
W.A. Brewer . . . . 12 February 1971
S.J. Hatch . . . . 12 February 1971
P.J. Horrocks . . . . 12 February 1971
S. King . . . . 31 March 1970
R.A. Knight . . . . 12 February 1971
S.G. Lidbetter . . . . 12 February 1971

P.J. Lockwood . . . . 12 February 1971
R.C. Morgan . . . . 12 February 1971
R. Proctor . . . . 12 February 1971
I.M. Watson . . 12 February 1971
J.D. Young . 12 February 1971

Course 693C
Joined on the **2nd September 1969** and **81.82%** of them graduated 528 days later.
I.E. Baggott . . . . 12 February 1971
A.F. Best . . . . 04 February 1970
I.W. Bilson . . . . 12 February 1971
N. Harris . . . . 12 February 1971
J.A. Holland . . . . 12 February 1971
H.G. Jones . . . . 12 February 1971
P.W. Kelly . . . . 26 May 1970
P.J.C. Moores . . . . 12 February 1971
N.J. Walford . . . . 12 February 1971
P.D. Whetham . . . . 12 February 1971
D.G. Winter . . . . 12 February 1971

Course 694A
Joined on the **21st November 1969** and **87.5%** of them graduated 532 days later.
S.M. Bailey . . . . 30 July 1971
K.M. Bastard . . . . 28 April 1971
N.K. Bennett . . . . 17 July 1970
J.G. Boxall . . . . 07 May 1971
T.J. Buckland . . . . 07 May 1971
C.J. Dalgleish . . . . 07 May 1971
P.J. Dunglinson . . . . 07 May 1971
S.P. Gray . . . . 07 May 1971
M.A. Holtom . . . . 07 May 1971
M.M. Ingram . . . . 07 May 1971
S.M.W. Leniston . . . . 07 May 1971
G.J.W. Lomas . . . . 07 May 1971
J. Maxwell . . . . 07 May 1971
M.R. Potter . . . . 07 May 1971
J.W.F. Russell . . . . 07 May 1971
R.V.A. Toovey . . . . 07 May 1971

Course 694B
Joined on the **21st November 1969** and **73.33%** of them graduated 532 days later.
B.R. Baker . . . . 07 May 1971
C.M. Brewer . . . . 20 March 1970
D.W. Brydone . . . . 04 September 1970
R.P.J. Childs . . . . 07 May 1971
R.M.J. Eley . . . . 23 March 1970
M.J. Harley . . . . 23 July 1970
G.E. Howard . . . . 07 May 1971
C.G. Humphrey . . . . 07 May 1971
R.L. Matthews . . . . 07 May 1971
P.M.J. McEwen . . . . 07 May 1971
D. Millerin . . . . 07 May 1971
R.J. Phillips . . . . 07 May 1971
P.A. Prior . . . . 07 May 1971

C.L.R. Seaman . . . . 07 May 1971
C.N. Spink . . . . 07 May 1971

Course 694C
Joined on the **21st November 1969** and **64.71%** of them graduated 532 days later.
R.G. Baylis . . . . 07 May 1971
P.H. Bright . . . . 07 May 1971
A.C. Cassells . . . . 07 May 1971
R.L. Evens . . . . 07 May 1971
C.F. Garrod . . . . 07 May 1971
D.P. Higgins . . . . 07 May 1971
C.M. Jenkins . . . . 28 September 1970
J.G. McKinstrie . . . . 07 May 1971
A.G. Newton . . . . 04 August 1970
M. Page . . . . 13 July 1970
A.J. Proctor . . . . 27 February 1970
J.M. Skellon . . . . 27 February 1970
D.W. Stealey . . . . 07 May 1971
M.P. Thorne . . . . 29 June 1970
M.J. Walbourn . . . . 07 May 1971
M.F. Welling . . . . 07 May 1971
R.M. Westray . . . . 07 May 1971

Course 701A
Joined on the **16th February 1970** and **80%** of them graduated 529 days later.
D.R. Campbell . . . . 30 July 1971
P.C.B. Capron . . . . 30 July 1971
F.J. Carver . . . . 30 July 1971
T.J. Cox . . . . 30 July 1971
D.C. Curgenven . . . . 25 January 1971
S.W.A. Dolby . . . . 30 July 1971
J.W. Gibney . . . . 30 July 1971
D.R. Guiver . . . . 30 July 1971
B.C. Jellett . . . . 30 July 1971
A.J. Joseph . . . . 30 July 1971
A.J. Lockwood . . . . 30 July 1971
T.J. Parrott . . . . 30 July 1971
H.N. Robson . . . . 26 October 1970
E.J. Vidler . . . . 30 July 1971
P.D. Warren . . . . 17 November 1970

The CAT and the Hamsters

Course 701B
Joined on the **16th February 19**70 and **62.5%** of them graduated 529 days later.
L.E. Agnew . . . . 16 September 1970
R.V. Blake . . . . 30 July 1971
W.M. Calder-Potts . . . . 30 July 1971
J.R. Charley . . . . 26 November 1971
J. Gardner . . . . 31 July 1970
D.J. Gass . . . . 30 July 1971
R.E.J. Graham . . . . 26 October 1970
M.R. Green . . . . 07 July 1970
S.P.S. Haddock . . . . 30 July 1971
D.A. Jack . . . . 30 July 1971
A. MacDonald . . . . . . 03 December 1970
G.W.K. Maule . . . . 30 July 1971
R.C.G. Pugh . . . . 15 October 1970
M.D. Siddell . . . . 30 July 1971
S.F. Taylor . . . . 30 July 1971
I.R. White . . . . 30 July 1971

Course 701C
Joined on the **16th February 19**70 and **78.57%** of them graduated 529 days later.
R.G. Balchin . . . . 16 December 1970
S.E. Burrett . . . . 30 July 1971
M.S.A. Capaldi . . . . 30 July 1971
M.A. Cleland . . . . 30 July 1971
W.J. Hair . . . . ?
D.W. Lawes . . . . 30 July 1971
B.A. Miller . . . . 30 July 1971
S.C. Nicholson . . . . 30 July 1971
G.D.M. Rees . . . . 30 July 1971
C.B. Rigby . . . . 30 July 1971
J.A. Sitkowski . . . . 30 July 1971
A.N. Sizer . . . . 30 July 1971
G.C. Uren . . . . 30 July 1971
A.M. Weir . . . . 30 July 1971

Course 702A
Joined on the **15th May 1970** and **62.5%** of them graduated 560 days later.
A.W. Ashburner . . . . 12 October 1970
J.r. Brandvik . . . . 26 November 1971
R.M.J. Carey . . . . 03 December 1970
J. Christian . . . . 12 November 1970
C. Dudley . . . . 26 November 1971
J.S. Foster . . . . 11 January 1971
C.J. Henry . . . . 24 September 1970
G.S. Holloway . . . . 26 November 1971
M.J. Lisby . . . . 26 November 1971
A. McNay . . . . 29 September 1970
J. Phillips . . . . 26 November 1971
A.L. Russell . . . . 26 November 1971
W.G. Scott . . . . 26 November 1971
J.H. Siddall . . . . 26 November 1971
D. Smethurst . . . . 26 November 1971
S.P. Smith . . . . 26 November 1971

Course 702B
Joined on the **15th May 1970** and **80%** of them graduated 560 days later.
W.K. Benzinski . . . . 23 July 1971
T.P. Cale . . . . 26 November 1971
M.B.B. Caston . . . . 26 November 1971
A.C.E. de Tourtoulon . . 26 November 1971
R.A. Field . . . . 26 November 1971
P.J. Hamblin . . . . 26 November 1971
R.E.J. Hocking . . . . 26 November 1971
J.W. Keighley . . . . 26 November 1971
D.A. MacDonald-Lawson 26 November 1971
M.F. Middleton . . . . . . 02 December 1970
P.G. Roper . . . . 26 November 1971
J. Shaw . . . . 26 November 1971
C.J. Slater . . . . 28 September 1970
P.H.S. Smith . . . . 26 November 1971
D.G.T. Thomas . . . . 26 November 1971

Course 702C
Joined on the **15th May 1970** and **68.75%** of them graduated 560 days later.
L.J. Ayres . . . . 26 November 1971
D.W. Baker . . . . 26 November 1971
L.C. Bolton . . . . 26 November 1971
I.I. Finlay . . . . 02 September 1971
V.B. Fitzgerald . . . . 17 February 1972
A.C. Graham . . . . 26 November 1971
C.D. Hayward . . . . 02 February 1971
G.H. Kean . . . . 26 November 1971
P.T. Nalson . . . . 17 November 1970
M.V. Potts . . . . 26 November 1971
C.H. Read . . . . 26 November 1971
H.M. Seed . . . . 26 November 1971
M.F. Selwood . . . . 25 May 1971
M.C.A. Simpson . . . . 08 February 1971
S.C. Stephenson . . . . 24 March 1972
D.A. Such . . . . 24 March 1972

Course 703A
Joined on the **7th August 1970** and **62.5%** of them graduated 595 days later.
K. Clarkson . . . . 24 March 1972
D. Dicketts . . . . 19 April 1971
A. Dobbie . . . . 24 March 1972
R. Graham . . . . 02 June 1971
D.G. Hirst . . . . 24 March 1972
G.J.W. Holdaway . . . . 24 March 1972
G.T. Legge . . . . 21 June 1971
S.R. MacGregor . . . . 24 March 1972
A.C. Monro . . . . 24 March 1972
C.P. Murray . . . . 24 March 1972
R.A. Pattie . . . . 24 March 1972
D.J. Summers . . . . 24 March 1972
M.J. Thomas . . . . 28 April 1971

The CAT and the Hamsters

D.A. Trewin . . . . .24 March 1972
J.P. Watson . . . . .08 March 1971
J.R. Wilson . . . . .09 March 1972

Course 703B
Joined on the **7th August 1970** and **87%** of them graduated 595 days later.
C.M. Barnes . . . . .24 March 1972
I.C. Brydone . . . . .24 March 1972
I.J. Cartwright . . . . .24 March 1972
D.C. Corfield . . . . .24 March 1972
D.J. Farley . . . . .24 March 1972
K. Fraser . . . . ?
K.M. Grant . . . . .24 March 1972
J.F. Irish . . . . .24 March 1972
M.O. Lewis . . . . .24 March 1972
R.E.J. McLaughlan . . . . .24 March 1972
I.S. Munro . . . . .24 March 1972
I.R. Murray . . . . .24 March 1972
L.A.J. Playford . . . . .24 March 1972
S.A. Taylor . . . . 21 April 1971
C.A. Timmins . . . . .24 March 1972
D.L. Vaughan . . . . .24 March 1972

Course 703C
Joined on the **7th August 1970** and **50%** of them graduated 595 days later.
S.J. Bevis . . . . 30 July 1971
R.A. Brown . . . . .24 March 1972
R.T. Brown . . . . .24 March 1972
B.P. Butlin . . . . .24 March 1972
P.A. Galistan . . . . 02 July 1971
W. McL-Gibson . . . . 16 April 1971
J.H. Mitchell . . . . 05 July 1971
A.F.S. Prior . . . . .24 March 1972
P.W. Ritchie . . . . 10 December 1970
S. Smith . . . . .24 March 1972
T.T. Steele . . . . .03 March 1971
A.C. Stephenson . . . . 26 November 1970
J.H. Thompson . . . . .24 March 1972
I.C. Vokes . . . . .24 March 1972
C.S. Williams . . . . .24 March 1972
P.J. Wright . . . . .01 June 1971

Course 704A
Joined on the **25th October 1970** and **75%** of them graduated 628 days later.
N.J.A. Banks . . . . 17 November 1972
A.J. Bird . . . . 17 November 1972
J.M. Bounden . . . . 17 November 1972
K. Buckeridge . . . . 17 November 1972
S.I. Bunce . . . . .27 September 1971
C.V. Catherall . . . . 14 July 1972
R.J. Chittenden . . . . 14 July 1972
N.M. Clarke . . . . .07 September 1971
R.M.J. Craft . . . . 14 July 1972
D.P.A. Duguid . . . . 14 July 1972

M.A. Dunning . . . . .14 July 1972
P.J. Egging . . . . .14 July 1972
S.R. Habgood . . . . .14 July 1972
M.D. Hastings . . . . . . 07 December 1970
G.J.W. Kinsey . . . . 28 April 1971
G.G. Leask . . . . .14 July 1972

Course 704B
Joined on the **25th October 1970** and **93.75%** of them graduated 628 days later.
P.J. Mallinson . . . . 14 July 1972
A.F. Millar . . . . 14 July 1972
D.J. Millin . . . . 14 July 1972
A.R.L. Pike . . . . 14 July 1972
R.R. Pilcher . . . . 14 July 1972
S.F. Russell . . . . 13 July 1971
S. Sheterline . . . . 14 July 1972
R.G. Thomas . . . . 14 July 1972
J.C. Thorne . . . . 14 July 1972
C.J. Tipney . . . . 14 July 1972
J.P. Towell . . . . .14 July 1972
D.S. Watt . . . . .14 July 1972
R.F. Weidner . . . . .14 July 1972
B.J. Whitehead . . . . .14 July 1972
R.A. Willetts . . . . .14 July 1972
G.C. Worden . . . . .14 July 1972

Course 704C
Joined on the **25th October 1970** and **81.25%** of them graduated 628 days later.
D. Archibald . . . . .13 May 1971
A. Baillie . . . . .17 November 1972
J.M. Barrowman . . . . .17 November 1972
R.S. Beetham . . . . .07 May 1971
M.J. Broom . . . . 02 June 1971
J.P. Dennaford . . . . .14 July 1972
G.S. Foxon . . . . .14 July 1972
C.P. Lewington . . . . .14 July 1972
M.K. Maiden . . . . .14 July 1972
R.J. Marshall . . . . .14 July 1972
N.V. McClune . . . . .14 July 1972
R.M. Price . . . . .14 July 1972
P.N.A. Rees . . . . .14 July 1972
A.G. Skuse . . . . .14 July 1972
R. Webster . . . . .14 July 1972
C.N. Yeoman . . . . .14 July 1972

183

The CAT and the Hamsters

Course 711A
Joined on the **18th January 1971** and **75%** of them graduated 669 days later.
D.R. Allam . . . . 10 November 1972
C.J. Bailey . . . . 17 November 1972
P.J. Biddlecombe . . . . 17 November 1972
P.J. Boulding. . . . . 17 November 1972
T.R. Brymer. . . . . 19 October 1971
C.R. Calder-Potts . . . . 17 November 1972
A.R. Cotton . . . . 17 November 1972
T.A. Dennis . . . . 20 July 1971
R. Fortey. . . . . 17 November 1972
P.E. Frisk. . . . . 17 November 1972
G.T. Gimblett . . . . 17 November 1972
D.C. Hanlon . . . . 17 November 1972
R.K. Hoult . . . . 17 November 1972
D.H.R. Jones . . . . 17 November 1972
P. Martin-Dye . . . . 17 November 1972
D.K.A. Minto . . . . 17 November 1972

Course 711B & C
Joined on the **18th January 1971** and **66.67%** of them graduated 669 days later.
P.H. Allen . . . . 12 November 1971
J.R. Beckitt . . . . 17 November 1972
G.W. Brennan . . . . 17 November 1972
T.D. Brocklehurst . . . . 17 November 1972
D.I. Coombes . . . . 17 November 1972
R. Greenhalgh . . . . . . 30 September 1971
P. Harrison . . . . 17 November 1972
C.A.I. Hickling . . . . . . 17 November 1972
B.J. Holliday . . . . 17 November 1972
A.J. Hunt. . . . . 19 January 1972
N.G. Jones . . . . 17 November 1972
A.J. Mole . . . . 17 November 1972
A.J. Moore . . . . 17 November 1972
J.D. Owen. . . . . 17 November 1972
C.B. Vosper . . . . 20 July 1971
T.M. Winsland. . . . . 04 October 1971
E.J. Daszkiewicz . . . . 02 August 1971
M.J. Flint . . . . 17 November 1972

Course 711C
Joined on the **13th April 1971** and **71.43%** of them graduated 703 days later.
S.G. Hunt . . . . 16 March 1973
R.D.W. Huskinson. . . . . 13 July 1971
S.B. Lane . . . . 16 March 1973
E.M.H. Murphy . . . . . . 16 December 1971
M.R. Nunn . . . . 25 October 1972
S. Parker. . . . . 16 March 1973
N.T. Pennington . . . . 16 March 1973
D.R. Phillips . . . . 16 March 1973
P.M. Revill . . . . 16 March 1973
C.J. Roberts . . . . 16 March 1973
S.J. Sharpe. . . . . 16 March 1973

A.J. Stimson. . . . . 05 July 1972
N.E. Tetchner. . . . . 16 March 1973
D. Yeomans . . . . 16 March 1973

Course 721A
Joined on the **10th January 1972** and **93.75%** of them graduated 648 days later.
R.W. Ball . . . . 19 October 1973
R.J. Broad . . . . 19 October 1973
L.D. Brodie . . . . 19 October 1973
R. Clarkson . . . . 19 October 1973
P.E.C. Farrands . . . . 19 October 1973
D.J. Farrow . . . . 19 October 1973
T.F. Fisher. . . . . 19 October 1973
W.A. Forbes . . . . 19 October 1973
R.T.H. Harris . . . . 19 October 1973
M.S.D. Holroyn . . . . 19 October 1973
T.J. Keeler . . . . 19 October 1973
A.M. Marchant. . . . . 28 July 1972
D. Melvin . . . . 19 October 1973
J.M.L. Pepper . . . . 19 October 1973
M.G.G. Rust. . . . . 19 October 1973
A.G.G. Sutherland . . . . . 19 October 1973

Course 721B
Joined on the **10th January 1972** and **87.5%** of them graduated 578 or 648 days later.
G.A. Broughton . . . . 23 May 1972
M.A. Clark . . . . 10 August 1973
N.J. Collyer . . . . 10 August 1973
D. Crook . . . . 10 August 1973
N.C. Druce. . . . . 10 October 1973
J.E. Fitch . . . . 19 October 1973
M.A. Gibbs . . . . 10 August 1973
R.C. Griffiths . . . . 10 August 1973
P.J.N. Harvey . . . . 10 August 1973
J.A.B. Higginson . . . . . . 10 August 1973
S.J. Hurst. . . . . 19 October 1973
R.J. McKeown . . . . 10 August 1973
R.C. Owens . . . . 19 October 1973
M.L. Robson . . . . 10 August 1973
A.J. Street . . . . 10 August 1973
R. Walton . . . . 19 October 1973

Course 721C
Joined on the **10th January 1972** and **92.31%** of them graduated 578 or 648 days later.
R.G. Brown . . . . 19 October 1973
G.J. Cathcart . . . . 10 August 1973
C.J. Clarkson . . . . 19 October 1973
S.N. Dalton . . . . 19 October 1973
P.J. Dunning . . . . 19 October 1973
F.J. Epstein . . . . 10 August 1973
J. Graham . . . . 19 October 1973
R.J. Kimber . . . . 10 August 1973
M.H. Robson . . . . 19 October 1973

G.C. Roy. . . . . 10 August 1973
S.H. Shepherd . . . . ?
M.L. Smith . . . . 10 August 1973
V.C. Wood. . . . . 10 August 1973

Course 724A
Joined on the **4th September 1972** and **80%** of them graduated 578 days later.
C. Acutt . . . . 02 May 1973
W.N. Charleton . . . . 05 April 1974
W.S. Davison . . . . 05 April 1974
D.G. Finnemore . . . . 05 April 1974
T.W.G. Harbord. . . . . 05 April 1974
M.D.D. Lindsay. . . . . 26 April 1974
J.D. Lunn . . . . 05 April 1974
A.G. Madley . . . . 05 April 1974
G.L.C. Revell . . . . 05 April 1974
P.T. Russell . . . . 05 April 1974
K.C. Sheen . . . . 30 September 1972
T.M. Steeds. . . . . 05 April 1974
I.M. Sykes. . . . . 05 April 1974
G.N. Wheeler . . . . 05 April 1974
R.J. Williams . . . . 05 April 1974

Course 724B
Joined on the **4th September 1972** and **92.86%** of them graduated 578 days later.
J.V. Astle. . . . . 05 April 1974
K. Barker . . . . 05 April 1974
P.G. Colwill . . . . 05 April 1974
B.I. Cox. . . . . 05 April 1974
P.W. Davis. . . . . 05 April 1974
T.J.F. DeSalis . . . . 05 April 1974
V.E.D. Fitzgerald. . . . . 05 April 1974
J.L. Guizzetti. . . . . 01 April 1974
R. Hamilton. . . . . 05 April 1974
D.A. Hodkinson . . . . 05 April 1974
R.J.S. McMillan. . . . . 05 April 1974
D.A. Radmore. . . . . 05 April 1974
P.H. Tanner . . . . 05 April 1974
P.A. Tiner . . . . 05 April 1974

Course 724C
Joined on the **4th September 1972** and **100%** of them graduated 599 days later.
G.J. Bressey. . . . . 26 April 1974
G.S. Cooper . . . . 26 April 1974
M.J.D. Cotes. . . . . 26 April 1974
A.J. Duggan . . . . 26 April 1974
G.H. Florence. . . . . 26 April 1974
P.J. Hughes . . . . 26 April 1974
P.G. Lloyd. . . . . 26 April 1974
P.E. Mason . . . . 26 April 1974
G.W.J. Medcalf. . . . . 26 July 1974
P.J. Parsons . . . . 26 April 1974
A.S.C. Robson . . . . 26 April 1974
M.R. Routh . . . . 26 April 1974

C.J. Schwaner . . . . 26 April 1974
N.G.R. Stephenson . . . . 26 April 1974

Course 725A
Joined on the **13th November 1972** and **100%** of them graduated 620 days later.
G.J. Bates . . . . 26 July 1974
M.A. Claydon. . . . . 26 July 1974
D.A. Edmondson . . . . 26 July 1974
D.W. Filshie . . . . 26 July 1974
D.G. Gray . . . . 26 July 1974
A.J. Green . . . . 26 July 1974
C. Hulley . . . . 04 December 1974
P.J. Morley . . . . 26 July 1974
D.A. Nicoll . . . . 26 July 1974
P.C. Price . . . . 26 July 1974
A.N. Sawrey-Cookson . . . . . . 26 July 1974
J.D. Stoddart . . . . 26 July 1974
D.G. Thomas . . . . 26 July 1974
S.C. Thompson . . . . 26 July 1974
S.J.K. Walker. . . . . 26 July 1974

Course 725B
Joined on the **13th November 1972** and **85.71%** of them graduated 620 days later.
D.J. Brown. . . . . 26 July 1974
J.L. Clifford . . . . 26 July 1974
P.M. Douglas . . . . 26 July 1974
M.I. Fotherby . . . . 26 July 1974
S. Grier . . . . 26 July 1974
P.S.E. Hegan . . . . 10 October 1973
R.S.C. Hockly . . . . 26 July 1974
M.C. Honnor . . . . 26 July 1974
N.H. McDowall. . . . . 26 July 1974
R.A. Patrick . . . . 26 July 1974
A.G. Race . . . . 09 July 1974
K.A. Roberts . . . . 26 July 1974
A.M. South . . . . 26 July 1974
C.G. Winders-Whitmarsh. . . . 26 July 1974

Course 725C
Joined on the **13th November 1972** and **92.31%** of them graduated 620 days later.
A.R. Darke. . . . . 26 July 1974
T.G. Davies . . . . 26 July 1974
L.R. Fort. . . . . ?
D. Gage. . . . . 26 July 1974
A.M. Gill. . . . . 26 July 1974
G. Hetherington. . . . . 26 July 1974
S. Lorraine . . . . 26 July 1974
C. Matthews. . . . . 26 July 1974
A.C.A. Pike . . . . 26 July 1974
S.E. Robottom . . . . 26 July 1974
D.P. Smith . . . . 26 July 1974
A.V. Stealey . . . . 26 July 1974
C.W. Wood. . . . . 26 July 1974

The CAT and the Hamsters

Course 731A
Joined on the **2nd April 1973** and **92.86%** of them graduated 606 days later.

N.A. Aitken . . . . 29 November 1974
A.J. Burge . . . . 29 November 1974
I.G. Carrick . . . . 29 November 1974
P. Everitt . . . . 29 November 1974
B. Hamilton . . . . 29 November 1974
N.M. Humphries . . . . . 29 November 1974
J.A. Hunter . . . . 29 November 1974
A.J.R. Jackson . . . . . . 29 November 1974
C.A. Jones . . . . 29 November 1974
M.C. Lilly . . . . 29 November 1974
A.S.C. Pickering . . . . . 29 November 1974
J. Quick . . . . 29 November 1974
J.C. Ratcliffe . . . . 29 November 1974
D.J. Turner . . . . 29 November 1974

Course 731B
Joined on the **2nd April 1973** and **85.71%** of them graduated 606 days later.

J.G. Black . . . . 03 December 1974
S.W.A. Buzdygan . . . . 29 November 1974
J.D.C. Deloford . . . . . . 10 December 1974
C.T.D. Hawkes . . . . . . 29 November 1974
K.R. Jones . . . . 29 November 1974
D.R. Keen . . . . 23 October 1973
C.L.R. Luscombe . . . . 29 November 1974
J.B.J. Massey . . . . 29 November 1974
P.D. Rae . . . . 03 December 1974
J. Read . . . . 10 December 1974
P. Varty . . . . 13 December 1973
P.M. Whitaker . . . . 06 December 1974
J.S. Wingrove . . . . 05 December 1974
N.J. Winspear . . . . 29 November 1974

Course 731C
Joined on the **2nd April 1973** and **86.67%** of them graduated 606 days later.

G.A. Beaton . . . . 29 November 1974
K.M. Brennan . . . . 29 November 1974
B.G.M. Connell . . . . . . 29 November 1974
J.I. Dudgeon . . . . 04 July 1975
P.R. Heaver . . . . 29 November 1974
D.T. Hoy . . . . 18 November 1974
S.J. Hunter . . . . 29 November 1974
N.J. King . . . . 29 November 1974
A.W. Morgan . . . . 20 September 1974
A.T. Mundie . . . . 29 November 1974
T.J. Orchard . . . . 29 November 1974
M.D. Shiels . . . . 29 November 1974
P.M. Twose . . . . 10 December 1974
R.M.E. Wilmot . . . . 31 December 1974
F.A. Zubiel . . . . 29 November 1974

Course 732A
Joined on the **2nd July 1973** and **75%** of them graduated 634 days later.

R.A. Albon . . . . 05 February 1975
N.A. Bennett . . . . 28 March 1975
D.S. Burgum . . . . 28 March 1975
A.G.W. Easton . . . . 28 March 1975
A.E. Eaves . . . . 02 April 1975
P.C.B. Elliott . . . . 28 March 1975
J.M. Ellis . . . . 28 March 1975
C.W. Fletcher . . . . 28 March 1975
J.D. Hodges . . . . 28 March 1975
G.C. Jarvis . . . . 28 March 1975
J.F. Nash . . . . 28 March 1975
R.I. Richardson . . . . 14 March 1975
S.M. Rogers . . . . 28 March 1975
P.M. Scowen . . . . 28 March 1975
G.W. Thomas . . . . 05 February 1975
J.S. Warham . . . . 28 March 1975

Course 732B
Joined on the **2nd July 1973** and **81.25%** of them graduated 634 days later.

P.I. Appleton . . . . 30 March 1975
A.D. Berryman . . . . 28 March 1975
J.P. Corcoran . . . . 28 March 1975
T.C.G. Doughty . . . . 28 March 1975
M.R. Emery . . . . 31 January 1974
P.E. Gascoigne . . . . 14 March 1975
S.B. Gibson . . . . 28 March 1975
D.G.P. Green . . . . 25 January 1974
R.J. Hunt . . . . 28 March 1975
T.R. Inge . . . . 28 March 1975
M.W. King . . . . 28 March 1975
P.M. Krause . . . . 28 March 1975
D.A. Lister . . . . 28 March 1975
C.W. Monsell . . . . 28 March 1975
M. Smith . . . . 28 March 1975
R.J. Ward . . . . 28 March 1975

Course 732C
Joined on the **2nd July 1973** and **81.25%** of them graduated 634 days later.

I.G. Bannister . . . . 28 March 1975
C.J. Burgess . . . . 28 March 1975
R.A. Creek . . . . 18 October 1973
R.G. Edmunds . . . . 28 March 1975
A.D.B. Evans . . . . 28 March 1975
D. Fenton . . . . 28 March 1975
D.A.W. Hamilton . . . . . . 31 October 1974
A.J. Houghton . . . . 28 March 1975
D.V.W. Johnson . . . . 06 March 1975
A.G. Mattick . . . . 28 March 1975
C.J. Nicholls . . . . 28 March 1975
M. Poole . . . . 28 March 1975
S.G. Smith . . . . 28 March 1975

The CAT and the Hamsters

S.J. Threlfall . . . . .28 March 1975
J.P.C. Watkins. . . . . .28 March 1975
J.A. Wicks. . . . . .28 March 1975

Course 733A
Joined on the **15th October 1973** and **80%** of them graduated 627 days later.
C.B. Amor. . . . . 04 July 1975
P.G. Argyle . . . . 08 July 1974
W.B. Barc . . . . 04 July 1975
A.A. Brember . . . . 04 July 1975
D.H.W. Commerford . . . . 30 October 1974
B.A. Cornook . . . . 04 July 1975
R.P. Doyle. . . . . 04 July 1975
M.G. Ferguson . . . . 04 July 1975
M.D. Grievson . . . . 04 July 1975
P.D. Heritage . . . . 24 January 1976
N.G.R. Moffat . . . . 04 July 1975
S.T. Reed . . . . 04 July 1975
J.P. Sutcliffe . . . . 04 July 1975
D.J. Watkins . . . . 04 July 1975
P.E. Wilson . . . . 04 July 1975

Course 733B
Joined on the **15th October 1973** and **86.67%** of them graduated 627 days later.
R.G. Aston . . . . 04 July 1975
D.W. Cuthbert. . . . . 04 July 1975
S.H.J. George. . . . . 04 July 1975
M.R. Hull. . . . . .01 April 1975
D.M. Kirkland . . . . 04 July 1975
R.E.J. Kosh. . . . . 04 July 1975
E.F. Lord . . . . 01 November 1975
C.P. Munday . . . . 04 July 1975
J.R.Q. Newth . . . . 04 July 1975
I.R. Patterson . . . . 04 July 1975
W.R.H. Pryce . . . . 04 July 1975
B.M.O. Robinson . . . . 04 July 1975
S. Ward. . . . . 04 July 1975
J. Watts. . . . . 04 July 1975
D.T. Wood . . . . 04 July 1975

Course 733C
Joined on the **15th October 1973** and **93.33%** of them graduated 627 days later.
N.N. Barnes . . . . 04 July 1975
T. Davies. . . . . .07 March 1975
R.C. Hall . . . . 04 July 1975
P.V. Hammonds . . . . 04 July 1975
D.K.A. Jones . . . . 04 July 1975
D.J. Lamb. . . . . 04 July 1975
A. Pass. . . . . 04 July 1975
H.A. Piercey . . . . 04 July 1975
S.H.M. Rayner . . . . 04 July 1975
M.C. Scott. . . . . 04 July 1975
C.A.J. Simmonds . . . . 04 July 1975
D.L. Taylor . . . . 04 July 1975

N.B. Webster . . . . .04 July 1975
I.L. Wilkinson . . . . .04 July 1975
M.A. Wratten . . . . .04 July 1975

Course 741A
Joined on the **7th January 1974** and **100%** of them graduated about 683 days later.
L.G. Allan. . . . . 21 November 1975
M.C. Bassett . . . . 21 November 1975
N.C.D.R. Best . . . . 21 November 1975
S.J. Carpenter . . . . 21 November 1975
W.S. Fairclough . . . . . . 21 November 1975
D.W. Friend . . . . 21 November 1975
J.D. Gold . . . . 21 November 1975
A.E. Newport . . . . 21 November 1975
R.B. Pursey . . . . 21 November 1975
D.F. Scrimshaw . . . . . . 21 November 1975
J.F. Turner . . . . 21 November 1975
G.P. Unwin . . . . 21 November 1975
P.J. Wild . . . . 21 November 1975
J.N. Wilson. . . . . 21 November 1975

Course 741B
Joined on the **7th January 1974** and **92.31%** of them graduated about 683 days later.
S.M. Aitchison . . . . .21 November 1975
D.C. Battery . . . . .21 November 1975
P.G. Benson. . . . . .21 November 1975
M.S. Brown . . . . 24 April 1975
M.A. Cooper . . . . .21 November 1975
G.L. Joseph. . . . . .21 November 1975
D.E. McGookin . . . . . . .21 November 1975
D.J. McRorie . . . . .21 November 1975
A.J.C. Plowman . . . . . . .21 November 1975
W.R. Prince . . . . .21 November 1975
F. Ramage . . . . .21 November 1975
E.T. Smith. . . . . .21 November 1975
P.M.F. Ward . . . . .21 November 1975

Course 741C
Joined on the **7th January 1974** and **78.57%** of them graduated about 683 days later.
M.D. Albrecht . . . . .21 November 1975
J.C. Beecham . . . . .21 November 1975
J.L. Berrisford . . . . .21 November 1975
M.G. Burt. . . . . .21 November 1975
A.M. Dormon . . . . .21 November 1975
P.F. Jessiman . . . . 09 August 1974
M.L. Joseph. . . . . .21 November 1975
R.C. May . . . . .21 November 1975
T.P. Neale. . . . . .21 November 1975
P.J. Sadler . . . . 08 March 1974
J.C.H. Schofield. . . . . . .21 November 1975
K.F. Strocchi . . . . .21 November 1975
P.M. Webster . . . . .21 November 1975
P. Weston. . . . . 24 June 1974

The CAT and the Hamsters

Course 742A
Joined on the **8th April 1974** and **92.86%** of them graduated 753 days later.
R.T. Bennett . . . . 22 April 1976
J.C. Chalmers. . . . . 14 April 1976
D.W.F. Collett . . . . 06 May 1976
T.J. Davis . . . . 30 April 1976
M.R. Dicks . . . . 30 April 1976
A.S. Holling. . . . . 30 April 1976
R.P.N. Izon . . . . 30 April 1976
S.A. Ledger . . . . 30 April 1976
D.P. Medhurst. . . . . 30 April 1976
S.A. Moffat . . . . 30 April 1976
A.T. Richards . . . . 30 April 1976
B.W. Stephens . . . . 28 April 1975
J.P. Stokes . . . . 30 April 1976
A.C. Wheeler . . . . 30 April 1976

Course 742B
Joined on the **8th April 1974** and **92.86%** of them graduated 753 days later.
A.M Backhouse . . . . 30 April 1976
S.G. Collyer . . . . 30 April 1976
C.A. Cox. . . . . 30 April 1976
J.F. Diggory . . . . 30 April 1976
A.R. Evans . . . . 30 April 1976
L. Fox . . . . 30 April 1976
B.C. Hutchinson . . . . 30 April 1976
T.D. Lock . . . . 30 April 1976
A.J.C. McDonald . . . . 30 April 1976
E. Neil. . . . . 30 April 1976
L.J.P. Printie . . . . .07 March 1975
E.M. Scott. . . . . 30 April 1976
M.J. Thrower. . . . . 30 April 1976
J.B.T. Wood . . . . 30 April 1976

Course 742C
Joined on the **8th April 1974** and **100%** of them graduated 753 days later.
P.M. Coots . . . . 30 April 1976
K. Dawson . . . . 30 April 1976
N. Garlick . . . . 30 April 1976
J.D. Goodsell . . . . 30 April 1976
J.L. Knight . . . . 30 April 1976
C.A. Marren . . . . 30 April 1976
C. McHattie . . . . 30 April 1976
J.L. McMillan . . . . 30 April 1976
S.F. Newbould . . . . 30 April 1976
S.A. Sheridan . . . . 15 April 1976
A.M. Slaney . . . . 30 April 1976
M.A. Walker . . . . 30 April 1976
J. Wiles. . . . . 30 April 1976

Course 743A
Joined on the **1st July 1974** and **100%** of them graduated 767 days later.
A.S. Barnett . . . . 06 August 1976
G.M. Brown . . . . 06 August 1976
C.D. Cain. . . . . 06 August 1976
M.J. Clark . . . . 06 August 1976
R.J. Dobson. . . . . 06 August 1976
M.D. Granshaw . . . . 06 August 1976
P.E. Griffiths . . . . 06 August 1976
D.R. Heath. . . . . 06 August 1976
J.P. Legat. . . . . 06 August 1976
T.B. Maskell . . . . 06 August 1976
J. Norden. . . . . 06 August 1976
K.R. Sherwood. . . . . 06 August 1976
M.T. Skeels . . . . 06 August 1976
C.G. White. . . . . 06 August 1976

Course 743B
Joined on the **1st July 1974** and **85.71%** of them graduated 767 days later.
M.A. Attenborough . . 10 December 1974
S. Bates . . . . 06 August 1976
A.R. Buchan . . . . 06 August 1976
R.G. Callaghan . . . . 06 August 1976
M.J.I. Freeman. . . . . 06 August 1976
J.D.J. Galpin . . . . 06 August 1976
P.J. Green . . . . 06 August 1976
G.B.G. Hingley . . . . .26 February 1975
D. Matthews. . . . . 06 August 1976
J. Nicholls . . . . 06 August 1976
D.C.J. Payne . . . . 06 August 1976
A.J. Scoffom . . . . 06 August 1976
C.D.L. Smith . . . . 06 August 1976
A.W. Stoneham . . . . 06 August 1976

Course 743C
Joined on the **1st July 1974** and **100%** of them graduated 767 days later.
B.A. Bisdton. . . . . 06 August 1976
J.E. Bowie . . . . 06 August 1976
J.E. Brown . . . . 06 August 1976
J.W. Dickie. . . . . 06 August 1976
P.D. Gosherton . . . . 06 August 1976
T.J. Hughes . . . . 06 August 1976
P.A.P. Jillians . . . . 06 August 1976
M.A. Lee . . . . 06 August 1976
P.M. Noonan . . . . 06 August 1976
J.G. Roberts . . . . 06 August 1976
G.M. Sharps . . . . 06 August 1976
G.M. Turner . . . . 06 August 1976
R.M. Wilkinson. . . . . 06 August 1976
N.M. Yeo . . . . 06 August 1976

Course 744A
Joined on the **14th October 1974** and **100%** of them graduated about 767 days later.
R.J. Cawthorne . . . . .late 1976
P.J. Collins . . . . .late 1976
W.I. Condy. . . . . .late 1976

The CAT and the Hamsters

A.J. Emery . . . . .late 1976
R.J. Hall . . . . .late 1976
N.A. Hilton . . . . .late 1976
C.P. Nash .late 1976
J.E. Paulley. . . . . .late 1976
M.L. Pound . . . . .late 1976
G.L.C. Sanders. . . . . .late 1976
A. Sharrott . . . . .late 1976
A.C. Stewart . . . . .late 1976
C.M. Taylor . . . . .late 1976
T.J.R. Williamson . . . . .late 1976

Course 744B
Joined on the **1st July 1974** and **92.86%** of them graduated about 767 days later.
D.W. Adam . . . . 19 November 1976
G. Gault . . . . 19 November 1976
P.L. Harrison . . . . 19 November 1976
N.G. Hassell . . . . 19 November 1976
C. Heritage . . . . 19 November 1976
N.S. Humphries . . . . . 19 November 1976
J.S. Kingsford . . . . 19 November 1976
J.T. Masters . . . . 19 November 1976
K.V.S. Morton . . . . 03 February 1977
D.G. Sanders . . . . 19 November 1976
C.D. Turner . . . . 19 November 1976
J.A. Vincent . . . . 19 November 1976
P.A. Watkins . . . . 19 November 1976
C.A. Young . . . . 19 November 1976

Course 781
Joined on the **13th February 1978** and **94.12%** of them graduated about 600 days later. **NB:** Graduation dates for this intake vary between 29/9/79 & 24/10/79.
D.W. Burns . . . . 28 October 1979
R.J. Davie . . . . .29 September 1979
J.T.J Fisher . . . . 05 October 1979
A.R. Foote . . . . .28 September 1979
C.M. Hendry . . . . .29 September 1979
P. Lister. . . . . 14 February 1978
K.J. McGhee . . . . 10 October 1979
E. McGreevy . . . . .29 September 1979
D.F. Marshall . . . . 24 October 1979
A.P.S. Maynard . . . . . .29 September 1979
P.H. Morris . . . . 12 October 1979
M. Reaveley . . . . 05 October 1979
A.M. Rocliffe . . . . 12 October 1979
R.K. Sedgwick . . . . 10 October 1979
A. Stokes . . . . .29 September 1979
R.D. Watts . . . . .29 September 1979
N.H. Williams . . . . 25 October 1979

Course 782
Joined on the **26th June 1978** and **100%** of them graduated about 600 days later.
NB: Graduation dates for this intake vary between 12/2/80 & 3/4/80. Two cadets apparently graduated in 1982.
G.W. Beard . . . . .22 February 1980
E.D. Carrington . . . . 03 April 1980
N.H.T. Cottrell . . . . .18 February 1982
A.C. Gaskell. . . . . .20 February 1982
J. Hobden . . . . .22 February 1980
M. Hogge. . . . . .14 February 1980
J.R. Jones . . . . .12 February 1980
D.E. Lawson . . . . .29 February 1980
D.P. Mowat. . . . . 03 April 1980
C. Newton . . . . .22 February 1980
A.W. Paterson . . . . .20 February 1980
S.J. Penn . . . . .21 February 1980
J.R. Pike. . . . . .15 February 1980
A.N. Smelt . . . . .25 February 1980
I.D.E. Turner. . . . . .29 February 1980
C.J. Wassell. . . . . .12 February 1980

Course 783
Joined on the **9th October 1978** and **100%** of them graduated about 600 days later.
NB: Graduation dates for this intake vary between 2/5/80 & 10/8/80.
R.M. Cochran . . . . .02 May 1980
J.A. Cuff . . . . 14 July 1980
A.J. Davis . . . . 21 July 1980
M.A. Johnson. . . . . 14 July 1980
E.J. Kettell . . . . 21 July 1980
A.A.I. Matheson . . . . 25 July 1980
N.J. Newbold . . . . 14 July 1980
N.M. Newport . . . . 21 July 1980
P. Perry . . . . 21 July 1980
G.J. Ridley . . . . 10 August 1980
R.J. Robinson . . . . 08 August 1980
T.E. Rushton. . . . . .22 July 1980
P.C. Swinscoe . . . . .14 July 1980
R.H. Tardrew . . . . .15 July 1980
J.P. Trillwood . . . . .18 July 1980
P. Welton . . . . .22 July 1980

The CAT and the Hamsters

Course 784
Joined on the **20th November 1978** and **100%** of them graduated about 611 days later. **NB:** Graduation dates for this intake vary between 15/7/80 & 5/8/80.

K.A. Beattie . . . . 15 July 1980
J. Godfrey. . . . . 02 August 1980
M.J. Hagon. . . . . 15 July 1980
R.J. Halloran. . . . . 23 July 1980
M.A. Langford. . . . . 23 July 1980
M. Osbaldeston . . . . 02 August 1980
M.D.P. Rostron . . . . 05 August 1980
C.P. Simpson . . . . 23 July 1980
K.R. Snell . . . . 21 July 1980
R.J. Tarling . . . . 28 July 1980
A.G. Taylor . . . . 15 July 1980
P.B. Tuffley . . . . 24 July 1980

Course 791
Joined on the **2nd January 1979** and **100%** of them graduated about 650 days later.
NB: Graduation dates for this intake vary between 23/9/80 & 24/10/80

S. Bloxham . . . . 07 October 1980
G.P. Clark . . . . 03 October 1980
T.J. Davies . . . . 16 October 1980
I.J. Fleming. . . . . 23 October 1980
J. Fox . . . . 03 October 1980
P.J. Gibney . . . . 02 October 1980
R.J. Hill . . . . 30 September 1980
M.L. Hitch. . . . . 03 October 1980
C.H. Lawrence . . . . 10 October 1980
K.S. Milne . . . . 13 October 1980
P.W.M. Mooney . . . . 23 October 1980
J.O. Oxenham . . . . 06 October 1980
H.M. Roberts . . . . 29 September 1980
M.C. Stephens . . . . 15 October 1980
K.J. Sumner . . . . 23 September 1980
D.A.C. Voak . . . . 24 October 1980

Course 792
Joined on the **12th February 1979** and **88.24%** of them graduated about 600 days later. **NB:** Graduation dates for this intake vary between 13/11/80 & 22/1/81.

L.M. Barton . . . . 21 November 1980
J.R. Bleazby . . . . 25 November 1980
P.D. Bowles . . . . 22 January 1981
G.I. Clark . . . . 13 September 1979
P.H. Collins . . . . 13 November 1980
L.N. Evans . . . . 12 December 1980
O.J. Hanmer . . . . 03 December 1980
R. Lucas . . . . 13 December 1980
T.J. Nicholson . . . . 13 February 1980
D.C. Parsons . . . . 21 November 1980
G.P.J. Rowden . . . . . . 03 December 1980
S.L. Shepherd . . . . 05 December 1980
M.C.R. Sims. . . . . 28 November 1980
C.D.R. Smith . . . . 13 December 1980
R.I. Stanley . . . . 03 December 1980
D.G. Stephens. . . . . . . 03 December 1980
R.D. Watson. . . . . 03 December 1980

Course 793
Joined on the **2nd April 1979** and **92.86%** of them graduated about 661 days later.
NB: Graduation dates for this intake vary between 8/1/81 & 29/1/81.

M.J.R. Adams . . . . 08 January 1981
F.J. Donnachie. . . . . 19 January 1981
M.C. Frost . . . . 23 January 1981
R.D. Gurney. . . . . 29 January 1981
N.P. Halliday . . . . 20 January 1981
R.J. McBrien . . . . 22 January 1981
? MacLeod. . . . . 06 January 1981
S.O. Morgan . . . . 22 January 1981
P.S.E. Mount . . . . 22 January 1981
A.C. Oliver . . . . 22 January 1981
P.G. Sharp . . . . 22 January 1981
T.G. Wareing . . . . 22 January 1981
R.J. Wilkins . . . . 16 January 1981
G.B. Wilson . . . . 27 January 1981

Course 795 (Last course)!
Joined on the **25th June 1979** and **93.75%** of them graduated about 710 days later.
NB: Graduation dates for this intake vary between 29/5/81 & 15/6/81.

P. Allcock . . . . 29 May 1981
C. Brooke . . . . 09 June 1981
P. Chick . . . . 05 June 1981
G.T. Chisnall . . . . 15 January 1980
P.J. Elliott . . . . 29 May 1981
W.A. Fleming . . . . 02 June 1981
P.A. Goldsmith . . . . 15 June 1981
M.W. Hutchings . . . . 04 June 1981
D.C.K. Jenkins . . . . 09 June 1981
D.G. Parkinson . . . . 08 June 1981
M.G. Roast. . . . . 08 June 1981
K.P. Rutherford . . . . 08 June 1981
L.G. Sealey . . . . 04 June 1981
C. Tann . . . . 08 June 1981
W.S. Vestentoft. . . . . 03 June 1981
D.R.N. Walker . . . . 09 June 1981

The CAT and the Hamsters

In 1965 CAT introduced a shortened graduate course to Hamble but later courses were based at Oxford (Kidlington). The selection of the graduate courses was still carried out at Hamble and listed below are the two carried out in situ.

Course G1
Joined on the **9th July 1965** and **100%** of them graduated 371 days later.
T.E. Barber . . . . 15 July 1966
P.G. Foster . . . . 15 July 1966
A.R.L. Gilbert . . . . 15 July 1966
B.I. Godbolt . . . . 15 July 1966
C.R. Knowles . . . . 15 July 1966
I.L. McGrath . . . . 15 July 1966
D.I. Tolley . . . . 15 July 1966

Course G2
Joined on the **9th July 1965** and **100%** of them graduated 371 days later.
R.N. Collings . . . . 15 July 1966
R.J. Hillson . . . . 15 July 1966
M. Lodge . . . . 15 July 1966
I. Logan . . . . 15 July 1966
D Tunnicliffe . . . . 15 July 1966

… The CAT and the Hamsters

Appendix 2

CAT instructors

THE following alphabetical list of Flying Instructors.is compiled from the CAT prospectus of 1966-67 and from information kindly supplied by the flying instructors I interviewed while researching the book. Although the prospectus listed military decorations, my other sources did not so I have take a decision not to include any, rather than omit some. Suffice to say that many of CAT's instructors gave illustrious service to their country before they went to Hamble and a few had even fought in the Battle of Britain. Where a complete set of initials is missing it is because I cannot discover it.

Latterly the College appointed Flight Managers but the following were the men 'in charge'.

George Webb Chief Flying Instructor until 1965.
Peter Duff-Mitchell CFI 1965 until 1972.
Cecil Pearce Director of Flight Training 1972 until 1980.
Tommy Thompson DFT 1980 until 1984.

Flying Instructors

W.H. Anderson	G.H. Farley	R.H. Kerswell	P.D. Pritchett
B.D. Batty	A.W. Farrell	W.V. Kinnin	D.J. Purcell
J.D. Beech	L.A. Fieldhouse	E.E. Kortens	P. Reed
J.A. Bennett	R.N. Frost	W. Lamont	J.I. Rees
A. Blackburn	D Greenland	J.D. Lewry	B. Sercombe
A. Blythe	J.C. Hall	M.A. Liskutin	A.E. Smith
B.D. Buswell	J.A. Hardman	A. Margetts	R.K.W. Snell
B.N. Byrne	D. Henderson	G. Mulholland	D. Steel
A. Cole	P. Hicks	L.S. Naile	R. Swann
J.T. Collyer	B.D. Hopwood	J.G. Neale	R. Street
E. Connell	M. Holmes	P.A. Nelson	H.E. Tappin
P.I.H. Courtney	A.J. Humphrys	V. Nightingale	A.W. Thompson
L.S. Craven	C. Hussen?	R. J. Noyes	F.J. Vickers
W. Crick	B.D. Ibison	L.J. Otley	D.K. Watburton
O.C. Douglas	D. Ilsley	S.R. Offer	G. Webb
J.C. Douse	A. Jackson	N.E. Pash	H. Wheldon
P.O.M. Duff-Mitchell	G.W. Jones	G.A. Patrick	K. Williamson
M.E. Edwards	N.L.D. Kemp	C. Pearce	P. Wreford
D.C. Evans	P. Kennett	A. Peddell	

Other Instructors.

This list is compiled from the CAT prospectus of 1966-67 and from College papers viewed whilst researching the book. My apologies for any omissions.

FLIGHT PROCEDURE TRAINER AND LINK OR SIMULATOR INSTRUCTORS

J. Hatfield	N.W. Slipp	Capt. F.W. West	D.E. Bell
C.R. Brown	D.A. Brown	W. Bryniak	J.A. Cope
L.R. Ovenden	R.A. Thomas	A. Thompson	
E. Freeling-Wilkinson			

TECHNICAL LECTURERS AND TUTORS

Chief technical tutor
C.N. Hoy

Senior technical tutors

D.R. Grant	M.C. Johnson	A. Palmer	R.B. Underdown

Technical tutors

F.A. Garrad	D. Goodwin	D. Holmes	T.C. Lea
A.J. Lyne	R.J. Ray	S. Richards	H.W. Rumsby
R.A. Seymour	A.G.J. Smith	R.H. Steel	G.S. West-Jones
B.M. Wilkinson			

Liberal studies

R.E.M. Hughes **(Director of Studies)** B.A. Timbs
F.S. Barnes **(Chief Educational Tutor)** D.E. Baker
C.T. Priestley C.D. Crocker

Appendix 3

Apache flying exercises

The CAT and the Hamsters

TO BE USED IN CONJUNCTION WITH THE APPROVED
FLYING SYLLABUS

APACHE FLYING EXERCISES
w.e.f. 5th September, 1966. (FOR COURSES 654/5/6 ONWARDS)

Ex. 1. 1.00	Handling Dual		Introduction to aircraft, all normal manoeuvres. Basic stalls, clean and U/C flaps down.
Ex. 2. 1.00	Handling Dual		Introduction to asymmetric flight Critical/Safety Speeds. Circuit and landing, touch and go.
Ex. 3. 1.00	Handling Dual		Consolidation of 1 & 2. Steep turns and stalling in steep turns. Further asymmetric manoeuvres. Early use of ADF/VOR. Missed approach procedures.
Ex. 4. 1.00	Handling Dual		Asymmetric – use of emergency pump. Glide and flapless approaches and landings.
Ex. 5. 1.15	Handling Dual		Emergencies – See syllabus. Including EFATO, feathering S/E overshoot and landing.
Ex. 6. 1.00	Handling Dual		Consolidation of all types of circuit, including asymmetric, and full flap baulked landings.
Ex. 7. ½ Hr.	Handling Solo		First solo on type. 2 Complete full stop landings if time/traffic permits.
Ex. 8. 1.00	Handling Dual		Stalls. Runways – including cross wind circuits and landings. Use of Compass Repeater as a D.1. Consolidation of asymmetric circuits.
Ex. 9. 1.00	Handling Solo		Stalls and Steep Turns. Circuits and Full Stop landings.
Ex. 10. 1.15	Handling & I/F Dual		Consolidation of Stall and Steep Turns. Full Panel I/F. Recoveries from unusual attitudes. Checks on Instruments. Basic use of ADF/VOR. Bad Weather Visual Circuit. Short landing.
Ex. 11. 1.00	Handling Solo		As Exercise 9.
Ex. 12. 1.00	I/F Dual		Full, Partial, and Limited panel. Unusual attitudes and recoveries.
Ex. 13. 1.15	I/F Dual		I/F. Circuits, approaches and overshoots from 200' – ditto asymmetric after EFATO.
Ex. 14. 1.00	Handling Solo		Runway Circuit work including short, flapless, EFATO at 500' and zero. Thrust apps, o/s and landings.
Ex. 15. 1.00	Handling Solo		Circuit and stall, steep turn. Revision. Feathering and unfeathering at height.
Ex. 16. 1.00	I/F Dual		As Ex. 13.
Ex. 17. 1.30	Route Flying VFR Dual		Schedule to EAST MIDLANDS or SWANSEA or SOUTHEND or IPSWICH

The CAT and the Hamsters

Ex. 18. 1.15	Handling Solo	Stalling, steep turns. Feathering, asymmetric at height. Unfeathering, circuits, landings.
No. 1 Progress Test 1.00 P1 i/C		To include Runway Landings. General Handling and Emergencies. See Test Form.
Ex. 19. 1.30	Night Flying Dual	Normal & asymmetric circuits and overshoots. Normal and emergency Side landings etc.
Ex. 20. 1.00	Handling P1 i/c	Revision - Clearing Faults in No. 1 P. Test.
Ex. 21 1.30	Route Flying VFR Dual	Schedule to Swansea or Southend or Ipswich or Liverpool with Radar approach.
Ex. 22. 1.00 .30	Night Flying Dual Solo	Consolidation of Ex. 19. Include 1 landing without landing lights. 2 Solo Landings.
Ex. 23 1.00	Instrument Airways Dual	ADF Tracking/Holding ADF Let-down. OCL and Critical Heights. Circling Minima. Missed approach. Ops. Manual for Minima.
Ex. 24. 1.00	Instrument Airways Dual	Airways Gatwick or Hurn or Birmingham with ADF/ILS etc.
Ex. 25. .30 1.00	Night Flying Dual Solo	Circuit Consolidation
Ex. 26. 1.00	Instrument Airways P1 i/c	As for Ex. 24 Airfield Charts Ops. and Met facilities.
Ex. 27. 1.30	Route Flying (VFR) (Mutual) Solo	Swansea or Southend or E. Midlands
Ex. 28. 1.30	Instrument Airways Dual	R1 or ADR 158 Stansted. Brief on Radio Failure Procedures.
Ex. 29. 1.30	Night Flying Solo	Circuit Consolidation
Ex. 30. 1.30	Route Flying VFR Solo (Mutual)	Cranfield for ILS. Cadet to use screens above 1000'
Ex. 31. 1.30	Instrument Airways Dual	R1 or ADR 158 Birmingham or Manchester.
Ex. 32. 1.00 1.00 .30	Night Flying Dual P1 i/c Solo	Out & back. Route to Gatwick or Birmingham or Stansted or Southend for R/W landings. Solo circuits on return.
Ex. 33. 1.30	Instrument Airways P1 i/c	R1/A2 Stansted. Asymmetric after missed approach procedure.
Ex. 34. 1.30	Instrument Airways P1 i/c	R1 A1 or ADR 158 Birmingham or Manchester.

The CAT and the Hamsters

Ex. 35.	Night Flying	Route No 2 (Special VFR) and	
1.30	Solo	circuits on return.	
Ex. 36.	Route Flying	Schedule to Cambridge for	
	VFR	ADF. Use of screens above 1000'	
1.30	Solo (Mutual)		
Ex. 37.	Instrument Airways	VOR Hold	
1.00	Dual	ILS/ADF	
		Hurn	
		asymmetric	
Ex. 38.	Night Flying	Route 3	
3.00	Solo	(Special VFR) and Circuit consolidation.	
Ex. 39.	Instrument Airways	Manchester or	
1.30	Dual	Jersey or	
		Guernsey or	
		Cherbourg	
		Customs/Fuel Uplift	
		Turn Round.	
Ex. 40.	Night Flying	Circuit Consolidation.	
1.30	Solo		
Ex. 41.	Handling	General Revision for General	
1.45	Dual	Section of M of A Test. Includes Partial and Limited Panel I/F.	
Ex. 42.	Night Flying	Circuit Consolidation.	
1.30	Solo		
Ex. 43.	Instrument Airways	Manchester or	
2.30	Dual	Belfast.	
Ex. 44.	Night Flying	CPL Night X/C	
3.00	Solo	Away landing at Birmingham or Stansted or Southend.	
Ex. 45.	Instrument Airways	Jersey or	
2.00	P1 i/c	Guernsey or	
		Belfast or	
		Manchester.	
Ex. 46.	Night Flying	Circuit Revision.	
1.30	Solo		
No. 2 Progress Test		Any selected route Turn Round,	
2.00	P1 i/c	use of all terminal facilities, fuel management, customs, also check L/P and asymmetric I/F and General Handling for M of A GFT/IRT See Test Form.	
Ex. 47.	Night Flying	Short Nav Ex. and Circuit	
1.30	Solo	Revision.	
Ex. 48.	Handling	Revision on any specified general	
1.00	Solo	items.	
Ex. 49.	Instrument Airways	Routes:-	
2.00	Dual	Guernsey or	
		Manchester or	
		Belfast or	
		Prestwick or	
		Turnhouse	

Any time from now on M of A GFT/IRT subject to satisfactory No 2 Progress Test

The CAT and the Hamsters

Ex. 50, 2.30	Instrument Airways P1 i/c	Routes:- Manchester or Ronaldsway or Stansted or Belfast.
Ex. 51, 2.00	Instrument Airways P1 i/c	Routes:- Jersey or Guernsey or Cherbourg or Dinard.

Day/Night Type Rating from now on.
(1179)

Ex. 52. 1.00	Handling Solo	Revision as Ex. 48.
Ex. 53. 1.00	Handling P1 i/c	Instructor in <u>left</u> seat. Runway work precision, and high speed work.
Ex. 54. 1.00	Handling P1 i/c	As Ex. 53 + VDF Let Down (Instructor in <u>left</u> hand seat)
Ex. 55. .45	Handling Solo (Mutual)	Consolidation of 54 including VDF.
Ex. 56. 1.30	Handling P1 i/c	Final revision. Cadet in right seat + VDF Cadet in left.